Imogen Edwards-Jo

Hotel Babylon, *Air Babylo

Babylon and *Pop Babylon*, as well

My Canapé Hell and *Sl

London with h

Wedding Babylon

IMOGEN EDWARDS-JONES
& Anonymous

CORGI BOOKS

TRANSWORLD PUBLISHERS
61–63 Uxbridge Road, London W5 5SA
A Random House Group Company
www.rbooks.co.uk

WEDDING BABYLON
A CORGI BOOK: 9780552156936

First published in Great Britain
in 2009 by Bantam Press
an imprint of Transworld Publishers
Corgi edition published 2010

Addresses for Random House Group Ltd companies outside the UK
can be found at: www.randomhouse.co.uk
The Random House Group Ltd Reg. No. 954009

The Random House Group Limited supports The Forest Stewardship
Council (FSC), the leading international forest certification organisation.
All our titles that are printed on Greenpeace approved FSC certified paper
carry the FSC logo. Our paper procurement policy can be found at
www.rbooks.co.uk/environment

Mixed Sources
Product group from well-managed
forests and other controlled sources
www.fsc.org   Cert no. TT-COC-2139
© 1996 Forest Stewardship Council
FSC

Typeset in 11.5/16pt Sabon by
Falcon Oast Graphic Art Ltd.
Printed in the UK by CPI Cox & Wyman, Reading, RG1 8EX.

2 4 6 8 10 9 7 5 3 1

For Eugenie.
Please can I be a bridesmaid?

Acknowledgements

With very grateful thanks to the extremely talented, highly entertaining and delightfully naughty players whom I met within the wedding industry. I am wholly indebted to them for their humour, generosity, trust, patience, endless explanation, great anecdotes and, most of all, their time. I would very much like to thank my dear friend Anonymous, whom I have literally travelled to the end of the earth with, for his help, humour and advice with this project. I couldn't have done it without him. Thank you also to the handsome Doug Young, the fabulous Laura Sherlock, the dashing Larry Finlay and all at Transworld for their fabulousness. Nothing would get done, written or indeed published without you. Thank you all.

Prologue

All of the following is true. Only the names have been changed to protect the guilty. All the anecdotes, the situations, the highs, the lows, the excesses and the insanity are as told to me by Anonymous – a collection of some of the finest and most successful planners and players within the wedding business. However, for legal reasons, the weddings are fictionalized although the incidents are real and the celebrities play themselves. Narrated by Anonymous, the stories now all take place in a week in the life of a wedding planner. But everything else is as it should be. The brides take centre stage, the mothers try and steal the limelight, and the grooms are bit-part players in a show where everyone else takes their cut. It's just another week in the turbulent and stressful world of weddings.

Sunday a.m.

It's the birds that disturb me first. Their endless bloody twittering has been going on ever since I crawled into bed this morning. And now the sun's pissing me off too. No matter how hard I try to move my head, the glare still manages to bore right to the back of my addled brain. There's no point in trying to sleep. The fact that I don't have the option is, of course, neither here nor there. In a couple of hours I've got to be back on duty, all tits, teeth and Listerine, reminding everyone how fabulous they were yesterday. In the meantime I might try just lying here for another five minutes enjoying these crisp linen sheets.

I close my eyes, but am suddenly enveloped in a blancmange of sheets and pillows and cushions. I am quite literally drowning in comfort. What is it with these posh hotels that they feel the need to cover the beds with so many goddamn soft furnishings? A mop of expensive blonde highlights appears from under the bedding, rapidly followed by an acrid yawn of old champagne.

'Morning,' she mumbles through her pink-stained lips, rubbing black mascara circles around her eyes. 'D'you have any Nurofen?'

'No, sorry,' I say.

'Oh,' she coughs, hacking away at the contents of a whole packet of Silk Cut Ultra stuck in her throat. 'Call yourself a wedding planner?' she sniffs, before flopping back into the pillows.

I didn't mean to fuck the bridesmaid. I was forced to. It was a toss up between her and the matron of honour, and somehow I just couldn't bring myself to do it with Matron. A friend of mine did that once and it got him thrown out of school. But given the choice between tracking down a minicab at four in the morning and heading cross-country to seek out a two-star B&B with a dragon manning the door, or tiptoeing upstairs with Louise or Abigail, it was no contest. And she was keen. Very keen. It takes a certain type of girl to carry off the missionary position while wearing a baby-pink frilled taffeta dress, and Louise/Abigail did it with great style and gusto. She even broke the bedside lampshade in the process. However, as I sense her hands making their way rapidly towards me underneath the duvet with all the rootling enthusiasm of a bargain hunter at a jumble sale, I think it is time to make my excuses.

'So,' I say, leaping out of bed, butt naked. 'No rest for the wicked.'

'Where are you going?' she asks, propping herself up provocatively on the pillows and cocking a bare leg over the top of the duvet.

She has one of those figures you only ever seem to find in the Home Counties – narrow hips, long, slim legs with fine ankles, and the sort of enormous bosom that begins under the chin and ends at the waist. It's a combination that can prove mightily distracting when poured into pink taffeta and paraded down the aisle, as half the blokes at St Mary's Church, Walton on Thames yesterday will attest.

'I've got the brunch to organize and the clearing up to supervise. I'm working,' I say, searching through the debris at the bottom of the bed for my underwear.

'It's eight a.m.,' she sighs, eyeing up my backside. 'No one will be up for hours.'

'Shit!' I say. 'I am already late.'

I leg it down the corridor, avoiding the collection of untouched breakfast trays and crisp *Sunday Times* newspapers, and head straight down the main stairs of the hotel, buttoning up my shirt as I go. Squinting into the sunlight, I stride across the lawn pretending to exude efficiency, only to find a sturdy group of Gallowglass boys already hard at work.

Hewn from young, muscle-bound, usually Antipodean stock, the boys from Gallowglass earn about a tenner an hour crewing heavy stuff in and out of weddings, gigs and private parties – anywhere that can afford to pay for an extra pair of hands. Employed for their breezy nature and big muscles, they are cheap and charming, and I couldn't get through a wedding without them.

At last night's reception for 180 people we tried to create some sort of louche bar effect for the guests to retire to after the dinner. We set up a false wall between the dance-floor/bar and the dining room, only for the wall to drop away after the cake-cutting ceremony to reveal a relaxing area packed with sixties and seventies furniture: velvet sofas, glass tables and large free-standing lamps, as well as the couple of wicker swing chairs that I can see two strong-armed blokes are in the process of dismantling.

'Morning!' I nod towards them, pretending that I have been around for at least an hour and am firmly on top of things. 'Careful with that!'

The more bleached blond of the pair smiles through his goatee. 'Keep yer hair on, mate,' he says. 'It's lighter than a Bangkok lap-dancer.'

'And he'd know,' sniggers his mate.

'Good, excellent, keep up the good work,' I reply brusquely, heading towards the marquee.

In the cold light of morning, the tent doesn't look quite so glamorous and decadent as it did last night. The yellow silk lining looks a little jaundiced, what's left of the flower displays hang limp and dehydrated, half the lemon-coloured roses have been pinched, along with the tea lights, and there are hundreds of fag butts squashed into the hand-laid parquet floor. Slim Jim glasses full of half-quaffed cocktails clutter the tables and champagne flutes full of ash lie in all corners of the marquee. What is it with posh people? I rented thirty-five ashtrays and still no one seems to have been able to find one when they were pissed at two in the morning. There are a few tailcoat jackets left on the backs of chairs, I spot a rejected telephone number scrawled in eyeliner on the back of a menu card curled up under a table and a damp-looking lilac silk handbag lying next to where the ice bar was. Five grand's worth of fun, the slippery blocks were hauled outside by the poor caterers at just after three o'clock this morning in the hope that they would melt quietly around the back.

Walking through the marquee towards the back entrance into the garden, I kick over a high-heeled shoe. Bending down to reunite it with its other expensive-looking half, I notice a pair of black lace knickers underneath one of the tables. I was clearly not the only person to get lucky last night.

'You're late!' comes the startling bark of a familiar voice.

'Shit,' I say, hitting my head on the table. Crawling out, I quickly scrunch up the lace knickers in my hand. Too late.

'I can't believe you're collecting trophies this early in the morning,' says Bernard, shaking his head piteously.

'I am not,' I protest. 'I'm tidying.'

'Stop!' he declares, raising a manicured hand like he has heard it all before – which he has. 'Go and make sure there's enough drink for the brunch. Lord knows where the bloody caterers are.'

Bernard is very well preserved for a single man just the wrong side of fifty. Tall and slim, he exudes all the well-washed, powdered and puffed cleanliness of a homosexual with Obsessive Compulsive Disorder. Which he is and has. His shirts are handmade, his shoes are polished daily and his suits are the crème de la crème that Savile Row can produce. His golden cufflinks are monogrammed and his watch whispers a quiet elegance. He is very definitely old school. He has buckets of charm, a tongue as sharp as a Tungsten steel razor, and he can spot a misplaced fork at forty paces. His gimlet eyes are often so narrowed that you could mistake them for a couple of silverfish slithering across a sideboard. His worst vanity – and he has many – is his hair, which despite the constant oiling and combing and tweaking, he insists on dyeing himself. As a result it can shine a gentle plum purple in some – well, actually most – lights.

But he is one of the best in the business. He has been a wedding and party planner for twenty years and in that time he has matched most of the great and not so good in the country. He started back in the days when the most extravagant nuptials were tea, cakes and a flute at Claridge's and everyone was tucked up in bed by ten thirty. Now there isn't a lion-tamer, elephant-handler, pyrotechnic practitioner, sky-writer, ice-sculptor, martini man, bagpiper or flower-petal-wreath-maker whose details he doesn't have in his well-thumbed Rolodex in South Kensington.

There are only four of us at Penrose, in a first-floor office just off the Brompton Road. Bernard is in charge, obviously, and I am his number two. Camilla is our well-connected, somewhat dyslexic secretary, who can book a three-storey marquee almost as enthusiastically as her weekly manicure. The other is Jez, Bernard's slouching, twentysomething nephew with bouffed *X Factor* hair. He spends his days surfing the net, while furiously texting long-legged lovelies who look like they are channelling Peaches Geldoff, and has little or no interest in the wedding industry. Which is a shame, really, as last year the company had a turnover of more than £21.5 million and a profit of just under £2 million.

I can feel Bernard's eyes boring into the small of my back as I head back inside the hotel to check on the booze. All the bottles left over from last night were collected together and locked into a storeroom near the kitchens at the back of the hotel. You have to be so careful with alcohol in the hospitality industry because it is one of the easiest things for light-fingered staff to lift. It is normally counted in and counted out of the party by either Bernard or me, and locked up in a safe place overnight for use the next day. The host is usually informed as to what has been left over and where it is being put, so there is no accusatory confusion the following day. If the quantity in the cupboard doesn't tally with what the host is expecting, then at least neither the caterer nor anyone from Penrose is going to get the blame. Suspicion usually falls on the marquee team or the band, who are notorious for their ability to sniff out alcohol like meths-fuelled tramps, no matter how carefully it has been stashed away.

Hotel staff are just as bad, though. I should know.

I used to be one. Thieving was one of the perks we looked forward to when I was a deputy manager at a provincial luxury hotel and spa near Chipping Norton. The reasoning behind it was, we were working a full-on weekend to a capacity crowd of demanding, short-tempered London types, and the least we deserved was a complimentary bottle of champagne courtesy of the bride and groom. Thankfully, nearly two years ago, Bernard took me away from all that. He was impressed by my people skills (mainly female, apparently) and told me he needed a new right-hand man as his last sidekick was moving on to The Admirable Crichton, or Bentleys, Fait Accompli, Lillingstons, Party Planners, or another of his equally high-profile competitors. I didn't need asking twice.

So now I'm the one keeping an eye on the staff, making sure any leftover bottles of champagne make it through the night. Just the other day I managed to prevent the bar staff at a five-star hotel just off Hyde Park from 'clearing the bar'. I remember this swift move from the not-so-old days, when as the guests move through after their champagne and canapés, the staff very efficiently tidy everything away – quite literally, everything. You turn your back for five seconds and the last six bottles of Krug have magically disappeared. The staff, of course, very conscientiously offer to let you count the empties out the back. But as any booze thief worth his free bottle of Bollinger knows, you just bring in a few bottles from the day before to make up the numbers.

This morning, however, the stash appears to be untouched. There are a few cases of Veuve Clicquot still unopened and a couple of cases of wine. I remember at the first wedding that I did with Bernard I couldn't quite believe the amount of drink he ordered. While Camilla phoned the list through to Majestic, where we have an account, he explained that on a hot June afternoon you need to allow for between a bottle and a bottle and a half of champagne per person.

'What? Including Granny?' I said at the time.

'Especially for Granny,' he insisted.

He went on to explain that straight out of church, after a long service, the first glass of cold champagne barely touches the sides. It is chugged back in one and you need to refill immediately. The second glass is knocked back with almost as much speed as the first, and from then on, the guests don't care. Any waiter with a bottle will be asked for a refill. So that's a bottle before dinner. And the other half is for the toasts, cake and speeches. He added that a bottle of red and a bottle of white are about enough to get them through dinner, plus a litre of water per person to make sure they can stand up at the end.

'It's a long hot day,' he said. 'You don't want anyone to go thirsty.'

The booze order and quantity also differ from nationality to nationality. The Brits are all about wine and champagne, although there are a few weddings these days where we end up doing a full bar, and during these less affluent times, cocktails are making a huge comeback. More mixers and less alcohol means your cost per head decreases quite significantly. On the whole, the young Russians and their oligarch parents that Bernard appears to be particularly popular with want vodka. And lots of it. A bottle each, according to Penrose calculations. The Gulf guys want whisky and, as they are not supposed to drink, they get half a bottle each. Their wives are usually on the fizzy drinks or water. And the same goes for the huge Indian weddings, where we cater for half a bottle of gin each for the blokes to add to the same amount of whisky.

'I trust all is ship-shape?' says a nasal clipped voice. I don't need to turn around to know that it is Nigel. Extravagantly tall and exceedingly slim, Nigel has thinning baby-blond hair, a long nose and nostrils so flared that in strong sunlight you can almost see right up to his brain. His catering company, The Lilac Olive, is a well-oiled fine-dining machine that can produce a three-course culinary treat in a car park, ploughed field or any other equally inauspicious venue. Lilac, as it is known in the trade, is Bernard's first choice when it comes to weddings and, indeed, bar mitzvahs.

'It seems to have survived the night,' I say.

'Mmmm – which is more than I can say for you,' says Nigel, inhaling through his huge nostrils. 'You smell cheaper than a rent boy in King's Cross.'

'Really?' I say, sniffing my own armpit. 'It's not too bad,' I lie. It is all I can do to stop my eyes from watering. No shirt or indeed deodorant could survive a fifteen-hour shift at the sweaty coalface of the hospitality industry.

'Take it from me, you stink,' he says, taking one polished step backwards. 'Didn't you manage to shower this morning? Were they all out of water at the B&B?'

I can tell he is fishing. His pale-blue eyes are fixed on me, darting back and forth, searching my face for signs of an interesting story or a grubby anecdote that he can pass on. For Nigel, despite all his long vowels and clipped consonants, is as bad as any elbow-over-the-garden-gate gossip. In fact, he is worse. His catering company flits, week on week, from wedding planner to wedding planner, and with him and his pinky-in-a-blanket canapés comes the gossip. You may as well film yourself at it and put your bare arse on YouTube as let Nigel know, because if he gets to hear about something it is round the industry in minutes.

And our industry is quite small. Not fiscally – the UK wedding market is worth £7.5 billion a year (in the States it is a massive $120 billion) and the average British bride spends between £21,000 and £25,000 on her big day. The most expensive part is the reception hire and the catering, which cost an average of £3,500 and £3,700 each. The engagement ring is on average £1,970 and the dress about £1,200, with the cake costing £260, the flowers £522 and the photographer setting the average couple back £940. Plus a £3,880 honeymoon on top! Bearing in mind that the average yearly wage in this country hovers around the £24,000 mark, this is a significant amount of money. It is a multimillion, multinational market, but those who plan and organize it are few and far between. While there are many local fixers who can certainly put together a pretty good shindig, once you break the £150,000–£200,000 barrier for your nuptials, the bride tends to look towards the capital for advice, where the air is rarefied and populated by the likes of Peregrine Armstrong-Jones at Bentleys, who organized Peter Phillips and Autumn Kelly's wedding, or indeed the legendary Lady

Elizabeth Anson at Party Planners, who has been marrying the rich, the famous, the posh and the parvenu for over forty years. We at Penrose are somewhere in the middle. We've done weddings for £30,000 and huge five-day celebrations for £2 million.

Last night's reception will have cost in the region of £160,000, including today's brunch. Sarah, the bride, is David's only daughter, and as a solicitor he has been saving up for his little girl's big day ever since she was born. I don't know what it is about a wedding that makes parents and/or couples think that it is fine and, indeed, necessary to drop the price of a family home on one day – but they do. What seems an utterly indecent amount of money to spend on a dress, a tent, a cake, some food, booze and a bit of music appears to be totally fine and dandy when the girl is dressed in white and someone mentions love. Thankfully, Bernard and I are on hand to help them spend it.

'Oh, don't look now!' declares Nigel, raising his eyebrows as far as his Botox will allow him – who knew the man was so vain? 'Here comes the bride, here comes the bride.' His flat, nasal tones echo embarrassingly about the flagstone hall.

'Oh, good morning,' says Sarah, looking at us curiously. 'What are you doing here?'

'Just checking there's enough alcohol for the

brunch,' replies Nigel. 'You need something to wash down the fried quails' eggs, blinis and maple-cured back bacon.'

'Oh, right.' Sarah stops halfway down the corridor and grabs her head and stomach at the same time, obviously feeling a little queasy.

'Do you want me to find you something?' I ask, staring at her long slim legs in her tight white jeans.

'Would you?' she asks, fixing me with her large round baby-blue eyes. 'You angel.'

'Of course,' I smile straight back, thinking exactly the same thing.

Five minutes later, the brand-new Mrs Anderson and I are sitting in the Blue Sitting Room while she tries to down half a pint of fizzing Alka-Seltzer. Her bare French-polished toes are tucked up underneath her pert backside, which has spent the last three months having daily workouts at the local Power Pilates studio around the corner.

'I can't thank you enough,' she coughs, as the bubbles go up the back of her nose. 'It was the best day of my life.'

'Thank you,' I nod.

'But no, really,' she continues, holding her nose before taking another swig. 'It really was. I felt like a princess.'

'Good.' I smile. 'You're supposed to.'

'And I did.' She smiles back. Tears are welling up in her eyes as she gently shakes her head, somewhat incredulous at what she has just been through. 'I really did. It was amazing.' Two small tears edge gently down her pretty pink-flushed cheeks. She quickly brushes them aside with a flash of her large solitaire-diamond engagement ring. For a stocky bloke with early-onset male-pattern baldness, Mark Anderson has done rather well for himself. 'D'you think it went well?'

'Well' is perhaps not the word I would have chosen. The actual wedding itself was 'fine'. The service went without a hitch. The vicar got their names right, which is always a bonus, and the car got them to and from the church on time without crashing. Dad David got down the aisle, Sarah looked stunning and all the guests made it to the reception. There was enough food and drink to go around and the couple cut the cake (which these days is no longer a cake but a mountain of profiteroles or Ladurée macaroons), and they both managed to remain sober enough for a first dance, which was thankfully not to Chris de Burgh, or Bryan Adams, or indeed Celine, Robbie, Whitney or Shania, but a new one on me. A country shmaltzy number called 'Amazed' by Lonestar, which Nigel reliably informed me later by the cheese platter is the number-one wedding-song choice of the year. I really must get out more, as I've never even heard of it. And then everyone went on to enjoy the dulcet croonings of the Frank Sinatra and Dean Martin impersonators.

Anyway, the only thing that let the wedding down was the speeches. For Bernard, whose Obsessive Compulsive Disorder makes him always ask to see the speeches before the big day, this was excruciating. For not only did the groom refuse Bernard's kind and controlling offer to run through the speech with him a couple of times before the dinner, but he buggered it up. And to compound Bernard's itching and scratching and twitching fury at being told to mind his own business, I did manage to persuade the best man, Nick, to show me his speech and thereby avert one of the most tired and twattish openers there is: 'I have been asked to prepare a couple of lines, but I am afraid that I have snorted them both.' This amateur drugs reference joke usually goes over the heads of the parents, amuses those who have been on the stag weekend, and upsets the bridesmaids as well as the bride. It ranks up there with the other foolish best man favourite, which is how much they all enjoyed whoring in Barcelona/Riga/Prague. This sort of casual mention of prostitution tends not to go down well with anyone at the reception and usually leads to tension and rows later on the dance-floor, as the com-bination of alcohol and deep brooding anger erupts into a big old-fashioned punch-up.

But Mark's opening line was so gobsmacking, it had the whole party catching flies for at least five minutes.

'So she got me here eventually, I guess,' he said as he stood up and shuffled his cards. 'And it wasn't through lack of trying.' It was all I could do to stop Bernard hurling himself across his carefully arranged marquee and tearing the cards out of the bloke's hands. What sort of opening gambit is that? I held tightly on to Bernard's shoulder while he munched his fisted knuckles and the bride's mother, Gillian, started to cry. Abigail/Louise looked appalled. She drained her glass of champagne in one gulp and glared across the table at Matron, who got out of her seat and flounced out of the room in a swish of pink taffeta. In fact, the only worse reaction I have ever seen to the opening few lines of a wedding speech is when the best man at a society wedding I arranged in the South of France pretended to be reading a speech he'd written for a girl the groom had been previously engaged to. That time a whole table of guests had stood up in unison and left the balmy beachside terrace.

It usually takes more than a few sentences to

alienate the audience. But Sarah reacted in exactly the same way that the other bride did in the South of France. They both just carried on smiling, looking poised and charming throughout. Perhaps Sarah didn't actually hear him, although she was by far the closest. Perhaps she simply didn't want to.

And Mark didn't stop there. In the name of comedy he went on to detail just how desperate Sarah had been to marry him. He told of her romantic endeavours and her tragic attempts to ensnare him, which culminated in him joking that he had been terrified to kneel down and tie his shoelaces in front of her, for fear that she might shriek out 'Yes!' while he was down there. In terms of fuck-up Mark had gone way beyond the usual forgetting to thank her parents, forgetting to say how pretty his new wife was, or failing to call her Mrs XYZ – which is the usual crowd-pleaser, guaranteed to elicit a friendly cheer. I thought his speech was almost as excruciating as the best man who once congratulated the groom on the fact that his second wife was so much more attractive than his first – when no one else, least of all the bride and her mother, knew he had been married before. But somehow, when it actually came to toasting the bridesmaids, which is who he was supposed to be raising his glass to, Mark managed to get away with it. Like so many things that prove too difficult for the middle classes to deal with, the whole giant embarrassing episode was swept under the carpet. Along with, one hopes, Gillian's dreadful sexy dancing to '(You Make Me Feel Like) A Natural Woman'. And Mark's father's Mick Jagger funky chicken impression. And indeed my sleeping with Abigail/Louise simply because I couldn't face going back to my cold, miserable shoebox of a room in the neighbouring village.

I have to say, that is one of my major gripes in this business. You'd be amazed how tight people can be when they have a million-pound budget. They will happily spend £35,000 on flowers, but won't shell out on accommodation for the girls who have to get up at three a.m. to cut and water them and decorate the marquee with them. I know of a very talented florist who flew out to Skiathos for a wedding and stayed a whole week to decorate the church, the reception area and a boat which took everyone from one place to another, only for her and her assistant to be put up in a two-star backpackers' hostel. 'I didn't imagine I'd be in the Four Seasons,' she said. 'But I did sort of suppose that they might look after us a bit.' But then she hasn't been in the business very long. As anyone who has been on the circuit for a few years will say, the last people to be fed, watered and accommodated are those who make the whole thing happen.

Last summer, Bernard and I were running a three-day wedding in Sussex, where the florist and her team of eight had been working for five days, putting in one three a.m. to three a.m. shift. The hosts were supposed to be feeding them breakfast, lunch and dinner. Most of the time they managed to disappear off to the local pub for something, but on the day of the wedding they couldn't. They had been up since five a.m. and had had nothing to eat except some Haribo and coffee, but when the florist asked for some food and the chef handed her a packet of biscuits for her team of eight, the shit hit the fan – or rather the roses were dumped on the ground. After much cajoling and pleading, the girls finally sat down to a three-course dinner including champagne, while the guests were arriving out the front.

It is this sort of treatment that means staff play up. So instead of having everyone report for duty bright and breezy and well rested, we always have slackers who bunk off due to 'illness'. It is amazing how many waiters and kitchen staff can contract flu or a stomach bug after staying overnight in a B&B. Short of following them to the lavatory or actually taking their temperature, it is impossible to call their bluff. At a wedding we did last week, we lost three staff overnight. One had a migraine, which I read as a hangover, since at least one bottle of rum for the mojito cocktails had gone missing. Another was actually sick, I think for the same reason, and the third had proved impossible to wake. There is only so long you can pound at an unanswered door before both of you get the hint. The girl was obviously not coming out and I was clearly wasting not only my fist but also my time. I had a brunch for 250 to organize. Which is more or less the case this morning.

Sarah drains her glass and stares at me, awaiting my response.

'I thought it was a great wedding,' I say. 'One of the best.'

'Really?' she says, touching me on the back of my sweaty hand. 'You're just saying that.'

Yes I am, I think. But what's a bloke to do? Tell the bride she's married an arsehole when the ink isn't even dry on the register, or indeed the cheque?

'There was one thing,' I suggest.

'Yes?' she says, leaning forward, tugging anxiously on her white T-shirt.

'Actually, I don't think I want to know,' she says, covering her ears.

'It's not a big thing,' I say.

'What then?'

I'm about to tell her I slept with her bridesmaid, but then I think better of it. What is the point of putting a spanner in the works? She may not find it either witty or amusing or indeed clever. Some might say it was highly unprofessional.

'Mark's father . . .' I start.

'And his Mick Jagger impression?' she finishes. 'What is it with every man over the age of fifty? One too many bloody drinks and they think they're in the Rolling bloody Stones.'

'I know,' I say.

'Tragic,' she laughs. 'I am going to miss you,' she says, kissing me on the cheek. It's not a romantic kiss. It is a sweet one. The sort of kiss that pretty girls hand out by way of compensation if you hang on in there long enough, pretending to be their mate rather than wanting to go to bed with them. Even so, I can feel my ears going red. 'I am going to miss our chats. Our phone calls.' She smiles.

'Daily phone calls,' I add.

'Did I call every day?' She giggles.

'Almost,' I say, getting up from the sofa. Time to get out of here. 'But you know that's my job.'

'And you're very good at it.'

Back in the marquee, Bernard is spitting feathers as he marches around tweaking tablecloths on the trestle tables that have been set up for the buffet.

'Where the fuck have you been?' he hisses under his breath.

'Looking after the bride,' I say.

'Isn't that the groom's business?' He huffs a cloud of potent Listerine at me. 'Meanwhile, I have the hungover mother of the bride on my back, who is wondering where the buck's fizz table is going, what's happened to the quails' eggs and whose knickers you've got hanging out of your back pocket.'

'Oh shit,' I say, pulling the black lace pants out of my trousers. 'I'd quite forgotten about them.'

'Yes, well, get rid of them and get to fucking work.' Bernard strides off in another direction, asking if anyone has seen the bloody photographer.

It's eleven thirty and there are trays of buck's fizz circulating through an elegant, if somewhat hungover crowd, who are all exchanging stories about the night before. Fuelled by attention and adrenalin, Sarah is looking surprisingly fresh-faced as she flits from group to group, collecting compliments. Mark is knocking back flutes of champagne, ducking questions about where he is taking the bride on honeymoon. Suddenly I spot Abigail/Louise coming towards me through the crowd. I have to say, in the cold light of day, divested of her pink frills and salon curls, she scrubs down rather well. She is wearing a flowered wrap-around dress that shows off her slim

legs and narrow hips. I can't believe I got quite so
lucky after all.

'Hello there,' she says, plucking a glass of
champagne off the tray of a passing waiter. 'Working
hard?'

'Very,' I say.

'You look rushed off your feet,' she says, running a
pink frosted fingernail down the front of my white
shirt. I feel my heart suddenly beat a little faster.
Wow, Abigail/Louise is certainly a girl who knows
what she wants. 'So.' She pauses. 'Just so you
know, I had fun, I hope you had fun. But what goes
on tour, stays on tour. I don't want you phoning me
– OK?'

'Yes,' I squeak like a bloody mouse. I clear my
throat. 'Of course, whatever you want.'

'Just make sure Sarah doesn't find out,' she says,
narrowing her eyes like she is checking I haven't told
the bride already.

'Whatever you say.'

' "Whatever you say, Amanda," ' she imitates.
Amanda? Since when has that been her name? 'You
sound a little bit pathetic, if you don't mind me
saying so.'

'Amanda!' A pink-faced bloke with no chin waves
across the marquee.

'Not a word,' she hisses, smiling and waving back

across the marquee. 'Roger! Darling! How lovely to see you . . . Now tell me, how's the City?'

She leaves me standing next to the buffet, somewhat bemused and wondering where to put myself. I am thinking of sneaking off for a steeling cigarette before I start organizing the jazz band and making sure Gillian has enough to drink, when I see Bernard striding into view.

'Why are you still here?' he barks.

'Um, I'm in charge,' I say sarcastically.

'Well, actually, I'm the boss and you're my sidekick, so don't ever forget that,' he says, running his neatly filed nails through his plum rinse. 'Haven't you got a meeting in town?'

'Oh, fuck,' I say.

'Indeed,' replies Bernard. 'You'd better bugger off, hadn't you?'

Sunday p.m.

What sort of person makes an appointment at Claridge's on a Sunday afternoon in June? It's sunny and hot and a Sunday – who wants to discuss business on a hot, sunny Sunday?

'They must be very busy,' Camilla suggested at the time of booking.

'Or just bored,' Jez added helpfully.

Either way, I have driven like a bastard up the motorway, power-eating crisps and prawn sandwiches off my lap, while downing as many full-fat Cokes as my hungover and slightly acidic stomach will allow. I drop into my sad, neglected bachelor flat, which is clearly in need of the love of a good woman – or even man, for that matter. But as I tell my mum, who occasionally drops by to do my socks, I am almost never there, there is no point in buying food as it only goes off, I use the place to sleep and shower and that's it. I bought the flat because it was small and cheap and didn't need much looking after. Just over the river in Battersea, it is on a bus route, has reasonable views and a porter to sign for my parcels. I don't need much else. I had a girlfriend who once made the terrible mistake of giving me a gold-fish. I'm afraid it died quite swiftly afterwards. I had to oversee a five-day wedding in the South of France and by the time I got home I found it floating on top of the water. I am not sure what I'd done. I'd scattered a pile of food in the water in case it got hungry, but apparently that was the problem. My girlfriend told me I had poisoned the thing. But I am not sure what else I was supposed to have done.

Anyway, I am in and out as quickly as I can and head off to Claridge's, Richard James suited, Paul Smith booted and a hell of a lot more fragrant than when I arrived.

This will be my first meeting with the happy couple and probably the only time I will meet the groom before the last week's build-up to the wedding. Penrose don't advertise and generally work on word-of-mouth recommendations. Bernard and I did have a chat last week about maybe trying to do some sort of publicity to try and drum up some business in these cash-strapped times. But then Camilla pointed out that we were booked up throughout most of next year already so there didn't seem much point.

It was the groom, Bill, who called me to arrange this inconvenient meeting. It is usually the groom who calls first. Afternoon tea at Claridge's is not that unusual a venue for a meeting, but I do actually prefer going to the couple's place so I can have a good poke around and try to work out what sort of people they are as a starting point for the wedding – modern or traditional, and, not to put too fine a point on it, just how much money they might have to spend on the whole thing.

Bernard always insists on Googling the pair before he meets them. After so many years in the business, he is not fond of surprises. He likes to categorize his brides into groups – New Money, Old Money and No Money – so that he knows what he is in for. He says you can always tell by a girl's fingernails what type of bride she is going to be. 'If she has square-tipped acrylic nails and a Fox's Glacier Mint ring, then you know you are in trouble.' Not that he would turn such a customer away. Twenty per cent of total costs – which is what we charge – is, after all, 20 per cent, but he knows that he is in for a tough time. It is the No Money crowd that he is generally less keen on. I am of the opinion that you can do a great wedding for very little money. It just depends on the

atmosphere, having enough alcohol and lovely guests. But I remember asking Bernard what you can get for £25k and he smiled.

'Darling, you can't get *anything* for £25,000.'

Obviously you can. You can get quite a lot. But maybe you just don't need Bernard to take 20 per cent of it along the way.

Having said that, Bernard works extremely hard for his cut, a lot harder than the majority of the people who regularly carve off hulking great slices of the wedding pie, and there are plenty of those. Bernard's thing is that he will do anything for the bride and groom and they can call on him – or indeed me – twenty-four hours a day, seven days a week. Although obviously we don't encourage that sort of behaviour – no one wants a lilac- or pink-rose crisis call at four a.m., but that is not to say we wouldn't take it. In fact, I have taken many late-night and early-morning calls, but they are usually slightly more urgent. Like 'Have you seen the groom?' Which is one of the more bollock-sweating calls I have ever received.

I'd organized a wedding in Tuscany and the groom had taken himself off somewhere, Lord knows where, at five a.m. to find himself, steel himself, etc. The only problem was that no one knew where the hell he'd got to by ten in the morning. His phone was off, the best man was still in bed, and there was panic growing around the palazzo that he'd done a runner. Fortunately, moments before I was about to take the bride to one side and suggest that her beloved might be having second thoughts, he sauntered in at eleven a.m. stinking very slightly of grappa.

Bernard also needed a shot of grappa after that. In fact we both did. It is not the sort of conversation anyone wants to have with a bride on the morning of her wedding. Bernard's mantra when he first meets the happy couple is: 'We are in charge, from the first piece of printed matter to leave the office to the last piece of rubbish to be picked up off the floor at the end. We have total control.' Husbands-to-be going AWOL in the Tuscan countryside are definitely not part of his plan.

Walking through the revolving doors at Claridge's, I am surprised how busy it is for a sunny Sunday afternoon. The afternoon-tea service is in full flow and almost all the green chairs and banquettes in the foyer are occupied. There are plenty of Americans in relaxed slacks, tucking into three tiers of cakes and dainty scones, as well as flustered families up in town for the day. A collection of bored rich women are picking the bread off the sandwiches and sipping flutes of pink champagne, and there are a couple of aged aunts who have probably just taken in an exhibition. I stand in the middle of the room, scanning it for a hand-holding couple who look flush with love and a recent engagement. From underneath the huge central flower arrangement, which is packed with more pink peonies than the Chelsea Flower Show, a slim dark girl with a deep Tango tan waves.

'Clara?' I mouth. She smiles. Her teeth are shiny white and regular – the girl's had veneers. Bill, whose back is to me, gets up from his chair. Smoothing down his tie – I am now thankful I'm wearing mine – he takes a step towards me with his hand out-stretched. He looks nice. He has large brown eyes, dark close-cropped curling hair and a generous smile. 'Bill,' I say, taking his hand. 'Very nice to meet you.'

'This is Clara,' he says. 'My fiancée.'

'Oh God.' She laughs just slightly. 'It sounds so embarrassing.'

'Good afternoon to you both,' I say. 'I am terribly sorry I am a tiny bit late. I've just come straight from another wedding.'

'Whose?' asks Clara immediately, leaning forward and crossing her slim brown legs. I notice she's got red manicured fingernails and the Fox's Glacier Mint. My heart sinks slightly. This is a girl who certainly knows her own mind. 'Was it good? Any tips? Anything we can steal for our wedding?'

'Well actually,' I say, sitting down, 'I was just wondering when yours was?'

'Oh, right,' she says, rootling around her feet and bringing out one of those large, rather expensive-looking handbags that are so important they actually get christened: Nancy or Luella or Kate. 'We were thinking of maybe the first week in June and having it here.'

'Here? Claridge's?' I check.

'Yes. Why do you think we suggested meeting here?' She raises her finely plucked eyebrows at me.

'I meet a fair few of my clients here,' I reply.

'Oh, right,' she continues, unperturbed. 'Well – anyway – where's your file?' she asks suddenly as she pulls her own rather fat file out of her handbag.

'I haven't brought one. The first session is usually a bit more of a getting-to-know-you meeting. Finding out your likes, dislikes, what you might want from a wedding, what the time scale is – that sort of thing. So I know what sort of people you are and we can develop some sort of understanding, so that when it comes to the wedding I know you so well I can pre-empt your problems and know exactly what you might need before you do.'

'Oh?' she says, putting her file slowly back down on the table.

'For example, my first question is always how did

you guys meet, and then I usually follow that up with how did he –' I nod towards Bill, who smiles, 'the groom – propose?'

'Right,' says Clara, flopping back into her chair. 'We'd better order a drink then, hadn't we?'

Over a glass of champagne and a plate of smoked-salmon sandwiches that Clara doesn't touch, I learn they met at work. They are both lawyers. He is more senior than her, but only just, and he proposed on Valentine's Day, getting down on one knee in an Italian restaurant just off the Old Brompton Road.

'It was so embarrassing,' says Clara, wrinkling her short nose. 'And he didn't even have the ring!'

'I wanted you to be able to choose the one you wanted,' says Bill.

Clara flashes her hand. 'What do you think?' she asks me. Being a bloke, it looks to me like every other solitaire diamond set in platinum I have ever seen, although it is probably verging towards the larger end of the scale.

'It's nice,' I say.

'Tiffany,' she replies.

'Lovely.'

We all shift in our seats. I can feel my mobile phone vibrate in my pocket. This might be quite a long meeting.

'So here,' I say. 'And in a year's time?'

'Is that normal?' asks Bill. 'You know, to be think-ing about things this far in advance?'

'Average,' I say.

'Average!' exclaims Clara, who clearly hasn't been described as such since trying out for the school netball team.

I go on to explain that these days if you want a 'hot' venue – and Claridge's is possibly the hottest place in town to get married – then booking the place a year, a year and a half in advance is a good idea. English Heritage venues are booked up for most of next year already. Even the most inauspicious of stately homes are ridiculously busy and usually you can't guarantee the date you want. The shortest time I have organized a wedding in is twelve days, but that person had originally hired and then fired us, only to re-hire us when the whole thing had gone tits up. She had the caterer and venue, which are the two most difficult things to organize, so we were only really there for the trimmings. We have had brides call up three days before the wedding asking us to crisis manage something, which is just not in our interests to do, and a florist friend of mine was once called the day before and asked to do the church, the button-holes and the bouquet. The bride was furious when she was turned down. But normally it is advisable to

try and book us a year to a year and a half in advance.

Certain weeks are obviously more difficult than others. The last weekend in June is possibly the busiest, as that is the week before the schools break up. The first two weeks in September are always busy as that is when everyone has come back from being on holiday. The last two weeks in April are when things get going, as the weather is getting a little better and it's a tiny bit warmer. May is a big month, so you have to be flexible as to the weekend you want, and also June. It begins to trail off in July and no one really gets married in August, unless they want a small wedding with a few intimate friends, because on the whole the world and his wife have buggered off.

'I'll check with the wedding team here tomorrow about next June,' I say. 'Do you have any date in mind?'

'The twelfth,' she says. 'Which is the second Saturday.'

'At least if we are here we don't have to worry about the weather,' laughs Bill.

'That's true,' I smile.

'But we would like it to be sunny,' interjects Clara.

'I am not sure Penrose can quite stretch to that, darling,' says Bill, patting her on the back of the hand over the table.

'I am well aware of that,' she replies, her eyes narrowing as she withdraws her hand.

'Um, any other initial ideas?'

Clara gets out her fat file and, licking her index finger, starts to leaf through a large number of cuttings that she seems to have collected from a whole range of different wedding magazines.

'Oh,' she says, like the idea has only just occurred to her. 'We'd like St Paul's.'

'Cathedral?' I check. She nods. 'Sure,' I say. 'That's possible. Are either of your parents MBEs, OBEs or Knights of the Realm?'

'Sadly, no,' says Bill.

'Do you live in the diocese?'

'Sadly, no,' he repeats.

'Well, then I'm afraid that's your answer.'

'Oh well,' shrugs Clara. 'If we can't have that place then we want somewhere nicely lit. You know, with proper floodlights.'

'I am sure I can sort something,' I say. 'But you have to be careful with churches. As places of worship, they are not just venues and sometimes vicars don't like it when you come in and take over and start moving things around.'

'I know that,' says Clara, narrowing her eyes at me. 'I'm Catholic.'

'Are you?' asks Bill.

'Well, not really,' says Clara, her head wobbling from side to side. 'I'm lapsed.'

'Sorry,' I say, flicking imagined dust off my trousers. 'I suppose I should ask what sort of service you want, as that kind of dictates which church we should go to. Do you want a Catholic service? Do you have a local church that you attend?'

'Um, no to both,' says Bill.

'We just want a wedding service,' says Clara. 'How about that nice church just near *Vogue*? I know someone who got married there, it was very *Sex and the City*.'

'Right, well, that is something to think about, anyway,' I say.

'And we'd like an evening wedding,' says Bill.

'So that we can get straight from the church to the party,' says Clara.

'Well, you can't get married after six,' I say.

'Oh, we were thinking more like starting at six and then out by seven,' she says.

'Legally you can't, I'm afraid.'

Quite a few elements of the current Anglican Church service stem from the Middle Ages, when marriages were more about money and property than love, and when churches were lit with candles. Then, couples had to marry during the hours of daylight – eight a.m. to six p.m. – to make sure that the vicar could see the faces of the people he was marrying, just in case an impostor was slipped up the aisle under the cloak of darkness. Equally the posting of banns (reading out the couple's names and intention to marry on three consecutive Sundays within three months of the wedding) started out as an appeal to the community, all of whom of course attended church, to check that the couple could legally marry – that neither of them were already married or indeed related. First cousins, however, are allowed to marry in the UK, indeed in some communities it is the preferred option, with over 55 per cent of British Pakistanis married to their first cousins. These days it costs £27 to post banns, but there are doubts as to whether they will remain a legal requirement for much longer, as last year there were moves by the Church to abandon the practice altogether. You can also, for £100, apply to the archbishop to be married by licence, if you are in a hurry to get down the aisle. The only time I have had to do that was when the bride had very sadly been diagnosed with cancer, and she wanted to be married as soon as possible.

Church hire itself is usually around £250, which when you compare it to how much the cost of the actual wedding is seems a bit of a bargain. Although other donations are, of course, gratefully received and the organist, the choir and any other ecclesiastical frill you want on top of your basic priest does cost more. But you'd be amazed when it comes to actually paying the bills how difficult it is to get couples to cough up. It seems they will happily pay £30,000 for an arch of flowers to decorate the entrance to Claridge's ballroom, but getting them to give the church £500 is impossible. A few months ago I had a couple who just wouldn't pay up. I called their various secretaries and PAs and assistants, only for the cheque never to arrive. It was becoming increasingly embarrassing as I kept on bumping into the vicar and I also needed to re-book the church. Somehow owing money to the church when the budget for the wedding had exceeded £500,000 seemed really rather unpleasant. It wasn't until a tabloid newspaper started sniffing around the story that the couple finally paid up. I have to say I'd think twice about doing business with them again.

'So it is an evening wedding you're after. They are always good fun,' I say, trying to sound a little more enthusiastic. 'And definitely here?'

'That's right,' says Clara.

'If you do go ahead with Claridge's,' I say, 'you will have to use their caterers and their staff and one of their approved florists.'

Claridge's, along with most of the five-star hotels

in the UK, is fairly straightforward to deal with. They have their approved list of people and suppliers, who consist mainly of staff plus a short outside list of recommended people, and that's that. If your name is not down on the list you can't work there. Talk to any quality florists and they will tell you that you have to be approved to work in any of the posh hotels. They need to know that you are a responsible florist who doesn't chuck stuff all over the floors, furnishings and expensive furniture. In fact, most of these places ban vases of water altogether. Although quite how you get on to the list in the first place is anybody's guess. It's a closed shop. Even if you were the most talented new kid on the block you would not get a look in. The only way would be if a huge client were to book you, someone the hotel could not turn down, and they insisted that only you would do, then you might be able to break into the market. But otherwise you're left out in the cold.

Historical venues, including art galleries and museums, are even worse. They work on recommendation only and of course take a slice of the action. Most cream up to 10 per cent off the bill from their registered suppliers. Having said that, there are some less scrupulous wedding planners who get a cut from the venue for bringing the wedding there in the first place. There are so many palms being greased at any one time it is hard to work out exactly who is scratching whose back.

So if a planner books a venue for, say, £15,000, they might well be getting a kickback from the venue of 10 per cent, as well as their fee to the client of 20 per cent of total costs. Then the caterer might well be giving 10 per cent to the planner too, as well as another 10 per cent to the venue. The same goes for the florist, the lighting guy and the band. All the caterers' suppliers are also registered. So the wine suppliers and the blokes who provide the chairs and tables all pay up to be a part of the action. The list is endless. The venue explains away its charges by claiming that you are helping support a stately home or are paying for the use of their working kitchen, although over the course of a year they must make enough money to refurbish their piss-poor filthy facilities at least twice over.

If you have to use a venue's preferred list of suppliers you are also limited to the taste of the people in charge. A lot of historical venues have suppliers and caterers who deal mainly with corporate clients, so their stock and range is quite tired and limited. When you are organizing a high-end wedding, the guests expect high-end wine and often all you have to choose from is a list of plonk. The end result is that you have to outsource your upmarket sauce and then you have to pay an extra corkage or handling charge on top. The whole thing is a complete bloody rip-off. So whenever possible I try and steer my clients, particularly those who don't have money to burn, away from the particularly money-grabbing historical venues.

But both Bill and Clara agree that using the hotel's staff and caterers is exactly what they are after. They want the Claridge's feel and they want the Claridge's look.

'It's the detail of the wedding that we want you for,' says Clara. 'The little touches that make the whole thing that much more special.'

'Great,' I smile, taking a large sip of my champagne. Bernard will be delighted to hear this. After all, detail is his speciality. He's a man who once antiqued a whole house with moss because the client didn't think the place looked old enough. 'What sort of stuff did you have in mind?' I ask.

Clara shifts excitedly in her seat. This is clearly the question she has been dying for me to ask all afternoon. Out comes the file again and with a moistened index finger she begins to leaf through pages and pages of ideas, from how to tie sugared-almond favours to what floral designs she wants to have on the back of her reception chairs. Quite a few of her ideas will need to be cleared by the hotel. But there is no point in telling her that now. She is having far too much fun, and who am I to spoil it? Bill looks a little shell-shocked by the deluge of detail that's coming his way. His large brown eyes are beginning to glaze over and he is starting to pick fluff off his right trouser leg. Poor bloke. I bet when he went down on one knee and popped the question, he didn't expect this amount of fuss. I also suspect that the reason he has agreed to hire a wedding planner is to try and steer clear of all this sort of stuff.

'I want the wedding to look very *Breakfast at Tiffany's*,' babbles Clara. 'Which is my favourite film, so very twenties and elegant. Are you cool with an Audrey Hepburn feel to everything, right down to the bridesmaids?'

'Well, then you'd better disinvite your sister,' jokes Bill.

'Why?' Clara's head spins around with worrying speed to stare at her husband-to-be.

'Well, you know,' he replies, his voice beginning to fade somewhat as he sees the recklessness of his comment. But he makes it all the same. 'She's the size of Jabba the Hutt.' Silly boy.

'Well, your mother looks like Jabba the fucking Hutt,' spits Clara. 'At least my sister can go on a diet – which she will do,' she says, looking at me as if I care what any member of her family looks like. 'While your mother can't change a thing.'

'So, Audrey Hepburn,' I say breezily, trying to diffuse the seething tension that has broken out between the two of them. 'So quite traditional then?'

'Possibly,' hedges Clara, probably fearing that she's not sounding terribly hip. Judging by her bag, style clearly matters to her.

'It sounds lovely,' I enthuse. 'Any idea what sort of flowers or colours you might be after?'

I normally throw this sort of question in right at the end of the meeting, along with more obscure ideas. It comes as part of my 'things to think about or remember' speech, because obviously I have organized over sixty weddings and the client has normally only ever been to a few, and this one is usually the first they have attended as bride and groom. So I generally finish with a pep talk about details – how do they want their tables laid? How do they want their napkins folded? Do they want placemats? Do they want coffee cups on the table at the beginning – because the caterers will always try and persuade them of that? Do they want covers on the chairs? Flowers on the end of the pews? The idea is to make them think about everything, so that when the bride and I meet again, usually without the husband-to-be, we can start to hammer out some details. Although Clara, it seems, has been thinking about nothing but the details since Bill's knee touched the floor.

She continues poring through her file, pulling out feature after photo of exactly what she is after. She must have spent a fortune in the past month on glossy magazines. As I sit there, listening and nodding away, I can feel my hangover creeping up the back of my neck, giving me a thumping great headache. I start to frown hard, trying to concentrate. I look across at Bill, who is slowly sliding down in his chair. There really are only so many photographs of fancies a bloke can look at without losing the will to live.

'That all looks fascinating and is something to bear in mind for our next meeting,' I say, stepping in.

'Oh,' says Clara, somewhat shocked at being interrupted.

'Next time,' I say, patting the top of the scarily full file. There is clearly so much more she has to say. 'I'll look forward to it.' I smile, lying with total conviction, which has rather worryingly become one of my strengths since I started this job. Lying and drinking are two talents that I now have down to a tee. Oh, and surviving on three hours' sleep over a sustained period of time, which is another job requirement, particularly when working abroad.

'So.' I inhale, before cutting to the chase. 'How many guests are you thinking of inviting?'

'Two hundred,' says Bill.

'Two hundred and fifty,' says Clara at exactly the same time.

'Are you inviting two hundred and fifty in the hope of two hundred coming?' I suggest. 'Or did you have something a little larger in mind?'

'We want two hundred and fifty,' insists Clara.

'Do we have that many friends?' asks Bill.

'*I* do,' she replies.

'Good,' I say, rubbing my hands together. These two really need to sit down and actually have a conversation about what they want, I think, otherwise I am going to be used as a punch bag. 'Something for you to go away and think about as well. Add it to the list. And what sort of budget were you thinking of?'

Clara looks at Bill and Bill looks at Clara. 'One hundred and sixty,' they both say at the same time. At least they agree on something.

'Is that flexible?' I ask.

'No,' says Bill.

'Yes,' says Clara at the same time.

'Another thing for the list,' I smile. 'Oh, and one last question. Who's paying?'

Wedding planning is supposedly about keeping the bride happy, but more often than not it is all about satisfying the wants and whims of the person footing the bill. The amount of times I have sat through a meeting with the bride and her mother, only for the bride to leave the room and the mother to take me to one side and say, 'This is *my* wedding and don't you forget it.' To which my response is to tap the side of my nose and reply, 'Say no more, Madam, say no more.'

If the parents are paying, then the parents have a say. And more often than not the mother is living some kind of bridal fantasy herself. Giving her daughter the wedding she never had the money to have, or was never allowed to have. If the father is involved then there is a tendency for the nuptials to be turned into a corporate hospitality event, with him inviting clients and contacts, people he wants to show off to or people he needs to entertain. I remember witnessing a loud and lippy shouting match between a bride and her mother over the guest list. The parents were paying for the wedding and wanted to invite some of their friends and their families, people the bride had grown up with. The bride insisted she didn't want the friends' children as they had nothing in common and she hadn't seen them for fifteen years. She stamped her foot and declared that if they were invited then she wouldn't come to the wedding. The mother hit the roof. She cried and screamed and then shouted at her daughter at the top of her voice, 'You are ruining what was supposed to be the best day of my life!' To which the daughter yelled back, 'I thought it was supposed to be the best day of *my* bloody life!' It took all my UN negotiating skills for a whole week to get the two sides to speak to each other again. But eventually the wedding was a huge success. The bride won out in the end and her mother forgave her.

But normally in that sort of situation I would advise a little compromise. Or perhaps I'd give the mother a job to do – taking care of the flowers or the marquee or bridesmaids – something to make her feel important while she carries on signing the cheques.

'My parents are paying half,' says Clara.

'And we are putting up the rest,' adds Bill.

'Excellent,' I say, thinking anything but. 'And will your mother be coming to the meetings?'

'You try and keep her away!' laughs Clara. I nod. It just gets better and better.

'I am her only daughter and she's been looking forward to this for years,' she says.

I drain my glass and contemplate gently passing this couple on to Bernard. He specializes in high maintenance and he's so good with the mothers. I heard him talking to one of them at a reception the other day. 'Don't tell me you're Alexandra's mother!' he exclaimed as he handed her a glass of champagne.

'But darling, where are your chins?' She of course hooted with laughter, took a sip of champagne and said he was the most charming man she'd ever met. I am beginning to think these two might be better looked after by him.

'Well that all sounds great,' I say, getting out of my chair and leaning over to shake Bill's hand. Clara offers one of her cheeks without getting up. I am definitely handing them over to Bernard. 'Lovely to have met you both,' I smile tightly.

'So when is the next meeting?' asks Clara, taking out her iPhone and tapping away.

'Why don't you give me a call tomorrow?' I say. 'I think we should try and sort something out then. In the meantime I'll get my assistant to check on availability here.'

We exchange a few more pleasantries; Bill pats my back a few times, like he's handing Clara over to me – passing the buck, so to speak. I smile and nod some more and hot-foot it out of there, blinking in the golden sunlight of a balmy June evening.

It feels good to be outside. People are smiling, a group of pretty girls with bare legs and open-toed shoes giggle past on their way into Claridge's bar. I stretch and breathe in the warm air. Christ, I need another drink. I am just contemplating who I should call and which pub I might grace with my presence when my mobile goes. It's Bernard.

'Have you heard the gossip?' he asks, cutting straight to the chase. Oh shit, I think. My heart beats a little faster and my hands begin to sweat. My secret is out. The bridesmaid will be furious. I have got so many excuses to make.

'Um, no?' I bluff, buying myself an extra few seconds. 'What?'

'Dean Martin beat the shit out of Frank Sinatra and now Frank's in hospital!'

'What?'

'Last night,' he continues. 'He deserved it,' he sniggers. 'He was the worst fucking impersonator we've ever had. "My Way"? Bloody no way.' At which point he starts to laugh.

Monday a.m.

When Bernard comes into the office just after nine, he is still full of the battle of the crooners. Sitting behind his immaculate green baize desk, which is devoid of clutter and sports only a brace of Mont Blanc pens, a blotting pad and a gold Rolodex plump with neatly written contact cards, he holds forth on the subject for the next hour at least. Camilla thinks it's a scream. She comes in and plonks her not-so-slim hips down in the leather armchair in front of Bernard's desk and sips her skinny latte, all ears.

'Oh – my – God!' she exclaims through her glossed lips. 'So he like hit Frank Sinatra and everything?'

'It was a proper punch on the nose, darling,' smiles Bernard. He's a man who loves a bit of violence, if only from the sidelines. 'Apparently there was blood everywhere! Splattered all over the walls of the B&B.

The harridan in charge was furious – she had to get her Cif out at four in the morning.'

'Do you think he broke it?' asks Camilla, hunched over her paper cup, cradling it in both hands.

'It was flat as a supermodel's breasts,' says Bernard, arching an eyebrow. 'I wouldn't be surprised if he's got to have the whole thing reconstructed from scratch.'

'That's got to hurt,' suggests Camilla, feeling her own rather delicate nose. 'My friend Esther had hers done the other day and said it was agony. It wasn't because she had a crap nose; in fact hers was rather pretty. But she was knocked unconscious by a ski lift after too much gluhwein in Val d'Isère.'

'Really?' Bernard wrinkles his own rather long hooter in sympathy.

'I know,' she agrees. 'Cost thousands to fix.'

'Does anyone actually know why Dean beat the shit out of Frank?' I ask, joining in.

'The usual reason,' declares Bernard.

'What's that?' asks Camilla.

'A girl,' replies Bernard. 'You know the one,' he says, looking at me. 'That waitress.'

'The sexy one?'

'Well, so everyone thinks,' shrugs Bernard. 'She does nothing for me, with her cheap short legs, but no one ever gets beyond the breasts and the pout.'

'Emily?' I say.

'That's the one,' he agrees. 'Apparently they were playing drinking games in the B&B, Dean had stolen a bottle of Bourbon—'

'Where from?' I ask.

'The hotel bar,' he replies.

'Cheeky sod.'

'And apparently she was playing one off against the other,' says Bernard, in a gently appalled tone of voice. 'I think Dean thought he was in with a chance, as did Frank, and swords were drawn at about four a.m.'

'Must be the first time Dean has beaten Frank at anything,' I say.

'You think?' says Bernard. 'I'm a Dean man myself.'

'Frank every time, for me,' I say.

'Do you know, I had a friend who sat opposite Frank Sinatra all night at a party in Hollywood a few years back now? He said it was terrible. So frustrating. He could hear the voice all night long, but he never got to see the eyes. There was some bloody flower arrangement blocking the view. Can you imagine how goddamn irritating that must have been?'

'Not a party you organized,' I say.

'I know.' He nods. 'Nothing I hate more than

fucking flowers blocking the view and inhibiting conversation. Who wants to stare at bloody roses all night? The florist should have been fired!'

My phone goes on my desk on the other side of the room. Our office is the whole of the first floor of an elegant Georgian house not far from some of Knightsbridge's more upmarket shops and watering holes, a stone's throw from Chanel and Bibendum. Bernard wanted to create a sort of luxury drawing room, where brides-to-be would be able to relax and discuss their forthcoming nuptials between fitting in a spot of lunch and a touch of shopping. And for those who are coming up from the country for the meeting and want to kill a couple of birds with one stone, we also have one of the capital's foremost wedding-list shops just down the road.

The office is divided in half by white panelled double doors. They remain open most of the time, with Bernard and his large immaculate desk in one section and Jez, Camilla and me in the other. Both sides of the office boast stunning chandeliers and most of the furniture is genuine Georgian antique, which Bernard picked up from various markets and auctions around the country.

Over on our side of the office Camilla holds fort at the front. Brunette and curvy, she is supposed to be the first face of the company, meeting and greeting and offering up cups of coffee or tea in fine Royal Worcester china. There is a selection of surprising nursery-type biscuits on offer, but Jez has usually swiped all the Bourbons by midday. There's a large fat flowered sofa to the right of Camilla's desk, and a table laid with the latest bridal magazines. I am to the left of Camilla. My desk is not quite so streamlined as Bernard's, to put it mildly. I am much more of a paper man. In fact, there are piles of it everywhere. It makes Bernard itch to come anywhere near it. I have a view out into the street below, and more often than not of the soles of Jez's feet. He is prone to putting his feet up on the desk whenever he is texting, which is most of the time. Bernard, because he has an extremely soft spot for his errant nephew, lets him get away with it. The only proviso is, as soon as clients come into the office he has to sit properly at his desk.

I slip in behind my desk and pick up the phone.

'Good morning!' comes the pseudo-husky voice of a girl trying to sound sexy. 'It's me.'

'Caroline,' I say as breezily as I can. 'How are you this morning?'

'All the better for hearing your voice,' she purrs.

'Tell me what can I do for you.' I exhale slightly, picking up my pen. Camilla looks across from her desk and raises her large dark eyebrows.

Caroline is famous in the office for her constant

calling. I organized her wedding over three years ago now and every week, sometimes more, she manages to find some reason to call me. I call her my stalker bride, which I suppose is a little unfair as I do enjoy her company, but I just wish she would leave me alone. And she is not the only one. It happens quite often after I have organized a wedding for someone that they keep on calling way after the whole thing is over. You can kind of see why it happens. I have been their confidant, their friend, their ally throughout one of the most stressful and extraordinary times of their lives. We have shared a lot. I have spoken to them anything up to ten times a day, particularly towards the end. I have listened to them talk about their families, their lives and whether they want lily of the valley as a bouquet, or a dome of roses. And I have cared. The problem is that they get married, go on honeymoon, and when they come back things have moved on. I am on to the next bride, giving her all my attention, and often they find it a little difficult. They mostly call up a few weeks afterwards. I always have a drink with them, a glass of champagne, so we can talk about the wedding and look at the photos. I tell them how pretty they looked and we usually get some sort of closure.

Occasionally I get a stayer, who wants to talk about her big day a little more. Or question if she has married the right man. The first year of marriage is supposed to be quite a shock to a girl's system. A lot of brides only think about the wedding day and not at all about what it might be like actually to live with the bloke. There's a phenomenon called Post Nuptial Depression that can set in once the happy couple have come back from their honeymoon, or even on the honeymoon itself. The come-down after all that fabulous wedding euphoria can be hard for some women, no longer being the centre of attention, when the reality of life, the big bills and the bloke they have chosen to spend the rest of their life with actually hits home. There are no more hours of chatting about matching shoes with dresses; it's all about the mortgage, the TV licence and taking out the rubbish. The sense of anticlimax can be so huge that apparently one in ten brides experience some form of PND. There is supposed to be a chemical explanation as well. Women experience a drop in phenylethylamine – the so-called love drug – immediately after marriage, but men do not. How else can I explain the number of slightly drunk brides I have had make a lunge at me after a few glasses of bubbles and announce that I am their Plan B?

'If it all goes tits up,' slurred one, admittedly at two a.m., 'I'm marrying you. You're the only person that really understands me.'

Caroline, however, is a little more persistent. Three years is a long time to blame it all on the hormones and PND. She has even become slightly devious during this period. She has started to get me to organize parties for her so that she can carry on calling up. So far I have done two baby showers and a first birthday party. I did think £10,000 on a baby's birthday party was a little bit excessive, but she insisted on all the trimmings so that she could come into the office for a few lunches to discuss everything – at length. I suppose she is only marginally less attention-seeking than the serial Vera Wang bride who I heard got married three times in the space of four years, wearing a different Vera Wang dress each time. I have to say that is good going, as it usually takes a girl rather longer than a year to meet a bloke and get him to propose. 'I think she just likes going down the aisle,' said the shop assistant who sold her the dresses, with remarkable understatement.

Caroline doesn't particularly want to be a bride, I don't think. She just wants attention. My attention.

'Are you busy?' she asks. 'Because I am around the corner and I was wondering if I could pop in?'

'I have a meeting in a few minutes,' I reply, lying about the time but not the meeting.

'Five minutes?' she says. 'That gives me ample time to drop by.'

'I'm afraid not.' I stammer slightly trying to think of something. 'I need to prepare.'

'Oh – OK then. Tomorrow then?' she suggests.

'What, you might be in the area again tomorrow?'

'I might be.'

'Right then—'

'So that's a date – see you at eleven.'

'What?' Shit. She's hung up.

'Another meeting with Caroline,' smiles Camilla, who likes to spend much of her time eavesdropping on my calls.

'Get your own stalker,' I say, bloody irritated at how I managed to talk myself into that situation.

'Temper, temper,' she replies.

'Haven't you got a holiday to organize?' I hiss across my desk.

I can see Camilla trying to think of some sort of smart response. Sadly it is not forthcoming. She has more weekends away and minibreaks than any resting actor or detoxing popstar I have ever come across. Not that I have come across an exhaustive amount of either, but you understand what I mean. And it's not as if her job is that taxing. She answers the phone, writes a few letters and occasionally gets sent on a cake- or wine-tasting. She buys the magazines for the office table, a job that judging by her voracious consumption of *Closer*, *Heat*, *Hello!*

and *OK!* she doesn't find too taxing. Due to her exhaustive knowledge of the famous, the infamous and the orange women who are endlessly photographed endlessly shopping, Camilla is an excellent asset when it comes to getting the full low-down on some of the brides-to-be who come into the office. We have a footballer's wife-to-be coming in this afternoon, and while I could tell you which club her fiancé plays for and how many goals he scored last season, I couldn't tell you anything about the bride, other than that she's been on some sort of reality TV programme and that she is stunningly pretty. Jez and I had a good look at her bikini snaps in a not-so-glossy magazine last week after her PA rang up and made the appointment. I can't imagine Jez will miss her arrival in the office for a minute, although I see he appears to be rather cleverly bunking off most of the morning.

Camilla takes a call from what I presume to be a groom, hoping to set up a meeting for a wedding in early 2011. He is clearly on charm factor ten, because Camilla is talking of squeezing him in with Bernard some time next week. Bernard won't enjoy that. He likes to have all his appointments cleared with him in advance. But he is otherwise occupied at the moment, hooting with laughter in the next-door office, sharing his crooner's punch with his other industry mates.

I decide to make a start on the mountain of envelopes on my desk. Being at the cutting edge of the hospitality industry, we are constantly being leafleted and sent press releases about new and fantastic things to make your party go with a swing. We get samples of new drinks – flavoured vodkas, different grappas. Absinthe was a big party spirit about ten years ago. I gather there was many an usher who lost his dignity after too many Green Meanie cocktails and ended up hurling his guts up, before falling fast asleep in a hedge. But one of the trends at the moment is putting things in glasses of champagne. I did a wedding a couple of weeks ago where we put hibiscus flowers in the champagne – they slowly open up in the bubbles and are rather beautiful to see. I had an oligarch's bash last month where we put edible gold leaf in the Cristal. It caught the light as it floated around in the flutes and made them look just that bit more expensive, which is, let's face it, the raison d'être for most of those blokes.

One of the latest things we have been looking at is a tornado in a box, made out of a humidifier and a fan. Perhaps not the most tactful thing for a wedding the other side of the pond, but it went down rather well at a do we did in Sussex a few weeks ago. Some people just want drinks and canapés, but the idea is to wow them a bit too, otherwise our reputation could become a little dull, and quite frankly what's the point in hiring a wedding planner if they don't bring a little razzamatazz to the event?

So along with drinks and trimmings, we are also constantly on the lookout for new venues – private spaces or indeed open-air spaces that we can turn into something special. We were rather bizarrely called in the other day to organize a fortieth birthday party in a car park. It was kind of liberating to have nothing to go on, but we ended up with two thousand square metres of black marquee with a fairy-light ceiling and large ice bars at either end. The tables were perspex, as were the chairs, and there were thousands of white flowers in huge ten-feet-high displays. It cost over £250,000, but the bloke is a confirmed bachelor and, quite frankly, what else is he going to do with all his cash?

My phone goes again and I manage to shift through the piles of paper to find it. 'Penrose,' I say. It is some bloke called Giles on the other end, asking about a winter wedding.

'Can you put something together in six months?' he asks. I say it shouldn't be a problem. 'And would the charge be 20 per cent of costs?' He tells me he has a £50,000 budget, and I reply that since it is such a short time span we could probably negotiate a flat fee of £7,000 and be done with it. He sounds pleased.

'The only thing I will suggest,' I add, 'is that you don't do it on Christmas Eve, Christmas Day, Boxing Day or New Year's Eve.'

'Why?' he asks. 'We were toying with the idea of New Year's Eve.'

'It triples your catering and staffing costs and therefore gives you a whole lot less wedding for your money. And half your guests would rather be somewhere else.'

'Right,' he says. 'I see where you are coming from.'

I personally rather like a winter wedding. The brides tend to be a little bit older, or 'uglier' as Jez so tactfully put it the other day when we were discussing it, and a little bit less high-maintenance. They are more often than not girls with a career who are paying for the thing themselves. They are usually more interested in getting married than the wedding day itself, and are generally a lot less fussy and tricky to deal with.

Winter weddings are much more fashionable than they were a decade ago. There are some churches I know in the capital where winter weddings outnumber summer ones by almost two to one. Also, what's liberating about a winter wedding is that no one gives a shit about the weather. We know it's going to be cold and grey and damp, so whatever else happens is a bonus. It does cut down on conversation on the morning of the wedding, though, when in summer I usually have my head out of the window, craning my neck towards the sky, checking for approaching dark clouds, promising things will brighten up later.

Winter brides tend to be a little bit more sartorially adventurous than their summer sisters, too. They have more interesting flowers, they are a lot less girly and much more likely to have individual touches like a fur trim, copious amounts of crystals or a long red train. But one of the main reasons why Bernard and I love a winter wedding is that we need some serious cash flow during the winter, and so they are a welcome sight in the diary.

'So would you like to come in?' I suggest, trying not to sound too keen.

'That would be great,' he says. 'It won't be me, obviously,' he laughs. 'Just my girlfriend.'

'That's fine.'

'What time are you open? Could you do a seven-thirty breakfast?' he asks.

'Well . . .'

'She's quite busy, you see, hence the need for a planner,' he adds.

'I am used to busy people,' I say. 'I once had a couple who had just two meetings and then more or less just tipped up ready to go down the aisle eight months later.' I laugh down the phone, but I can tell from his cool reaction that that's exactly the level of contact and involvement he's aiming for. 'Which of course is fine,' I add rather weakly.

'So a seven-thirty breakfast this week? Thursday?' he suggests.

'I have a wedding on this week,' I reply. He doesn't say anything. 'But I am sure I can fit it in.' He hangs up. What the hell have I let myself in for?

'Kathryn is here,' announces Camilla as soon as I have put my phone down.

I look up and my heart sinks slightly. My first meeting with Kathryn last month proved to be rather difficult. Her husband-to-be spent most of the meeting on his BlackBerry emailing clients or text messaging while we tried to battle through a few plans in the moments when he gave us a sideways glance of attention.

'Kathryn!' I smile, coming out from behind my desk to shake her hand and kiss her cheek at the same time. 'Lovely to see you. Would you like a cup of coffee? Tea?'

'Um . . .' She stares at me through her long pale eyelashes, blinking at me like a myopic dormouse. 'Tea?' she suggests, like she's not sure whether that's the best option.

'Great. Camilla – one tea, and I'll have a double espresso.'

'Milk and sugar?' asks Camilla.

'Oh, I have changed my mind,' Kathryn says suddenly. 'I'll have the same as you.'

'OK – great. Take a seat.'

Kathryn has the slim hips of a child and the flat stomach of a woman who has not had lunch since 1986. She is wearing a pair of skin-tight jeans, which were clearly designed with the eleven-year-old market in mind, and even then they bag slightly around the buttocks. She is sporting high-heeled black boots and an expensive-looking flowered shirt that's unbuttoned to show off her cleavage. Judging by the plumpness of her embonpoints, it looks like she's picked them out of a packet in Harley Street. She has glossy blonde hair, a glossy pink mouth and eyes that won't meet your gaze.

'So how have you been?' I ask, slipping back behind my desk.

'Not great,' she says.

'Oh?'

'I am having a few family problems,' she mumbles, pulling out a used tissue from her shirt-sleeve.

'Oh dear, I am sorry.'

'It's been going on for a while.' She starts to dab

the end of her small nose with the tissue. I suddenly realize that she's actually crying.

'Oh dear.'

My heart starts to race in panic. I can't bear it when girls start to cry. It makes me feel so embarrassed and useless and uncomfortable. What the hell is she doing? I wish she'd stop. I glance around the office, frantically looking for a box of tissues. We don't normally need tissues in here. We plan weddings. Weddings are happy occasions. I imagine tissues are in plentiful supply at an under-taker's, but we have no call for them. Well, actually, except for the final fitting of the wedding dress. If I hear the mother's coming along I normally have a fistful of Handy Andys for that occasion. But Kathryn's here to choose some tablecloths and glass-ware, which is normally quite a painless business.

I look around for some support. Jez has clearly found a better way of spending his morning and Bernard has miraculously closed his office door. Camilla is edging her way out of the door, mouthing the word 'coffee' at me. So I'm all alone, staring at this weeping woman, wondering what the hell I should do.

'It's my father,' she says, shaking her head. Her shoulders are moving up and down now. She's sobbing. 'He's been having an affair.'

'I am sorry to hear that.'

'With my best friend!'

'Right.'

'How could she?'

'Or he.' Shit, I think, why did I get involved?

'It's not his fault,' she says, staring at me.

'Right. I was just saying. It takes two to, you know . . .'

'Well, don't!' she barks. 'And she's supposed to be my bridesmaid, and if I don't make her my bridesmaid then she is going to know that I know and then my mother will know and then she'll ask my father for a divorce and the whole family will fall apart.' She takes a deep breath. 'And it will all be my fault.'

She looks up at me for a second, scanning my face like I might have all the answers. I smile weakly. What the hell am I supposed to do? She then opens her mouth wide enough for me to see her entire dental history and bawls her head off. Tears run down her cheeks, columns of snot pour from her nose. I am beginning to feel a little sick.

'There, there,' I say somewhat pathetically, patting her hand over the desk. 'I'm sure it will be fine. Just keep quiet about it, have your friend as the bridesmaid and no one will be any the wiser.' Terrible advice, I know, but what's a bloke to do in such a crisis?

'D'you think?' Her voice has all the last-gasp desperation of a drowning man.

'Well, it's a plan.' I shrug.

'Do you think I could do that?'

'I am sure you could.'

'It's my wedding day.' She sniffs.

'And that's all that matters.'

'It's my big day and I shall do what I want.' She looks at me and smiles through her tears. 'You are very kind.'

'Not really.'

'No, you are,' she continues. 'You're a good listener.'

'Not really,' I say again.

'This isn't the first time my father's done this, you know. He had an affair with another one of my friends when we were all still at school . . .'

I sit there for another twenty minutes, listening to her father's entire sexual history. And boy has the man been putting in the hours – three affairs with three of her friends and plenty more besides. She sits and snivels and shares her family secrets, and all I can think of is that we have a WAG coming in this afternoon and I have so many things I should be doing. I wish she would stop. But every time I inhale and try to open her file, she hits me with another revelation. I glance over her shoulder to see Camilla peering through the crack in the door, holding two cups of coffee. She too is waiting for the confessional to end.

'That's terrible,' I say, apropos of nothing. 'Oh, look!' I feign surprise. 'Here is Camilla with our coffees.' Camilla takes this as her cue to make an entrance. Kathryn looks up. Her eyes are puffy and her nose is a little pink.

'Oh, right,' she says, taking the proffered cup of coffee. I am not sure she remembers asking for one.

'So,' I say breezily, rubbing my hands together, trying to change the subject. 'Have you thought about tablecloths?'

'Sorry?' She looks completely confused.

'Tablecloths? Long? Short? With a trim? Without a trim? Sage is very fashionable at the moment.'

'What?' She dabs her pink nose.

'Sage.' I bring out a sample from under the pile of paper and crap I have on my desk. 'Here.'

'Oh,' she says. 'That's nice.'

'Isn't it?' I agree. 'What do you think? With chair covers to match?'

In the last five minutes of the meeting I manage to get Kathryn to make some sort of decisions on the wedding. I was hoping to get through a whole list of things, trying to move her nuptials on to a more ready footing, but sadly her father's persistent bed-hopping put paid to that. We arrange for her to come in again later in the week, as she only has a few months to go and there are certain things that need finalizing before we can press ahead.

'Jesus,' says Camilla as soon as Kathryn closes the door. 'My God, what's her problem?'

'She appears to have quite a few.'

'They always come out from under the carpet just before a wedding,' declares Camilla. 'Weddings and funerals are always full of family secrets. I went to a funeral of a bloke the other day where another family appeared from nowhere. It transpired that the man was a bigamist and had two families, which he commuted between. Neither one knew about the other and they lived about twenty miles apart. He used to buy both his wives the same perfume at Christmas so they smelt the same.'

'The canny bastard.'

'I think the whole thing sounds exhausting,' says Camilla, before answering her ringing telephone. But then Camilla finds paying the many hundreds of parking tickets she picks up a month very tiring as well. It is only when the bailiffs arrive and tow her Mini away that she finally coughs up.

She puts the call through to me. It's a bloke calling up about getting married abroad. We are getting more and more enquiries like this – couples who have no attachment to a place or a country, choosing to get married there. It is partly to do with money. You get much more bang for your buck abroad. The catering is cheaper and the food is normally better. Also the weather is usually much more predictable, which negates the need for hiring a marquee or a great big overpriced venue. You can have the whole thing outside with flowers and lights in the trees and it will cost a fraction of what it would over here. As Bernard puts it, 'Weddings abroad are for those cash-strapped couples with all the ideas and the taste but none of the money to back them up. They wouldn't dream of having less than two hundred to their wedding, so Tuscany is the only place they can go.'

He is also of the opinion that couples marry abroad when they don't want half their guests to come. They feel obliged to invite aunts and uncles but suggest they fly to Nice, which means half the family don't come. He also thinks couples are a bit flashier when they get abroad. They hire drivers and smarter cars, which is all a little more amusingly ironic in Italy than it would be in Hampshire.

There is also the added problem of international weddings. If the girl is from London and the boy is from Canada, where should they get married? In the old days her parents would have paid for the lot in London, but these days the couple choose Cape Town and those they want come, and they are in control.

We have links and contacts in destination spots all over the world. The most popular are Cape Town, the South of France, Italy and Spain. We have done a couple on the beach in Bermuda and a few five-day events in the Bahamas. Bizarrely, we had an enquiry back in February for a wedding in Germany. Bernard got his knickers in a twist about the menu consisting entirely of bratwurst; fortunately we were called a couple of days later to cancel. Bernard was thrilled – I have never seen anyone more pleased at losing 20 per cent.

Anyway, these guys are interested in Ibiza in May, which I gather is one of the most perfect months to get married there. The countryside is still lush, the wild flowers are out, and the sea is just warm enough to swim in. He's a photographer, she works in fashion; it sounds like they are planning quite a party. I have never done a wedding in Ibiza, but I don't let this bother me. I start suggesting house parties and private chefs and a beach party and he seems keen on my pitch. I get them to book in for a meeting next week.

'Of course,' I say before hanging up, 'I don't mind coming out to Hoxton.'

Jez finally slopes his way into the office just as Bernard opens up his double doors.

'Nice of you to pop in,' says Bernard.

'I've been here for ages,' Jez replies. 'Look, here's my jacket.'

'We all know the jacket-on-the-back-of-the-chair trick, pretending you've just popped out. I was using that one before you were even conceived. Anyway, make yourself useful now you're here,' he adds, pulling out a crisp twenty from his crocodile-skin notecase. 'Go and get me some WAG snacks.' Jez looks blank. 'I don't know – some edamame beans – that's what they all live on, don't they?'

'Well actually, I think some nice chocolate biscuits would be best,' suggests Camilla.

'Don't be ridiculous,' says Bernard. 'The woman is getting married in a year. A carbohydrate won't pass her lips until well past "I do".'

'Ice?' I suggest. 'I knew a bride who snacked on ice.' Bernard glares at me. 'At least she had something to crunch on.'

'Have you called Alice yet?' he barks. 'She's getting married on Saturday – she might have a few things to discuss. Anyway, when are you going down to the venue?'

'Thursday afternoon.'

'Cutting it fine, aren't you?'

'I don't think so.'

'Better not,' he says, tapping the side of his nose.

'Give her a call – now! You!' He turns to Jez. 'Why are you still here?'

I get Alice on the phone and she seems delighted to hear from me. Apparently, she was just about to call to make sure that I am coming to her final dress-fitting tomorrow. I suggest maybe she would like to go with just her mother, but she won't hear of it.

'I wouldn't have got this far without you,' she announces. Her voice sounds so excited it is a little contagious. 'This is going to be the greatest week of my entire life and it's all down to you.'

'Don't be silly,' I reply. I love the last-week build-up to a wedding. It's chaos, it's hard work, but the bride is giddy with happiness and if you have planned it all properly, everything should just fall into place. 'See you tomorrow.'

'Love you,' she says, and then hangs up.

I sit back in my chair and look out of the window. I spot Jez wandering up the street looking for snacks for a girl who won't eat, and I think this is going to be a good week. Who wouldn't want this job?

Camilla interrupts my thoughts. 'Call for you,' she says. I nod and she puts it through.

'Hi, it's Clara here,' comes a vaguely familiar, slightly bossy voice.

'Clara?'

'From yesterday?'

'Oh right, of course.'

'Now . . . about the cost of the wedding. Bill and I are planning to buy the flat next door. It's quite expensive, actually. Two million pounds. So we were wondering if you'd mind reducing your price by five hundred.'

'Five hundred pounds?'

'Yes.' She sniffs. 'Do we have a deal?'

Monday p.m.

I found myself agreeing to Clara's request, if only to get her off the phone. There was no point in arguing with her about five hundred pounds, and quite what that had to do with the fact that she was shelling out another two million I have no idea. All I could do was put the phone down on her. Thank God she's having a London wedding and there'll be no need to accommodate the staff, as Lord knows what tightwad hell-hole they would have put us up in.

Anyway Keeley, the footballer's wife-to-be, will be here within the hour and Jez has been instructed to sort out the office. Under Bernard's watchful eye, the old magazines are chucked, any droopy blooms are culled from the crystal vase of peach roses on Camilla's desk, and any loose papers are piled behind the fern, where no one can see them. Fresh bottles of

Evian are put on ice in the silver bucket with tongs in Bernard's office, the cut glasses are polished, and Jez finally reveals his WAG snacks to the office.

'Grapes?' says Bernard.

'Yeah, they're healthy,' shrugs Jez.

'She is not in hospital,' sighs Bernard. 'And I don't even have any scissors in the office.'

'I've got some scissors right here,' says Jez, snapping a yellow plastic pair at Bernard.

'Grape scissors, you moron,' spits Bernard. 'Honestly.' He huffs his way back to his desk. 'You employ monkeys . . .'

The buzzer goes downstairs. Everyone stares at Camilla.

'Come right on up – first floor,' she says. 'Courier,' she replies to the unasked question. Everyone relaxes for a second.

There is nothing like a celebrity wedding to get the office on edge. We have done a few and they have all been exciting and a nightmare at the same time. Firstly, all celebrities, no matter how Kate Winslet bangers-and-mash low-key they say they want their wedding to be, always manage to take over. You become their ultimate sidekick. It's much worse than with a normal bride, because they are used to people running around after them and obeying orders at the click of a finger. They also have so many whims to pander to, so if on Monday you decide you are having a low-key spit-roasted-pork event, it could quite easily become a sit-down dinner for a thousand by Friday. They're weather vanes to fashion. Victoria and David decided to have their wedding dinner à deux with Brooklyn next to them in a matching crib, because that's what Mel B and Jimmy Gulzar had done a few months before at their wedding. There was no top table, just a small table for two and a couple of matching thrones. Not conducive to a rip-roaring riotous night of jolly conversation – but when you spend most of your reception posing for photos for a reputed million-pound *OK!* magazine deal, you can kind of see that the dinner is not that important.

Talk to Nigel about celebrity weddings and he says they bring him out in hives. Firstly, no one eats the food because they are either anorexic, bulimic or on drugs, and secondly, you never actually get to serve dinner properly. At the last celebrity wedding he did the party was kept waiting for two and a half hours while the famous and photogenic couple got snapped. Eventually the guests gave up waiting for their supper and went through to the marquee and started helping themselves. He, of course, was horrified, as he didn't get to announce the dinner.

Interestingly, weddings have become much more fashionable recently in celebrity circles. It used to be a little un-hip to tie the knot, but now everyone from Pink to Peaches Geldoff, and from Liam Gallagher to Katie Holmes and Tom Cruise have got married. Even someone like Cheryl Cole is standing by her vomiting adulterous footballer husband, despite his fateful night out with the lads. Celebs are always sharing how they want the happy ending and are looking for 'the one', which is a far cry from groovier days when ladettes had partners and no one would be seen dead walking up the aisle in a big white dress.

But now big frocks are everywhere. The bigger the better. The smaller the bodice, the bigger the skirt, the more marvellous they are. A girlfriend of mine who works in bridal wear blames Jordan. Actually, everyone who works in the wedding industry blames Jordan for everything. She really embraced the idea of a fairytale wedding and thereby gave the rest of the country carte blanche to do so. Bernard turned down the chance to do her wedding, and I kind of wish he hadn't. Although the company would never have lived it down, it would have been quite fantastic to have been involved in such a ridiculous extravaganza. I can't believe a gay man turned that chance down, but maybe his good-taste radar wouldn't have been able to cope.

Before Jordan, it was considered embarrassing to want a big dress. The pink coach is obviously still embarrassing – Bernard was offered it recently for some wedding we were doing in Hertfordshire and he said he'd rather kill himself than send out any of his brides in that thing. But the dress was revolutionary. The meringue was dead and Jordan resuscitated it and spawned an army of big-frocked imitators. Hers was a Swarovski-decked puffball by Knightsbridge designer Isabell Kristensen, but Hollywood Dreams, a shop which stocks similar huge gowns, has been doing sterling business ever since. Never has the pink-net-and-satin business been so busy.

The door buzzer goes again and Jez practically chucks his cup of coffee down his front in shock.

'Good afternoon, Keeley,' says Camilla down the intercom. 'First floor. We've been expecting you.'

We all hold our breath. Jez wants to see if Keeley's breasts are quite as fabulous close-up as he imagines. I am secretly hoping that she has brought her premiership footballer husband-to-be with her. Camilla wants to check out her outfit, and Bernard just wants to look at her nails.

She knocks gently on the door and all four of us say, 'Come in!' Bernard gives us a group glare and hisses, 'Get the fuck back to work.' It is not quite as under his breath as he hoped. 'Keeley!' he declares a little too loudly by way of compensation. 'Come in, come this way, come to the inner sanctum.'

Keeley is a veritable symphony of honey. She is a little taller than I imagined her to be, not the usual disappointing short arse that every celeb seems to be. And she is beautifully put together, with her honey-coloured hair and her honey-coloured skin and her honey-coloured terry tracksuit. I know it is Juicy Couture, but there is nothing couture about a track-suit. She is wearing honey-coloured Chanel pumps and is sporting a matching handbag. She has a sock-ing great Fox's mint on her left hand, which appears to be the same size as the diamonds in each ear. Hubby-to-be must have bought the whole set when he was down at Hatton Garden – I wonder if he got some sort of stash discount.

'Hiya,' she says to everyone, flashing a bright white smile at each of us in turn, showing us the results of a clearly rather recent bleach. 'Lovely to meet you all.' She turns round. 'And this is my sister, Danni. Keith couldn't come along today, so she's taken his place.'

Looking from Keeley to Danni, the phrase 'the Lord giveth and the Lord taketh away' comes to mind. The poor girl. What must it have been like growing up with the honey goddess as your sister when, let's just say, you were missed out when the pretty stick came tapping?

'Hiya,' says Danni, her shoulders all hunched.

'Hi, Danni,' I say, coming over and shaking her hand. 'Can I get you anything to drink? Tea? Coffee?'

'A Coke,' she replies.

'Absolutely,' I smile. Shit. None of us had thought of those. 'Keeley, would you like the same?'

'No, thanks,' she says with a swing of her honey hair. 'I'd like a green tea.'

Jez is dispatched at speed to get a full-fat Coke and some green teabags, while I follow Bernard and the girls into the inner office.

'You've got a lovely place here,' says Keeley, sitting down on the dark-green leather Chesterfield sofa. 'Ever so chic.' She rests her hands on her knees and crosses one leg over the other. I clock Bernard checking out her nails. They are white tipped but not square. Sadly not quite so 'rich, thick and un-opinionated' as Bernard would have hoped.

'So, ladies, welcome. It's lovely to have you here at Penrose. I can't tell you how excited we are about working with you,' says Bernard, looking at both the girls. 'First things first. Do you have a magazine deal, and if so which one are we dealing with? One of those exclusives where we have to keep everything a secret and spend most of our time running away from the press?' Bernard sounds like he is being amusing and jovial, but in fact he is actually working out how much of a nightmare this wedding is going to be, and if he really wants to be a part of it. Sometimes even when the budget is huge and 20 per cent is really rather juicy, it's just not worth the hassle.

'Well, I'm not really sure at the moment,' Keeley says. 'My agent is talking to a few people.'

'Would you like a piece of advice from an old queen?' he asks.

'Any advice would be welcome,' she smiles.

'Don't.'

'Oh,' she says. This is clearly not what she wants to hear.

'If they haven't offered, then I wouldn't go looking for it.'

Bernard goes on to explain that normally on the announcement of the engagement the big offers come in. Sometimes the magazines will call in favours, saying remember the topless photos of you that we bought to keep off the market? Or the photos of you shagging on a sunbed in Spain that we paid a fortune for so that no one else could run them? Well, now it's payback time. And the control they have over the wedding can be extremely restricting.

The more famous you are, the more control you have. If you don't command many headlines, then you may as well sell your soul down the river as well. Not only can they tell you what to wear, where to stand and what the theme should be, but they issue edicts like 'No black, no red, no cameras, no mobiles.' So your guests feel like they are turning up to more of a theatre opening than a wedding.

They also ask you if you have any famous friends, and if you are short, they invite along their own guests to up the celeb count and make your wedding look more showbiz. Out goes plump cousin Lucy in her mint dress, and in comes some actress from *Emmerdale* you have never met, let alone spotted across a crowded room. Instead of Aunt Edith sitting next to Uncle Fred, suddenly the likes of Bonnie Langford creep into your family snaps. The strangest bridesmaids turn up at the most star-studded events – how else did Martine McCutcheon end up at Liza Minnelli's side when she was marrying David Guest at their seven-figure-deal, ten-page-spread wedding?

And then of course there are the photographs. Who takes them? Are they any good? Can you have picture approval?

'No one wants to end up in the same situation as poor Peter Phillips and Autumn Kelly,' says Bernard.

'I'm sorry?' says Keeley.

'I mean, did he sell the photos without telling the Palace because he needed the money? Who knows?' says Bernard. 'But Peregrine Armstrong-Jones, who organized the wedding, must have known what was going on and should have made it clear.'

'Right,' nods Keeley.

'*Hello!* magazine has never been invited to a private royal reception before and no one knew who they were, because no one was introduced, and there are certain rules and regulations when photographing the royals. You can't snap them eating or drinking. All pictures have to be approved for publication and these weren't. And the magazine was told to leave the major royals alone, so those girls Kate and Chelsea really got it.' He sighs. 'And now, of course, if they bleat about press intrusion they don't have a leg to stand on. It's a mess. So,' he looks across the table at Keeley, 'if you don't have to sell your big day, then don't. If you can't afford the most expensive caterer, then don't have them. If you can't afford to have five hundred guests, have three hundred.'

'It's not about the money,' she interrupts.

'Although it's not to be sniffed at,' he replies. 'In the olden days the most you'd get was £400,000, which is what Emma Noble and James Major managed to pocket for their wedding. Before then it was more like £250,000. But Posh and Becks broke the barrier. They got a million, but that's only because Richard Desmond was convinced the *Sun* had offered the same. Their agent apparently fell off his chair when the call came in. Catherine Zeta and Dinosaur

Douglas got a million as well, and now everyone's hoping for those sort of figures.'

'Wayne and Colleen got £2.5 million,' declares Danni.

'But their wedding set them back just under £5 million,' I say. 'She spent £85,000 on trips to New York for dress fittings.'

'And the dress was £200,000,' adds Bernard. 'And Westlife were another £400,000. Old Colleen was hardly holding back, was she? All those hand-stitched pearls and private jets for all their mates. Even the venue, Villa Durazzo, is a sackful of euros these days.'

'Look, Keith's on over £90,000 a week, so we really don't need the cash,' says Keeley a little sharply. 'I just thought it would be nice.'

'Trust me – it will be nicer without,' smiles Bernard. 'We can always release some photos to the press if you want.'

'For a spread?' She smiles, liking the sound of that.

'Or you could do what Claudia Schiffer did and sell off your honeymoon,' I add. 'Much more sensible. You do a morning in bikini and shorts and then they leave you alone for the rest of the time.'

'Well, if Claudia's done it,' says Danni, 'it must be a good idea.'

'Mmm,' agrees Keeley.

'So, do you have any ideas that you'd like to share first?' says Bernard, taking up his Mont Blanc fountain pen and smoothing down a sheet of paper on his blotting pad.

'We were thinking abroad is nice,' says Keeley.

'Wayne and Colleen Lake Como abroad?' I ask.

'Oh no, not that abroad,' she replies, holding her stomach.

'Posh and Becks abroad?' I say.

'Yeah, David and Victoria.' She nods. 'Like that.'

'So, Luttrellstown Castle, Phoenix Park?' says Bernard, jotting it down. 'Outside Dublin. It's currently closed for a refurb, I'll have to check when it opens again. How many people?'

'How many did David and Victoria have?' asks Danni.

'Actually theirs was quite small,' I say. 'They only had two hundred and fifty.'

'You've got more mates than that!' says Danni, giving her sister a gentle shove.

'I am sure you have,' smiles Bernard. 'But the question is, do you want to entertain them all? How wide do you want to spread the net?'

Bernard is a great believer in only having your nearest and dearest at the wedding. He is always saying if you want to invite the masses then you should have an engagement party and be done with it. But you'd be amazed how many people invite celebrities to their weddings over and above their real friends. Much like everyone who has ever met Elton John asks him to be godfather to their child, so anyone who has even so much as sat next to a celeb always invites them to their wedding. Bugger Uncle Jim if you can have Denise Van Outen turn up for an hour on her way to perform in *Chicago*. One of the worst cases Bernard and I ever witnessed of brown nosing was when we were asked to invite the US ambassador to a wedding. There was something quite odd about the couple anyway. They appeared a little mismatched. He was a rich dumb-arse American and she was some Far Eastern babe with a trick pelvis who exuded ambition. Anyway, she asked us to invite the American ambassador, to which we both agreed and asked for the man's private address. She knew neither his name nor his address, but was insistent that we invite him. The terrible thing was that he came! He arrived with three bodyguards and stalked the room, looking very lost indeed. After about half an hour, he sidled up to me and whispered out of the side of his mouth, 'I am terribly embarrassed. I wonder, could you remind me where I might have met the happy couple?'

'You haven't,' I said.

'What? Neither of them?' he checked.

'Neither of them.'

'Oh,' he said. 'That is even more embarrassing. The only reason why I came was because I thought we might have met and I didn't want to appear rude.'

Needless to say, the poor man didn't stay for dinner. He made his excuses. But the bride looked pleased. She had had a VIP at her wedding, even if it was only for half an hour, and that's exactly what she'd wanted.

Inviting people you don't know never makes for a good party. We organized an amazingly elaborate wedding for a Russian oligarch a few months ago. There were 180 guests and no budget. We were told to spend as much as we wanted. Bernard thought the evening was going to be fabulous; we had enough vodka to drown a small Greek island and enough caviar to sink the *QE2*. We'd gone to town on ice-sculptures – we had swans, dancers, bears everywhere – we'd had the centrepieces made by Aynsley China in Stoke, and there were flowers on the backs of the chairs as well as a £60,000 arch of flowers for the bride and groom to walk through. The Cristal flowed freely, but the conversation was dead in the water. No one knew anyone. They were all the bride's father's business associates, so everyone was too scared to put a foot out of line. It was not so much that they didn't have anything to say, more – am I talking to the right person? The result was a damp squib of a party where no one let their hair down and no one enjoyed themselves. We were packing up by around midnight, having been convinced that we might have to ask the hotel if they'd mind if we went beyond three a.m. What a waste of a million pounds.

Keeley and Danni sit on the sofa drinking their various beverages, staring at the bunch of grapes, while Bernard suggests weekends for the wedding. Keeley has suggested the end of July and Bernard is persuading her otherwise.

'The first week, like Posh and Becks, is fine,' he says. 'The fourth of July was their date.'

'Around then,' nods Keeley. 'Should be good.'

'Great,' says Bernard. 'Any other ideas? Food? What's your favourite dinner? Your favourite meal?'

'Oh, it's got to be Christmas dinner with all the trimmings,' she replies.

I look at Bernard and I can see him wince. What is it with WAGs that they all love 'Christmas dinner with all the trimmings' so much? Maybe it's the only dinner they allow themselves to eat. Every time we do a footballer's wedding, Bernard asks that question and we get the same reply.

We know the guys who did Posh and Becks and apparently she said the same. She wanted roast turkey for 250, which of course is impossible to do in a marquee without the meat tasting like a dried-out old slipper. Eventually they plumped for a spicy tomato soup served in hollowed-out pumpkins, and guinea fowl with a selection of vegetables and dauphinoise potatoes. Apparently, they both took some persuading on the guinea fowl, as neither of them knew what it was. They were very dubious at the tasting and it wasn't until Victoria pronounced it was 'just like chicken' that it got the go-ahead. The desserts were David's favourite sticky toffee pudding for the boys and summer fruits in Laurent Perrier pink champagne jelly for the girls. Except, of course, on the day the boys ate the jelly and the girls tucked into the puddings. My friend said it was as if they hadn't eaten for weeks. He is convinced they had all been so determined to get into their size-zero frocks they hadn't allowed themselves anything sweet for months. He says it's the same at all the celeb weddings he does. The girls all make a beeline for the pudding and chocolate.

Chocolate is a big thing. We haven't had a reception without it. And it is always the brides who are insistent. I guess because for the past six months it's been verboten – the bridal equivalent of crack cocaine. But what always makes me laugh is the moment when you see the bride totally let go. She has agonized over the menu, the dress, the seating plan, the flowers, and then come the day you'll find her in a quiet corner with her flip-flops on underneath her dress, shovelling chocolate down her throat like there's no bloody tomorrow. It's hilarious. I do remember one bride who just wouldn't stop eating on her wedding day. She just sat down at the top table, opened her throat like some foie gras goose and went for it. I queried her demand for seconds of profiteroles and she whispered in my ear, 'Listen, I've got the bloke. All bets are off now. Just get me another plate. I haven't seen solids since bloody March!'

Usually the celeb wedding is not really about the food and wine. They are not likely to serve 1964 Cheval Blanc to their guests because they are unlikely to know about wine. They will know their Cristal from their Veuve Clicquot, but that's about it. It takes an older star like Michael Douglas to have a seven-course dinner at his wedding. One only hopes that Catherine had left some room in her Lacroix dress for New England clam chowder, foie gras and apple pie.

Keeley looks a little disappointed by the idea of Christmas dinner being off the menu, but Bernard consoles her by saying that it is perhaps not the best supper to be serving at the beginning of July.

'It would sit a little heavily in the stomach,' he says. 'And no one wants to dance with a heavy bellyful of food.'

'Yuk,' agrees Keeley. 'I get what you mean.'

'And I presume you want dancing?'

'And a band,' she says. 'How much do you think for Take That?'

'I'm not sure,' says Bernard. 'Elton and Rod are a million each. Robbie is the same. You can get Girls Aloud for about half of that, but I would guess Take That are up there with Elton and Robbie.'

'If not more,' I add.

'They are really very popular at the moment,' says Danni.

'It depends if they want to do it and can fit it in, or if they are on tour,' says Bernard, making a note.

'I love Take That,' says Keeley rather wistfully.

'Don't we all, darling,' says Bernard. 'Let's just see what we can do. Anything else?'

'I'd like a white carriage to take us to and from the church, with four white horses with plumes,' she enthuses.

'Plumes are for funerals and circuses,' says Bernard, without even bothering to look up from his pad.

'I'm sorry?' says Keeley.

'You will be, darling, if you turn up at the church with a horse-drawn carriage with plumes. You'll be a laughing stock.'

'Really?'

'Absolutely. There are rules, and that's one of them.' Bernard smiles, but he is not budging.

'Well.' Keeley pauses. 'Thank God you're here, because the last thing I need is to be laughed at. I want a proper princess wedding, but I also want it to be tasteful.'

'That's great,' agrees Bernard. 'But I am happy for you to have a coach if you want, as it is your big day.'

'That's true,' interrupts Danni, rather over-supportively.

'But have a think about it,' Bernard continues, ignoring her sister. 'Animals.' He shudders like a man who is congenitally allergic to anything with fur. 'They are just another thing that can go wrong. I will never forget this poor bride I know who turned up two hours late for the church. The horse had bolted on the final approach and ditched the driver, and she ended up going round and round in circles on Clapham Common with about ten people trying to catch her. Sometimes you just don't need the stress.'

'I think horses should be avoided altogether. If you arrive in a carriage there's always a danger you won't make it, and if you arrive riding on one horse you end up looking like Lady Godiva,' I say.

'Or worse still, Trudie Styler,' says Bernard, rolling his eyes. 'Lord above! Who can forget her smug mug on the back of a grey horse being led around by Sting as if she was on a donkey on Blackpool beach? What was she thinking? Trailing that £20,000 Versace dress through the Wiltshire countryside on the back of a horse. Purlease!'

'OK then!' laughs Keeley. 'No horses!'

'Seriously, if you want horses, you can have them,' says Bernard, leaning back in his chair and putting his hands in the air, pretending to be defeated.

'No, no, you're all right,' she says.

'Right then.' He smiles. 'We're nearly done, I think, for today. You've said when and where and how many. Anything else?'

'About the flowers . . .' she starts.

'We have a few select florists who we can recommend. They normally work with us on everything and are really charming,' he replies.

'That's good. I was thinking red and white carnations and lots of that stuff . . . what's it called, Danni?' She turns to her sister.

'Baby's breath?' says Danni.

'Gypsophila?' says Bernard.

'The little tiny white flower,' she suggests.

'Gypsophila,' Bernard repeats.

You can almost hear the tumbleweed blow through the office. Bernard looks like he might just come out in a fit of itchy scratchy hives. Baby's breath or gypsophila is his bête noire. He says it belongs on a garage forecourt and even then it's gone up in the world. Personally, I think if it is done in the right way and there is masses of the stuff, then you can get away with it. But to those in the know, it is the most unstylish of flowers and to be avoided at all costs.

'Keeley,' starts Bernard, 'the budget for this wedding is going to be around a million, of which a good £30,000 to £40,000 is going to be spent on flowers. I think the best thing you can do is to meet some of our florists and see what they have to say. Keep an open mind and see where it takes you. You have employed a wedding planner to save you from certain pitfalls. I think you should let us do our job.'

Keeley looks like she is on the verge of tears, the poor girl. But Bernard is really only being cruel to be kind. If Keeley wants her wedding to appear in the press, then it is better for us to help her get it right, so that she doesn't make any huge faux pas, because otherwise she will only garner pages of derision from journalists who will pore over the details with a fine tooth comb.

After all, it took the Beckhams the best part of five years to get over the terrible smirking of the style press over their wedding. The crowns, the thrones, the purple outfits they changed into later are etched on the minds of commentators. Jordan will be forever cast in pink and Peter Andre is the man in the white suit. Planning it right and getting the right look can also reap their own rewards. Colleen Rooney's wedding was surprisingly well done. Fleet Street's pens were poised to have a field day with the flashy vulgar bad taste on show, but they were disappointed. Colleen looked fabulous, the venue was decked out very beautifully – although there were a few too many white roses – and by the end of the day a new style queen was born.

I look across at Keeley, hoping she is not going to be the second weeping woman I am going to have to deal with today, and she puts her head down and composes herself. She's a smart, ambitious girl and she knows this is her big moment, her chance to step out of her husband's shadow. Get it right and style columns and publishing contracts will beckon, and there will be guest appearances aplenty.

'No, you're right,' she says, running her manicured fingers through her blow dry. 'It's your job to know what's right for a wedding, and that's why Keith and I are employing you.'

'Absolutely,' agrees Bernard.

'So Keith and I will have a chat about it all, and I'm due in again on Thursday, right?'

'Correct.'

'And you'll have some things for me to look at then?'

'Absolutely,' he agrees again.

'Excellent,' she says, getting up from the sofa and smoothing down her tracksuit over her perfect backside. 'Well, I look forward to that.' She picks up her honey-coloured padded bag and hooks the gold link chain over her shoulder. 'Come, Danni, I could murder a champagne.'

She sweetly shakes everyone's hand in the office, including Jez, who has been hanging around like a bad smell all afternoon in the hope of seeing her leave. As the door closes behind her, Bernard lets out a loud yawn.

'She's a smart cookie, that girl. Did you see the way she contemplated getting pissed off about those fuckawful flowers?'

'I thought you were a little harsh,' I reply.

'You've got to start as you mean to go on,' he counters. 'I am not putting my name to a wedding that has carnations and baby's breath, no matter how big the budget. I'd never live it down.'

'Your name and reputation are everything,' agrees Camilla, who lost both of hers last year dancing topless to 'It's Raining Men' at the Farm Club in Verbier.

'I have turned a WAG wedding down before,' says Bernard. 'The woman who insisted that the bridesmaids' dresses should match the napkins.'

'Was that after one meeting?' I check.

'She was thick, rich *and* opinionated – a very bad combination,' sighs Bernard. 'Anyone fancy a drink?'

Thankfully we manage to leave Jez and Camilla behind and head up the road for a couple of glasses. Bernard is not the sort of man to enjoy standing around in a pub nursing a large glass of warm beer, crunching nuts out of a bag. He enjoys a coaster for his drinks, and at least a saucer for his snacks. So he is limited to hotel bars or private members' clubs for refreshment. I remember him announcing one spring that he was giving up hotel bars for Lent. It was a pathetic attempt to save money and it only lasted three days. One look inside a pub, one step on the sticky carpet, one smell of the spilt beer and BO aroma and he was sent shivering straight to the Connaught for a restorative flute and some re-assuringly expensive Chinese crackers.

'I think Keeley's wedding will be fun,' he declares, pursing his lips as he takes a sip of bubbles. 'She looks like a nice girl.'

'Jez certainly seems to think so.' I smile, gulping my double vodka and tonic. I'm sure it is my fondness for alcohol that led me to be in this business in the first place. I think Bernard's excuse is that he's obsessed with luxury and he likes bossing people around – this job neatly combines the two.

'But the sister!' He smiles, crossing his legs and placing his hand on his smooth cheek. 'She's a fucking car crash!' Bernard is obviously not allowed to swear in front of his clients and as a result he tries to get as many 'fuck's and 'shit's out of his system when he can. 'Fuck me!' He giggles. 'It's always the family that lets the WAG down in the end. I have to say it is the *only* reason to buy a *Hello!* or *OK!* WAG spread. I'll have a gawp at the dress and then a good close look at the relatives. Derek and I used to spend hours going through the pages. It was a scream!'

Derek used to be Bernard's partner – business and sexual. They set up Penrose together over ten years ago now. But they split up after some God Almighty row about something very small and now Derek runs a rival planners to ours over in Soho. Banks & Co are often pitching against us for clients, much to Bernard's annoyance. Although I think it is a battle he secretly relishes.

'Don't you remember at Posh and Becks' wedding? One of David's relatives was caught popping the silver drinking goblets and tea lights into their Tesco's bag?' continues Bernard.

'No,' I say. 'But I remember hearing that half the guests couldn't work out whether it was a marriage or a piss-take. The Bishop of Cork in an Irish castle with a woodland-scene cake, and Victoria with hair and make-up and lighting all ready for her behind the stage – everyone was very confused.'

'Mmm,' agrees Bernard. 'I think we can do a little better than that, don't you?'

'I bloody hope so,' I reply.

'Let's fucking drink to that,' he replies, draining his champagne glass. He gets up from the table.

'Where are you going?'

'My puppy-training, of course.' He smiles. 'Where I go every Monday night.'

'But Sophie is ten years old!'

'One lives in hope,' says Bernard. 'Anyway, the trainer is a total sex god.'

Tuesday a.m.

Alice has called me six times already this morning and it is not even ten a.m. Our appointment at Annabel Rogers is at ten thirty and she can hardly contain herself. Her wedding is on Saturday and this is the final fitting for the dress. They are cutting it a bit fine, if the truth be told, but Alice's been away at some health farm in Austria in a last-ditch attempt to lose some pounds, and the shop seemed to be quite confident of the fit. Not that Alice needed to lose any more weight. She's been starving herself for months and, I think, is in danger of going over to the other side. Personally I like a girl with some curves. There is nothing attractive about those lollipop actresses with large heads and stick bodies who look like they haven't had a square meal in a decade. I remember a dietician once saying to me, 'Ever wonder why

Victoria Beckham doesn't smile? Because she is bloody starving!'

Anyway, Alice keeps checking I am on my way and that I have got her shoes. For some reason, Anello and Davide had them delivered to our office, after they had been dyed just a shade more cream to match the dress. I had a quick look at them this morning, all wrapped in tissue in their box, and they are beautiful. They have a small heel, which is wisely low, bearing in mind how long the day is and how much she will be standing, socializing or dancing. They are pointed at the front and have a small diamanté buckle on the side. Her feet are a tiny size four and the shoes look so sweet and virginal. It is kind of hard even for someone as well practised as I am not to get emotional as the big day approaches.

It is a beautiful, sunny morning as I walk up a pretty Mayfair side street looking for the Annabel Rogers shop. She is not a designer I am familiar with, she was Alice's call, and I am quite interested to see the place as we might recommend her to other brides.

The bridal dress market is an entire industry in itself. It ranges from the sublime to the monstrous to the rip-off. With prices and ranges to suit all pockets, you can spend as little as £60 on a wedding dress from Asda, or £20,000 on a couture frock from Versace. The first will be 100 per cent polyester with a net underskirt and ruched front; the second white satin with hand-embroidered gold roses. The workmanship is entirely different but they both get the job done.

It is in the middle market where things start getting complicated. Most of the dresses you can buy off the rack in boutiques and department stores these days are made in China. One of the reasons you have to order them so far in advance is because they have to get the orders back and forth. If you go to any of the bridal fairs from Earls Court to Harrogate you can see the same dress design offered up in fifty different places. Obviously these days it is all about cutting costs, which is why most of the wedding dresses you see going down the aisle in the UK are Chinese. They have marginally smaller mark-ups than most other bridal wear, being priced at five times the cost price, in comparison to seven or ten times cost price for British dresses. (The normal fashion retail mark-up is three times cost price.) So a £150 wedding dress made in China will sell at around £800 in the boutique. But should you want any last-minute alterations or beading, the Chinese dress is problematic. If you send the dress back to China then you can't be sure it will be returned in time, and the quality of the beading is not as good as it is here in the UK or Europe. For some that wouldn't matter, but for Alice it was not an option.

From her name and where she is situated, I am presuming that Annabel Rogers is one of the many bridal-wear designers who market themselves as couture but are anything but. There is a certain group of designers, including Vera Wang, Catherine Walker, Philippa Lepley, Vivienne Westwood, Jasper Conran, Ian Stuart and Jenny Packam, who all make dresses that are altered for you, but they are not couture, in the strict sense of the word. Their designs are not unique to you, and there is not a dummy at the back of the shop that has been padded up to your exact measurements. What usually happens is that a dress is designed and made up in various different sizes for the bride to try on. While she is in the dress, they tweak it to fit. So they might put together a size 14 top and a size 12 bottom half, or size 10 skirt and a size 8 bodice, and then it is stitched and re-fitted on the bride. Having said that, there are some designers who are so inflexible they won't actually dress a larger bride. I know of one very well-known designer in particular who won't have anyone larger than a size 10 wearing her clothes, because she doesn't want curvy girls being seen in her dresses. Fortunately, there are others who are more accommodating.

I know that Sarah's dress last Saturday cost £2,500 plus another £500 for alterations. But she shed so many pounds in the last few weeks before the wedding that the beading had to come off, and the dress was altered from the inside at least twice. That's one of the great catches when buying a bridal frock – you need to ask whether alterations are included, as they can add at least another 20 per cent to the price. Then again, I always think bridal wear is expensive anyway. Make anything in white and you may as well put a nought on the end of it. I remember Sarah being quite a canny bride. She refused to pay £75 for some hair clip and bought the same thing in a shop around the corner for £7. She also had a bit of a fight with the designer about a shrug for the church. Her mum was very keen for her to have her arms covered during the service, but Sarah didn't want the thing at all. The shop wanted to charge £200 for the shrug, which Sarah refused to pay, saying she was only going to wear it for forty-five minutes. Eventually they threw it in for free. But it took some negotiating on our part.

And these shops really can make quite a lot of money. One destination bridal place I know in North London gets about forty brides a month coming through their doors, spending anything from £3,000 to £8,000 on a dress, so you can see they are turning over some serious money. They can probably afford to give away a shrug or two.

*   *   *

I spot Alice tumbling out of a taxi at the other end of the street. The strawberry-blonde hair is distinctive even at this distance. She is followed by her mother, who is dressed to come up to town, and who has had her darker copper-coloured hair set nice and hard for the occasion. Alice is wearing jeans and a white shirt, with flat navy shoes, while her mother is sporting a floral wrap-around dress. She shouts and waves down the street as she spots me walking towards her.

'Hi there!' she yells. 'Have you got my shoes?'

'Yes!'

'Do they look OK?'

'Perfect.'

'This is my mum, Louise, by the way,' she says, pointing. Her mother cracks a stiff smile as I approach. Her dark-pink lipstick is bleeding into the lines on her top lip. 'Mum,' Alice continues, 'this is the boy who's done everything! Isn't he fabulous?' She squeezes me very tightly and kisses me on my cheek, just clipping my lips with hers. She is too busy chattering away and opening up her shoebox to notice what she's just done. But I can feel my cheeks flush with the wet warmth of her kiss.

Sometimes it is hard not to fall a tiny bit in love with the bride. For a start, she gets better looking every time you see her. Once the gym classes kick in and she starts having all those treatments that brides

119

think they should have, the transformation can be extraordinary. As I follow Alice's backside into the shop, she looks fantastic. Happiness is also, of course, one of the world's greatest aphrodisiacs. And no one is happier than a bride-to-be. Except Kathryn, of course, who can't stop bloody crying. But apart from her, brides are usually quite upbeat.

No sooner have we crossed the threshold of the shop than a stocking-footed assistant shoots out from behind a clothes rack and tells us to stop right where we are.

'This is a shoes-off shop,' she declares, looking down at our feet. 'No shoes in here at all.'

'Oh,' bristles Louise, 'but we are not just here to browse, we are here to collect.'

'We have a shoes-off policy,' insists the assistant. 'No exceptions. And anyone who wishes to handle the dresses must wear these gloves.' She hands us each a pair of white cotton gloves, the sort that are used to handle the fragile pages of rare books. My big man hands are obviously far too porky for them, so I hand them straight back. This puts the assistant in a spin. She looks from me to the gloves and then the dresses.

'I promise I won't touch anything,' I say. 'Anyway my hands are clean.' I hold them up for inspection.

'But these are wedding dresses!' she exclaims, like that was supposed to mean something.

'Good,' I say.

'Do you have an appointment?'

'No, we thought we'd just come here for fun!' I joke. It falls very flat indeed.

'You must have an appointment,' she reiterates.

'We're here for a final fitting,' says Alice. 'I am Alice Oxford.'

'And is this the groom?' asks the assistant. 'Because it is very bad luck for the groom to see the bride in the dress.'

'No, I'm the planner.'

'Oh, right,' she says, slightly taken aback. 'Come this way, please.' She smiles at me. I am now clearly part of her gang.

At the back of the shop there is a large white room with a long rack down the right-hand wall, packed with dresses covered in plastic. Some look like samples, others look like frocks that are awaiting collection. There's a long white-velvet buttoned chaise longue next to the rack and a couple more large white-velvet armchairs to sit in. Scattered around the room are various white-satin shoes in various sizes and at various heights. Over towards the long sash window is a white table with a large glass vase of white peonies. Just to the left of that is a large triple-view mirror, and above is a shelf of net veils and a small collection of tiaras. The floor is covered in a thick cream carpet and the room is redolent with the cloying smell of rose air freshener.

'I'll just go and tell Andrea that you are here,' says the assistant.

'I thought her name was Annabel?' I say.

'Annabel doesn't design full-time, she oversees from her house in the country.'

'Oh,' says Alice's mother, sounding a little put out.

'When you buy Vera Wang you don't get measured by Vera, now do you? The dresses get sent to the States and back,' she replies. 'It's the same here.'

'So Annabel makes the dresses in the country?' asks Louise.

'She oversees.' The assistant smiles. 'I'll go and tell Andrea you're here.'

Less than a minute later, a large woman with an even larger bosom that almost enters the room ahead of her arrives. She has a tape measure around her neck, a pin cushion strapped to the back of her left wrist and a mouthful of pink and white marshmallows.

'Morning,' she mumbles. 'Sorry – I was just finishing my breakfast. Anyway, how are we all today? How's the bride?'

'Fine,' grins Alice. 'I'm Alice, we met last time. You measured me.'

'Yes, yes,' replies Andrea. 'Has the bride brought

her shoes along? And is she in the right bridal under-wear? Exactly what she will be wearing on the day?'

'Yes, she has and is,' replies Louise, taking up residence on the chaise longue. She puts down her large red handbag and removes her silk scarf from around her neck. She crosses her ankles, placing them to one side, and prepares for the unveiling.

Andrea makes her way along the rack of dresses, checking the names tacked to the front of the plastic.

'Oh,' she says, spotting Alice's name and pulling the covered dress off the rack. 'I see you chose the Maria.'

'Yes,' smiles Alice. 'I thought it looked the nicest.'

'Much the best shape for a girl like you,' says Andrea, looking Alice up and down. 'Either that or maybe the Daphne.'

'The Daphne was great,' agrees Alice. 'But I just didn't fancy the square front.'

'But when the bride has a bosom I often find the Daphne works the best,' asserts Andrea.

'Funnily enough,' says Alice, turning around and starting to strip off, 'you and I discussed it the first time I came in, eight months ago.'

'And has the bride's mother seen the dress yet?'

'No, she has not,' Alice's mother replies.

'And the bride's friend?'

Alice suddenly turns around, devoid of all clothes

except for a rather expensive-looking white lace bra and matching pants, and all I can think of is lucky Richard – the groom-to-be – and it is all I can do to stop my voice from suddenly rising an octave.

'No,' I squeak, and then cough in a more manly fashion. 'I haven't seen the dress yet either.'

Andrea pulls on her white gloves, forcing her rather plump fingers as far as the fabric will stretch; the look has all the glamour of a butcher's window. She removes the transparent plastic cover from the dress with such reverence that all we are missing is the accompaniment of a heavenly choir.

'Would the bride like to step into the dress?' she whispers.

'Oh, sure,' says Alice. 'I can't wait.' She points a bare foot towards the open bodice.

'Careful! Bernadette!' calls Andrea. 'Can you help the bride?'

The fortunately already-gloved assistant leaps up from the corner and helps Alice into the stiff, heavy dress.

'It's just as well we made this a touch smaller,' says Bernadette, pulling the bodice up around Alice's waist. 'You've lost a bit of weight since your last fitting.'

Alice turns to face her reflection while the two women pull at the laces of the inner corset and then work on the row of tiny satin-covered buttons that go all the way down the back of the bodice. There is no quickly slipping in and out of this thing. A good three whole minutes later, when both Andrea and Bernadette have worked up quite a sweat in this airless white room, Alice finally turns around to give us the full effect, her eyes watering slightly with emotion. Her smile is so beguiling, I feel my heart tighten in my chest. She looks stunning.

The dress has a strapless bodice and is an A-line shape that is currently very much in vogue with the Home Counties bride. I think they sell more A-line dresses in Fulham than anything else. If the eighties was the decade of the Princess Diana/Elizabeth Emmanuel meringue dress with huge sleeves, and the nineties the cut-on-the-cross slip dress as designed by Narciso Rodriguez and modelled by Carolyn Bisset at her marriage to John F. Kennedy Junior, then this century has so far favoured the A-line, mainly because it flatters almost every figure, no matter how wide of hip or short of leg the bride happens to be. Not that Alice is either, of course.

Wedding-dress fashion is far more traditional and indeed slow-turning than high-street fashion. Bizarrely, from the twenties right through to the fifties it was far more cutting edge and reflective of its times. But for the last twenty years or so it has become more classic and static. Designers will do a yearly catwalk show, but unlike fashion designers they will also keep their bestsellers in stock from year to year. So Vera Wang will have a new collection, as well as dresses from several seasons back. Unlike a fashionista who would not be seen dead in something that is three or four years old, a bride goes into a boutique and chooses something that suits her figure, irrespective of whether it is old hat or hot off the cat-walk. Although Bernard has noticed – as this is more his department than mine – that high fashion is returning to the bridal market. Top designers traditionally used to finish their Paris and Milan shows with a wedding dress, but this stopped at least a decade ago. However, this tradition seems to be back, with Vivienne Westwood designing bridal dresses and Alexander McQueen producing a feathered wedding dress at the end of his recent show. And with Pronovias, the Spanish designer bridal specialist, recently opening its thousand-square-metre flagship store in the ultimate fashion location – Bond Street – big frocks are proving to be big business.

But some dresses become iconic by accident. The story behind the Emmanuel dress for Lady Diana is a case in point. Apparently the favourite to design the dress at the time was Hardy Amies, who was already sending half the nation's posh girls down the aisle, as well as being the Queen's couturier. But when *Vogue* magazine called up to say they were doing a round robin to lots of designers for an article about wedding dresses, Hardy Amies were caught on the hop. They sent in a few sketches of pretty summer organza dresses for nineteen-year-old country brides, not realizing what they had been asked for. It was neither show-stopping nor appropriate for a royal wedding. And it was Elizabeth and David Emmanuel who clinched the deal from under everyone's noses.

Former students at the Royal College of Art, David and Elizabeth had previously designed for HRH the Duchess of Kent, although Diana had worn one of their outfits (a pale-pink blouse and a pale-pink taffeta skirt) when she was photographed by Lord Snowdon for *Vogue* magazine. They had then gone on to design a black low-cut evening dress for her first official outing as royal fiancée. But when she called them up and asked them to design the actual wedding dress, no one could believe it.

With no brief from Buckingham Palace and no commission, they made it up as they went along. Talk to any bridal designers now and they'll tell you the huge leg o'mutton sleeves were hideous and the Emmanuels' biggest mistake was to use English silk from Lullingstone Silk Farm, the only silk farm in the UK. They should have used French silk rather than the English stuff, which crumpled like toilet paper. But they got away with it. Most people remember the twenty-five-foot train and the embroidery – which was done by Elizabeth Emmanuel and her mother using Carrickmacross lace, which belonged to Queen Mary and formed the 'something old' part of the frock. The whole dress featured ten thousand mother-of-pearl sequins and pearls and went on to put nearly every subsequent bride in a meringue for a decade to come. And all for the nominal cost to Raine Spencer of £1,000.

Alice's dress is three times the price. But she does look fantastic. She turns across the room to look at her mother for approval.

'That's dreadful. I knew I should have come with you in the first place,' announces Louise, after the longest of pauses.

The whole room turns to stare in shock. Can she be looking at the same girl, in the same dress, as we all are?

'You can't wear that!'

Alice's mouth is hanging ajar, her hand covering it. She is too overcome to say anything.

'The bodice is half an inch too long and it looks terrible. It pushes your bottom out of line and your waist looks too long.'

Alice starts to cry. Her shoulders shake and she

does small hiccups along with her sobs. She looks like she might actually throw up.

'Oh, don't worry,' says Andrea, spinning Alice around and squatting down on the floor. 'That is very easily fixed.' Her voice is singsong calm, like she is trying to soothe an overwrought child.

'Is it?' steams Louise. 'Because the wedding is on Saturday and I am not having my daughter walking down the aisle in that monstrosity.'

'As I said, it's easily fixed. There are thirteen buttons going down the back of the bodice. What I'll do is take the skirt off, remove one button, shorten the bodice and sew it all back together. The dress will be ready for pick-up tomorrow.'

'Really?' asks Bernadette, her eyes widening at the amount of work she has just been asked to do in such a short space of time.

'No problem at all,' insists Andrea.

'I really love it,' declares Alice weakly, staring at her tear-stained face in the mirror.

'Well, you would, wouldn't you?' replies Louise. 'You've never been one for the details in life and you've always had rather poor taste. How else do you explain Richard?'

'You've never liked him,' mumbles Alice.

'No, I haven't, and I haven't made a secret of it either. Once you've met the mother,' she says to me, trying to recruit an ally, 'you'll see what I mean. Terrible family.'

'Well,' interrupts Andrea, 'just imagine the dress is fixed, shall we? And shall we have a look at the veil?'

'Mum?' snivels Alice. 'Did you remember?'

'Oh, of course,' says Louise, picking up her large red handbag. 'Now this,' she says with great portent, 'is the family veil. I got married in it. My sister, your aunt, got married in it, as did your cousin Emily. It's been in the family for a whole generation.' Out of the red bag she produces a Sainsbury's bag, and out of that she teases the veil. We all stand and stare, waiting for something along the lines of marvellous. Instead, out flaps a rather moribund ball of yellow net.

'Oh,' says Andrea, wrinkling her short nose. 'It looks like it might need cleaning.'

'Well, that shouldn't be a problem,' declares Louise, still flapping and billowing the musty fusty bit of tea-stained net.

As veils go, it is not the worst I've seen, but it is pretty shit. I don't know what it is about veils, but mothers of the bride often get quite belligerent and insistent that we use the 'family' veil, only for some moth-eaten square of crappy lace to be laid across the desk like it has been sanctified by the Pope.

A few months ago we had one very grand mother

at the initial meeting, who wanted the designer to use the lace off her own dress, which had been designed by the same company thirty years before. She went on and on about 'the lace, the lace, the lace'. In fact, there was such a tra-la-la about the lace that the designer was actually quite excited about using it. He called me a few times to ask if the mother had dropped it off. He was intrigued to see quite how wonderful and fabulous it was. Eventually a jiffy bag arrived and at the bottom there was a shitty little pile of crap that was yellow and gnawed by a mouse. It wasn't a complete piece – it was scraps. Each little bit had to be washed by hand and pieced together. Eventually the poor bloke managed to cobble together some sort of bodice with it, because there was bugger all else he could do with it. But that is typical of the sort of client who thinks they are very, very smart and chic. They are people of significance and substance; they have 'family lace' or a 'family veil'.

But talk to any decent couturier or designer and they will tell you that it is the 'dressing' or stiffness in a veil that makes it come alive. Veils don't like being stored in Sainsbury's bags in the loft, they become flat and floppy and they often don't last more than one wedding. Also something that looked fabulous in the 1930s doesn't necessarily translate to today's dress.

The example of the shower curtain worn by Victoria Lockwood when she got married to Charles Spencer is reason enough to ditch the family-lace look. It clung around her face and drowned her; it was surely not the image that Tomasz Starzewski was after when he designed her £12,000 medieval-style dress with gold lace and fur trim.

'Well, it might take more than a couple of cleans,' says Bernadette, picking the net up gingerly in her white-gloved hand. 'It is really very yellow.'

'I'm sure an overnight soak in some Vanish would do the trick,' insists Louise, the loose skin below her chin beginning to wobble like a pelican eating lunch. 'It has been in my family for a generation,' she says again, flapping it out. 'It's a tradition.'

'I know,' agrees Andrea, coming over and putting a gloved hand on Louise's shoulder. She is clearly used to dealing with such emotions in the claustrophobic confines of the rear of the shop. 'But sometimes these things might be for the best. I am sure you looked beautiful in it.'

'I did,' nods Louise, fondling the veil between her fingers. 'Everyone said so.'

'I know,' agrees Andrea again. 'But the bride's dress won't match the veil, and if you wash it, it will lose all its bounce. So,' she suggests, 'do you have another daughter?'

'Grace.'

'Well, if I were you, I'd give it a good old clean and save it for Grace.' Andrea pats Louise's shoulder.

'Yes,' she replies, shooting her daughter a look. 'I'll save it for someone who might actually appreciate it.'

Alice just stares at her mother, looking slightly defeated. I have to say, I have heard of Bridezilla rearing her monstrous head at about this point in the proceedings, demanding more jewels on the dress, prettier shoes, a different veil. But Mumzilla usually waits until after the final fitting before she starts getting critical. Either that or she has had her moment much earlier on, at the engagement or when it came to drawing up the guest list. Perhaps Saturday is not going to be as easy a ride as I had thought.

'Fortunately,' says Andrea, with the breezy efficiency of a saleswoman sensing a retail opportunity, 'we have a few lovely veils right here the bride can try on if she wishes.'

'Oh, thank you,' gushes Alice. 'Which one do you think would go with the dress?'

'Well, we usually team the Maria with Agnes.'

At this point I just have to get out. There is only so much anthropomorphism of dresses and veils I can cope with. They are not people, they don't have characters, and they don't need to be called girls' names. This is not the first time I have come across names for wedding dresses, but naming the veils sends me over the edge. I say I am just popping outside for a minute and all the women look at me in astonishment, as though I am about to miss out on the best bit.

Outside in the street, I spark up a cigarette, inhale deeply and start to pace up and down. I dial in for my messages on my mobile. There are a couple from Nigel at The Lilac Olive just checking what time he is allowed access to the site on Friday, and another from Steve the marquee man, asking what time I will be down at the venue on Thursday, when they will be striking the marquee. There is also another more intriguing one from Bernard. He sounds excited and wants me to call back ASAP.

'Hello, it's me,' I say when Bernard picks up.

'Guess what?' I can hear he is grinning.

'What?'

'We've got our first gay enquiry,' he beams down the phone.

'What, for a wedding?'

'Well, a blessing,' he corrects. 'You can't have a gay wedding in church, although that vicar at St Bartholomew's did one and ignited the wrath of the Anglican Church, but it is more usually a blessing.'

'So a gay blessing stroke wedding.'

'I know!' He giggles. 'The pink pound, here we come!'

Bernard has been keen to crack the gay-wedding market for a while, ever since he had a chat with a friend in Hatton Garden who said that the pink pound was making a huge difference down there. Heterosexual couples only shell out on one wedding band each, and it is usually something plain and simple in either platinum or gold. Gay couples apparently will buy a couple of rings each. One for the office, where they might have to appear a little more conservative, and another for the weekend, which will be a touch more flamboyant, with diamonds on the outside or even inside the ring. According to Bernard, the metropolitan gay couple have much more disposable income than their hetero counterparts. How else would things like embroidered white-leather jockstraps that sell at £1,800 each be so goddamn popular?

There are a couple of gay-wedding shows that are just beginning to get going. Held in Manchester and Brighton, they are small and staid and not quite reflective of the market, which is usually more high style and high concept than a straight wedding. Only the other day Nigel was telling us about a gay wedding he is catering next year, which is totally themed in black and white with art deco furniture being shipped in to the venue, plus a white and perspex grand piano. The couple have asked for an enormous glitter ball, plenty of caviar and a roaring band. Apparently photos of the desired wedding cake were sent over recently, only to reduce Nigel's pastry chef to tears. The details, the layers, the false layers – it all proved too much for him.

Even my friend Alex, the florist, finds it hard to keep up. He's done a couple of gay weddings recently and he says he had to keep himself very firmly on his toes. So far, he says, they have all really known their stuff. They buy flowers every week, they might have someone come in and do their flowers at home if they are having a party, or even a little intimate dinner. They know their dahlias from their daffs; in short, they know what they are talking about. Lesbians, he confided, are a little different. One of them usually knows what she wants and the other doesn't give a shit. He said that at the only lesbian wedding he's done, one had sublime taste and the other one thought it a huge imposition on her valuable time that she had to think about such irritations and distractions as bloody flowers.

'That's so exciting,' I enthuse back at Bernard. 'Have you booked them in for a meeting?'

'You bet I bloody have,' he says. 'Next week – Thursday. And you're doing it with me.'

'Brilliant.'

'Are you coming back to the office?'

'In about half an hour.'

'Good,' he says. 'We've got appointments,' he adds ominously.

'I know. I'll be there.'

'You'd better be.'

I stub out my cigarette and look around for a bin, but failing to find one, I kick it into the kerb.

Back in the changing room, the atmosphere is improved. Louise is sitting on the chaise longue nursing a cup of tea and a pink wafer biscuit, while Bernadette and Andrea puff out Alice's floor-length veil and adjust her diamond-studded tiara. Even from behind, the effect is breathtaking. She has to be one of the prettiest brides I have ever looked after. She doesn't notice me as I walk in and carries on chatting.

'I had a friend who was chucked at her final dress-fitting while wearing her wedding dress,' she says.

'Really!' exclaims Bernadette, fanning out the bottom of the veil while crouching on the floor. 'What, by mobile phone?'

'Yes.'

'Text or call?' asks Andrea.

'Text.'

'Coward.'

'I agree,' says Alice. 'I mean, if you are going to dump a girl three days before the wedding, then at least have the balls to call.'

'Do people really behave like that?' asks Louise, taking a sip of tea.

'Men do,' says Andrea. 'They're just not good at confrontation, they'd do anything to avoid it. I know a girl who'd been married for fourteen months. She'd had a big £60,000 wedding, which she was still paying off in instalments. Her husband told her he was leaving via text message while she was at work, and when she got home the flat was empty.'

'Take it from me, darling,' says Louise, crunching into her wafer, 'all men are shits. Oh, hello,' she says, turning to look at me. 'I didn't see you there.'

'Oh, hello,' says Alice, turning around. 'What do you think?'

'Stunning,' I say, feeling my cheeks flush slightly. 'Totally stunning.'

'Oh, thank you,' she says, coming towards me. She plants a kiss on my cheek and gives me an expansive hug. She smells so clean and fresh and delicious. 'Not all men are ghastly, Mum.'

Ten minutes later, after Louise Oxford has dropped another £750 on a veil and crystal tiara for her daughter, we prepare to leave the shop. Alice thanks everyone profusely and sweetly kisses the two plump women before hailing a cab with her mother. I'm left to sort out the final arrangements for the dress.

'So, shall I come and collect it tomorrow after the alterations have been made, or will you need another day just to be safe?' I say, consulting my schedule. 'I am not leaving town until Thursday, or Friday at the latest, and we can always get it couriered if you want.'

'It's ready to go now,' says Andrea.

'Sorry – but thirteen buttons down to twelve?'

'There are only twelve on the dress. It fits the bride like a glove. The mother doesn't know what she is talking about it.'

'Oh.'

'I just said it to keep her quiet. It happens all the time.' She shrugs, handing me the large dress in the transparent plastic cover.

'If you are sure,' I say, grabbing hold of the white satin hanger.

'Trust me,' replies Andrea. 'She won't notice a thing.'

As I load the dress into the car, I check the twelve satin buttons going down the back of the bodice, and pray silently that these two wily women are right.

Tuesday p.m.

I arrive back in the office with the wedding dress over one shoulder, a ham sandwich in one hand and a latte in the other. If either of those ladies could see me now they might actually need smelling salts.

'All right?' sniffs Jez. His feet are on the desk and his nose is in a men's glossy magazine that cunningly seems to combine boys' gadgets with girls' tits.

'Fine, thanks.' I plonk the dress down on the desk. I have a momentary panic that some black marker pen might be devoid of a lid, but the dress is covered in plastic – how dirty can it get? 'How's everything here?'

'Fine,' he replies, scratching his bollocks. 'Camilla is having her legs waxed or her pussy, I'm not sure which, and Bernard's gone out to get some lunch from the organic health-food shop around the corner.'

'OK.'

'Oh, and that mad bitch came to see you this morning.' He sits up and pats down a particularly troublesome frond of gelled hair, checking his reflection in his computer screen, which he only ever has on when he's looking for trainers or surf shit on eBay.

'Which one?' I laugh, like I have so many mad bitches chasing me.

'The blonde. Caroline.'

'Oh, her.'

'Apparently you, like, had an appointment?'

'Well, actually we didn't,' I reply. 'She said she might pop in and I made sure I wasn't here. Did she leave a message?'

'The normal one,' nods Jez. I look at him questioningly. He looks back at me as if I am a moron. 'You know – call her?'

'Right,' I say, putting my latte down on my desk and carefully removing the dress and hanging it on the hat stand behind me.

'You should just put the poor bitch out of her misery,' continues Jez. 'You know, tell her you ain't going to fuck her.'

'OK,' I reply, turning on my computer to check my emails. 'And how do you suggest I do that?'

'I don't know – just say, "Listen, I'm not going to shag you, get off my case, you nutter."'

'I suppose that might do it,' I reply, spamming all the offers for Viagra, 'ladies' and watches that persist on coming through on my account.

'Yeah, well,' he replies. 'Don't come crying to me when it all ends in tears.'

'When what ends in tears?' asks Bernard, breezing back into the office carrying a biodegradable bag of something equally ethical. 'Was there a fight at the fitting?'

'Well, actually nearly,' I reply. 'Alice's mother was not terribly cooperative and was a bit of a negative cow.'

'Right,' says Bernard, putting his neatly folded bag down on my desk. 'Well, I suppose it's a jealousy thing. Her daughter is more attractive and happier than her, she has it all ahead of her, while her mother is, let's face it, past it. And what's the father like?'

'I don't know – they're divorced, aren't they?'

'There you go then,' declares Bernard. 'It explains everything. What's the dress like?'

'Nice,' I say. 'The usual A-line job.'

'Oh, thank God for that!' he sighs.

Bernard can't stand it when a bride goes off piste and goes somewhere other than our recommended list of places to get a dress. He had heard of Annabel Rogers but neither of us had seen any of her designs, so he had been a little sweaty about what Alice might choose. He's been burnt before. Having spent a year organizing the most lavish wedding, with stunning flowers and touches aplenty, the bride went and spoilt the whole thing by going to some shocking boutique and buying some hideous dress. She went down the aisle with a throatful of Graff diamonds and the most terribly ill-fitting dress Bernard had ever seen. He had to eat his own fist to stop himself from screaming. Fortunately the groom didn't seem to mind; however, when he complimented his new wife on how stunning she looked as she came down the aisle, half the reception laughed.

Foreign weddings also make Bernard super twitchy, because there is always a danger that the bride might go local and find herself a neighbourhood seamstress who will cover her in frills and bows and little roses. The idea might be terribly sweet in principle, but in practice the result is often horrendous.

'It looks all right,' says Bernard, peering through the plastic.

'We had a veil moment,' I say.

'How shit was it?' He smiles. 'Totally fucking terrible?'

'Like a chewed-up mosquito net.'

'Excellent,' he says, picking up his paper bag and heading over to his office. 'It was ditched, right?' I nod. My phone goes. 'You'd better get that,' he nods. 'And eat up. We've an appointment in fifteen minutes.'

I pick up as he walks off. 'Hello?'

'Hi, it's me – Alice.'

'All OK?'

'I just wanted to thank you for earlier.'

'That's OK.'

'My mother was being a witch. She'd just found out that my father is bringing his girlfriend to the wedding after all.'

'Oh dear.'

'You can say that again. They haven't seen each other since my mother took a pair of scissors to all her clothes about ten years ago. She was taking it rather badly, I think.'

'I can't say that I noticed.'

'You're so diplomatic,' she laughs.

I have learnt in this business that it is generally not a good idea to get too involved in the minutiae of the bride's life. But it is hard to stop yourself, because everyone offloads their problems and shares their confidences with you. But woe betide you if you end up taking sides or passing comment or agreeing with someone, as it will only come back to haunt you. The last thing you want is to be at the centre of a pissed-up family shit storm.

'So you are bringing the dress down with you on Friday?' she asks.

'Absolutely.'

'Do you think it will be ready in time?'

'I shouldn't be surprised if it was finished a little bit sooner than that.'

'Really? Because that's the last thing I need to worry about, when I have Cold War breaking out at home and Richard has suddenly announced that his ex-girlfriend Daisy is coming.'

'Daisy?'

'She is on the list as one of the people who haven't bothered to reply. I mean, how bloody rude is that? I know we didn't put cards in, but you would have thought that she might have put bloody pen to paper. But oh no – that's too tricky for the likes of her.' Her sarcasm is making her cough and splutter down the phone. 'Daisy's too busy with her fabulous life to let us know if she is going to grace us with her skinny-arsed presence!'

'Is she a plus one?' I ask, calling up the guest list on the computer.

'Of course she isn't a bloody plus one!' Alice is steaming down the phone. 'She is after my fucking husband! She is in love with him and has been since they met at university.' She spits the word. 'Like all his friends from university – they are a little bloody gang of mates, with "in" jokes and "in" holidays and "in" parties that they've all been to. All except for me, of course, who has no fucking idea what they are on about half the bloody time.'

'I am sure that's why Richard asked you to marry him, because you weren't part of his old gang. You are new and different and exciting,' I say slightly nervously, not wanting to join in too much.

'It better bloody be,' she replies, sounding a little exhausted by her rant and indeed the whole thing. 'Anyway,' she sighs, 'don't put the bitch anywhere near Richard.'

'Well, he'll be on top table with you. So that shouldn't be a problem.'

'Not even on a next-door table to us. I don't want her in his fucking eye-line!'

'OK.'

'Get it?'

'Loud and clear.'

'Good!' she says and hangs up.

My ear is actually hurting. It is unlike Alice to be rude. She has been rather charming and undemanding so far. We had an initial meeting back in September last year in the pub around the corner from where they live in Paddington. Richard, her fiancé, struck me as rather a nice bloke. He was quiet and a bit on the skinny side, but was very generous with the vodka and tonics as we sat outside tucking into packets of dry-roasted peanuts. The best man, Andrew, came along too, which was a first for me, but apparently they have been mates for years and he only lives around the corner. And I have to say, I liked them all. I have had very little to do with Richard since that day, but I find it hard to believe that this quiet and unassuming chap can inspire such a catfight. Maybe he is a genius in the sack. Or tells brilliant jokes. Or is very kind to puppies. Who the hell knows? I have long since given up trying to work out what women find attractive in men.

Over the years I have seen the oddest couples get together. Stunning girls and dweebish boys. Hugely overweight women and drop-dead-handsome men. Paunchy middle-aged men and nubile young girls. It is obvious why fifty-year-old Derek is attracted to nineteen-year-old catalogue bride Lai Sue. You can see what's in it for both of them. Then there's the rich banker and the young Russian, Natasha, who they both know will take him to the cleaners within the next five years. But there are some people you kind of want to shake and say, "She doesn't love you," or "Are sure about this?" I will never forget the charming fortysomething bride who I think just wanted to get married, perhaps just to say that she had done it. The groom was a handsome thirty-year-old bloke who arrived at the wedding driving a Panda and left in a Porsche. The bride had his name written in the sky by a biplane at a cost of £60,000 and eighteen months later he left her for a younger model. But there was no telling her not to marry the cad. She had a lovely day, I suppose. And she's got some great photos to put on the mantelpiece, next to the pictures of her cat.

I tuck into my rather soft sandwich and tepid cup of coffee. I am not looking forward to this afternoon. Once a month we throw our doors open to all that the wedding industry has to offer, from cake-makers to sugared-almond distributors, just to make sure that we are not missing a trick.

And what an industry it is. It is the most competitive and yet at the same time the most provincial business I have ever come across. It is one of the few markets where shops and businesses that have been in families for generations, and have been handed down from father to son, compete head to head with international bestselling brands. An old friend of mine who used to work at *Brides* magazine told me that Condé Nast used to have an awards ceremony every year, where they invited the great and the good within the industry and handed out a few gongs over dinner and some champagne. It was meant to be a jolly and galvanizing experience, allowing like-minded and similarly interested people to gather and have some fun. In the end they had to stop it because the whole ceremony became so bad-tempered and acrimonious. The only people who were ever happy were those who won. The losers were so sore they would strop off and threaten to withdraw their advertising. One year the publisher was kicked in the shins in the toilet by some furious dress-shop owner who had lost out in the best-bridal-wear category. And the advertising head was sent a voodoo doll of himself imbedded with pins. They all took it so seriously and so personally it wasn't worth the yearly fallout for the magazine.

And the competition isn't just between those in the industry, but between the magazines themselves. *Brides* is the market leader, followed by *Wedding*, *You and Your Wedding* and *Wedding Day*, and it is a crowded market, with ever more esoteric titles such as *Wedding Cakes* or *Wedding Flowers* launching all the time. In the US, the bridal magazine market has expanded 98 per cent in the last five years, making it the most rapidly expanding glossy market. Also, somewhat surprisingly, the May edition of US *Brides* magazine is only surpassed in thickness by Italian *Vogue*, such is the scrum of companies keen to advertise between its pages. 'The book' is quite literally as thick as a book, and a bestselling airport bonkbuster to boot. With such a limited market and only one ideas pool to fish in, plagiarism is rife. A recent article in the UK *Press Gazette* compared the front cover of two of the leading bridal mags in the UK, pointing out that one had used the same model in the same dress with the same hair and make-up that the other mag had used three months previously. So you can imagine the competition between the editors is stiff, and the atmosphere is pretty frosty.

Bernard and I were at the Harrogate bridal fair last year, slurping glasses of free champagne and dipping foreign objects into the nearby chocolate fountain, when we witnessed a classic hair-flick, handbag moment between two editors. The more powerful of the two was walking towards the champagne bar to help herself to a well-deserved flute, when the other came flouncing and pouting towards her. The flouncing one leant over and very loudly whispered, 'Watch out!' into the ear of the other. The powerful one looked so confused she nearly dropped her rather expensive handbag. Then the flouncing one tapped the side of her nose in a 'if you know what for' manner, and flounced off. At which point Bernard could control himself no more and shrieked with laughter.

The powerful one looked as us both. 'Did you see

that?' she asked. 'That was about as scary as being threatened by H from Steps.'

All Bernard could do was shake his head gently from side to side and wipe away the tears. Then again, Bernard tends to get slightly hysterical at the Harrogate bridal fair – actually at any bridal fair. We used to go to them all – the Designer Wedding Show in February and October, and the National Wedding Show in February and September. But the National used to bring him out in hives. It was the explosion of silver-bell motifs, princess-cut tiaras and wedding packages to Ayia Napa that brought on the scratching and itching and self-doubt – how could a man of his taste and aesthetic values be involved in such a low-rent industry? So now he limits himself, and indeed me, to the Designer Wedding Show, which is pretty frocks and super cakes, and Harrogate, where the big manufacturers show their wares.

The biggest show in Europe, Harrogate has something like 150 exhibitors and they show over 200 collections. Bernard and I usually spend most of our time propping up the bar in the Hotel du Vin, sinking bottles of wine and watching the grumpy florid-faced manufacturers argue over the price of duchess satin and the mark-up on Swarovski crystal. I think he secretly looks forward to it every year.

Which is more than I can say for this afternoon.

This is something he hates. We have the owners of a bridal-wear boutique coming down from Manchester, plus a cake-maker from Norfolk. It is Bernard's idea that during these hard times we should put our feelers out a little more and try and get our name out and about to generate a wide customer base and not be so south-centric. So the first meeting is a couple from Big Day Frocks just outside Manchester.

'I think your next meet is here,' announces Camilla, coming through the door with pink shins, smelling of expensive salon creams.

'Really?' I ask, shovelling in the last of my sorry sandwich.

'Well, I presumed it was them. They were having an argument over which bell to press just outside the door.'

'Why didn't you invite them in?'

'I wasn't sure,' she says, parking her backside back behind her desk, just as the buzzer goes. 'There!' she declares, like she was right all along.

Not so fresh off the train, Lee and Patsy come blinking into the office. She is short, rotund and in her fifties, with immaculate hard maroon-coloured hair and matching maroon-lined lips. He is also short, rotund and in his fifties, but with no hair and a thick grey moustache that looks a little sticky along the edge, as if he keeps it as some sort of flavour-savouring device should he get nostalgic for his lunch.

'We're here to see Bernard,' says Lee.

'He knows we are coming,' adds Patsy, folding her arms underneath her ample bosom and raising her painted eyebrows.

'Of course I do! Please come through,' says Bernard, opening his double doors. 'Thank you for coming all this way. Would you like tea? Coffee? Something cooler?'

Pasty pulls at the neck of her green knee-length dress, and hoiks up a thick white bra strap. 'I'd love a cool drink,' she says. 'It's hot in London,' she adds, like she has come to a different country rather than just spent a few hours on the train.

'Still or fizzy water?' asks Bernard.

'A glass of still water would be great,' she huffs as she flops down on Bernard's green leather sofa.

'The same,' nods Lee, also doing the same.

'Hello again,' I say, coming in to shake their hands. 'I am the one who's been speaking to you on the phone.'

'All right?' nods Lee.

'Yes thanks,' I smile.

Bernard serves the drinks and then immediately launches into his speech about who we are and what we do. He is at his most charming and beguiling and flatters them at every possible moment. Surprisingly for such a roaring snob, Bernard is the first person to sweep his class prejudices aside when it comes to business. Well, these guys have been at the forefront of the Manchester bridal market for the last twenty-five years. Rumour has it that Patsy actually came into the shop to marry someone else, but when Lee came over to measure her for her dress, she ditched the bloke and married him instead. They are also famous for their sales pitch, or perhaps 'style' is the word. Their shop is on a main street but you have to go up an escalator to get in there. There used to be a red cord across the top of the escalator with a liveried doorman on rope duty. No sooner had mother and daughter crossed the threshold than the rope would be closed behind them and either Lee or Patsy would leap out and ask, 'Now when is Modom's big day?'

It was rare that anyone left without making a purchase. As a result, they have one of the most successful shops in the North.

'We've actually been diversifying of late,' shares Patsy with a purse of her lips.

'Oh, right?' says Bernard, crossing his legs to reveal a knee-length candy-pink sock.

'It was Patsy's idea to provide more of a full service. So along with the white Roller and a white taxi cab, we now do his and hers Botox and fillers out the back,' says Lee.

'I took myself on a course,' smiles Patsy. 'I wanted to do the veneers as well, but you have to be a qualified dentist for those, which is a shame because I saw a bride the other day who had had the lot done as part of a package. It was just over a thousand pounds for the lot, which I thought was very reasonable.'

'Very reasonable,' agrees Lee. 'She's done me – can you tell?' Lee moves his face from left to right for us to admire. 'Can you? Can you?' Now he mentions it, I can see that one of his eyebrows is a little higher than the other, and he does have the expression of a man who has just sat on a drawing pin.

'Very good,' says Bernard.

'You should let her have a go on that big frown of yours,' suggests Lee, pointing to the Grand Canyon furrows between Bernard's eyebrows.

'Yes,' smiles Bernard, a little tightly.

'Oh, I'd have those gone in no time,' asserts Patsy.

'Excellent,' says Bernard, trying to shift the subject on. 'And I understand that you have also dropped your appointments system in the shop?'

'Not dropped it exactly,' replies Patsy. 'We're still doing appointments and fittings in the afternoon, but the morning is open to anyone who wants to come in.'

'Don't you get a lot of time-wasters?' I ask.

'Not really,' she shrugs. 'You have to be nice to the Muriel market.'

'Muriel market?' I quiz.

'You know, the girls who aren't engaged yet, but who go shopping for dresses anyway,' says Lee.

'It happens all the time,' continues Patsy, looking at my surprised face. 'If I had a fiver for every dress that I've sold to a girl who is not even engaged, I'd be a rich woman. Sorry,' she adds, taking in her husband's irritated look, 'an even richer woman! They are always coming in to have a look, and you ask them when their big day is and they say their bloke hasn't asked yet, but they know he will, so they are just taking a look at what's out there.'

'But they are not engaged?' I check.

'Not even close. But it doesn't stop them from buying a dress and putting it in the wardrobe for when he does. You should see the shop when we have a sale. Clearing out old stock, we discount quite heavily sometimes, and girls come in and buy their dream dress, and keep it in the wardrobe until he pops the question. There are loads of them at the bridal fairs. We did the Asian bride fair in Manchester recently and it was exactly the same.'

'Although they kept on asking if any of our dresses came in colour or if we had any saris,' corrects Lee.

'Yeah,' says Patsy. 'Who'd have thought that? But we do have a new bestseller dress,' she adds excitedly, before standing up to demonstrate. 'It has Velcro all around the bottom, so you can have a long dress and then rip—' She pulls at an imaginary skirt in a manner reminiscent of Bucks Fizz at the Eurovison Song Contest back in the eighties. 'And there you have a dress ready for dancing. The modern bride wants to be comfortable, doesn't she?'

'She does,' agrees Bernard.

'I mean, you see this?' says Patsy, holding up her right hand and waving her little finger at both Bernard and me. 'I call it my crooked little finger. And you won't believe how I got this.'

'Try me,' says Bernard.

'If I had a penny for every bride who during a dress fitting says something like, "Jesus, my G-string is really irritating me," I tell you. So I get down there and I hoik it out of the crack with my finger like this.' She shows us the hooked little finger again. 'And I say, "Don't fart while I am down there, love!" I tell you,' she laughs. 'The relief on their faces! But look at my finger.'

I glance across at Bernard and for the first time in my life I see that he is genuinely lost for words. He is staring at the crooked finger, trying to work out what to say.

'Your customer service is unsurpassed,' he says eventually. 'No wonder you have one of the most popular shops in the North.'

'Well, I'm glad you think so,' smiles Patsy, bristling with pride on the sofa. 'We like to think that we care.'

'Well, thank you very much for coming all this way to see us,' says Bernard, getting up out of his seat.

'Is that it?' asks Lee.

'This was just a getting-to-know-you chat,' replies Bernard. 'So that when asked, we can recommend each other.'

'Oh, excellent,' says Lee. 'We will be sure to send some of our brides your way if they need a planner.'

'Great,' I smile.

'Not that we get much call for it,' adds Patsy. She leans over and snaps at the bunch of grapes left over from the WAG meeting yesterday. 'But you know,' she adds, chewing and spitting out the pips and bits and leaving them in a small saliva-covered pile on Bernard's mahogany desk. He twitches as he watches her. 'If we can, we'll send a few people your way. You scratch our back—'

'And we'll pull out your G-string!' hoots Lee.

How Bernard laughs as he ushers the pair out of the door! As soon as they've gone he rushes back to his desk, lets off a small shriek and removes the pips with a napkin.

'If I suggest another meeting like that again, just shoot me and put me out of my misery!' he says, before hurling the napkin and its half-eaten pip 'n' skin contents straight into the bin.

But before Bernard has too long to dwell on his encounter with Lee and Patsy, the second appointment arrives. She knocks on the office door and walks in, lugging a black portfolio. In her early thirties with a crown of blonde curls, Chrissie is rake thin, with alabaster skin, and smells of baking. Her eyes are sky blue and fringed with fluffy ginger eyelashes.

'I'm here to see Bernard,' she mumbles to Camilla in a soft, sugary voice.

'Come straight on through,' says Bernard, opening his double doors again. 'Tea? Coffee?'

'I'd love a cup of lapsang, if you have any,' she says.

The relief on Bernard's face is palpable. A woman who likes lapsang souchong tea is most definitely someone he can do business with, even if she does make cakes. Bernard has a hatred of wedding cakes, as indeed do I. They are the biggest rip-off in the industry and serve no real purpose other than being something to cut at a particular moment. I think Posh and Becks had the right idea. Their woodland-scene cake with models of the two of them as a naked Adam and Eve on the top was mainly made of polystyrene. In fact, there was only one place where the cake could be cut (between the green apples), using the ceremonial sword inscribed with the message from Brooklyn. It didn't matter that most of it was inedible, as most wedding cakes are inedible. They are made far too far in advance to be nice to eat. In the old days, when wedding cakes were fruit cakes and the top layer was traditionally kept for the christening of the first child, and pieces were sent in the post to absent relatives to sample or spinster aunts to put under their pillows in the hope that one day their handsome prince would come, it didn't matter that the cake was ten days or a couple of weeks old. In fact, it improved with age. But these days the only person who wants a fruit cake is Granny; the fashion is for a chocolate cake or lemon sponge, or even a pile of macaroons. The cake has turned into a pudding. If you talk to Nigel he'll say if you want to eat the cake, let the caterers make it; if you just want to cut the cake, then let a professional cake-maker do the job. Chefs as a rule don't like serving things they haven't made, so to prevent any argument it is better to let the caterers make the cake – and a whole lot cheaper.

If the caterer makes the wedding cake, the mark-up is around 15 per cent. If you get a cake-maker to do it, there is no telling what they'll charge. Bernard and I have regularly taken delivery of £2,000–£3,000 cakes. The most expensive and spectacular one we have ever seen was a £20,000 cake for a reception of 1,200 people. I think that took a couple of talented pastry chefs a week to put together. But with your average £2,000 cake, if you think that labour and costs for making and icing it come to about £175, that is some mark-up. We had a £1,000 cake the other day, where the couple were charged an extra £180 for the real roses they put on the top. And half the companies don't even make the actual sponge. They take delivery of it, and then simply ice the cake in-house. They like a nice hard cake to cover in soft rolled icing, hence them leaving it to stand for a couple of days.

'So,' says Bernard as he and Chrissie flick through her portfolio of iced cakes. 'Which other cake companies do you admire?'

'The Little Venice Cake Company,' she says.

'Expensive but good,' nods Bernard.

'Peggy Porschen.'

'Stella McCartney's wedding-cake-maker,' I say.

'And I quite like Choccywoccydoodah,' she laughs. 'Mainly for indulgence.'

'Who doesn't?' declares Bernard, his mouth watering slightly as he flicks through Chrissie's book.

She has cakes covered in rose petals, cakes designed to look like presents, cakes decorated with tiny lily-of-the-valley flowers. They come in all colours, including red and orange, and all sizes, from the cupcake to a seven-tiered one right at the back. While Bernard leafs through, Chrissie explains that she used to be the pastry chef at one of the top London hotels, but eventually got obsessed with afternoon-tea cakes. She made a couple of wedding cakes for her friends and has since moved to Norfolk to start up on her own.

'You have to have a very cold, steady hand,' she says. 'Hot hands are the death of the pastry chef. Thank God I have always suffered from poor circulation.'

'Can you do the pyramid of profiteroles?' asks Bernard.

'Easily,' she replies. 'But I think if you are going to use me, it should be just as a cake-maker, otherwise the chef might get a little pissed off.'

Chrissie leaves amid much handshaking and exchanging of cards. She has put a pile of well-presented booklets detailing her work on Bernard's desk and says that she will be in touch.

'Now you see,' smiles Bernard, awfully pleased with himself, 'that went well. That's the reason why we meet new people and spread our wings. She was nice – and talented.'

'And not too expensive,' I add.

'I know! That seven-layered job was only a couple of grand,' agrees Bernard. 'I think we will definitely use her.'

Much as I would like to stand around and talk about cakes, we are interrupted by Camilla telling me my next meeting has just buzzed up. I grab my coat and head down the stairs to suggest we have a nice cold drink out in the sunshine. Charlotte and Angus are delighted by my idea, and five minutes later I am sitting in the garden of a nearby gastropub with an ashtray of olives and a large glass of white wine.

'So how did you propose?' I ask Angus, a rather square-shouldered bloke in an England rugby shirt.

'Well, mate,' he grins. 'You'll enjoy this. I walked in with the ring on the end of my cock!'

'You must have a very thin penis,' I suggest.

'No – it was a fucking big ring!' He roars with laughter as he pours himself another glass of wine.

I watch Charlotte giggle away next to him, but I am willing to bet this was not quite the proposal she was after.

'Fucking big,' repeats Angus, laughing at his own

hilarity one more time. 'You should have seen the look on her face. She was so shocked.'

'I was,' smiles Charlotte, flicking her long brown hair. When she smiles she tries so hard her nose and chin almost meet in the middle.

'But she said yes. I couldn't bloody believe it.' Angus pauses for a large swig of wine and a deep breath. 'I tell you, what I am really looking forward to is the stag week.'

'Week?' I ask.

'Yeah, you've got to have a week these days,' he declares. 'Everyone's doing weeks in Cuba, five days in Las Vegas – Wayne Rooney went to Ibiza for a week in a villa with his mates.'

Angus is right that the days of a night on the town, with dinner, and a crotch in your face in Stringfellows, are over. These days you have to take out an extra mortgage and resign from your job to prove total stag commitment. Everyone also wants to go abroad. Post-communist cities like Budapest, Bucharest, Prague, Vilnius and Tallinn are some of the most popular venues, where the beer is as cheap and plentiful as the girls. I'm convinced it is because couples are getting married that bit older so they have more money, and the blokes have a greater desire to pretend they are footloose and fancy free instead of married, living with their girlfriend, or looking after young children. I suppose if you've been married for a while, a five-day shag fest somewhere cold with terrible food and even worse service might be tempting.

'Do you organize stags?' he asks.

'No, but we can recommend some companies,' I suggest. These companies will in turn be very nice to us, of course.

'I tell you,' continues Angus, 'my mate had the best stag. They were in Prague, right? And he got arrested on the street by these policemen, yeah? And he wasn't wearing his coat, he was wearing the best man's coat, which had two grams of Charlie in the pocket. He tried to tell the police that they weren't his drugs, but they said they'd take him down the police station anyway. So there he was, in the back of the van, and they said, "Let's not take him to the police station, let's take him to the woods." So my mate's in the back of the van, crying and saying his prayers. The police got their guns out as they arrived in the middle of nowhere and the groom was like pissing himself. And as they pulled him out of the van all the other stags were there and they shouted, "Surprise!" It was a stag arrest!'

'A what?'

'A stag arrest,' he says, taking another swig. 'Bloody funny, if you ask me.'

'Yes,' I say, looking across at Charlotte, who is quietly sipping her drink. Her face is devoid of expression.

'Oh, and my other mate, he went to Las Vegas. Now that sounds brilliant. They had this night when they had two hookers straddle two chairs while the groom shagged them with a dildo on his head!' Angus's whole body rocks with laughter. 'It's the Bill Clinton excuse, isn't it? I mean, he technically didn't have sex, now did he?' He grabs my knee and squeezes it. 'Don't you agree?'

'It certainly brings a whole new meaning to the phrase "dickhead",' I say, taking a large gulp of wine.

There are some engagements that are destined never to make it to the altar, and this is one of them.

'Anyone for an olive?' I smile, offering round the ashtray.

Wednesday a.m.

I crawl into the office with one of those cracking white-wine hangovers that can only be solved by a bacon sandwich and a vat of coffee. Angus and Charlotte would not let me go last night. The more I edged towards the door, the more bottles of white wine Angus insisted on ordering. It was about nine thirty before I managed to extricate myself from the pub garden, and considering that I had been there since about five thirty, it was quite some going. We drank at least a bottle of wine each and by the end none of us were making sense. Not that Charlotte spoke very much anyway, and I barely got a word in either. She and I were essentially an audience for Angus's stories. A sounding board with a human face. He would honestly have been happy with anyone. It just so happens that last night the two of us drew the short straw.

It was like listening to a monologue at the local rugby club dinner. I have never heard more stories involving alcohol, sex and vomit since Ashley Cole's night out on the tiles. Everyone he mentioned seemed to end up either naked on the floor of some public urinal, naked in the street, or naked in a skip in the street. Although I know in my heart of hearts that they will never make it to the altar, I just wish he'd put both Charlotte and me out of our misery by saying so. She needs to find a man who doesn't want to sink pint after pint while being lap-danced by three eastern European girls in a nightclub. And I need to be able to cross them off our client list, as the idea of organizing a wedding for him and his closest pals fills me with total dread. I am not sure if the hotel, the marquee or indeed I would survive.

I sit and chew on my bacon sandwich with the window wide open, as there's nothing that annoys Bernard more than the sweet smell of fried food in the office. He says it creates a bad impression. I think it's really because it makes his stomach growl with hunger. Thankfully, he is a little late this morning, as he's gone to collect Alice and Richard's wedding cake from a bespoke cake-maker in North London. I hope he has cleaned out his car as the back seat is always awash with ginger-and-white dog hairs courtesy of his King Charles spaniel, Sophie. In the early years

Sophie was allowed in the office; she'd sit underneath Bernard's desk and he'd hand-feed her dog chocs all day long. Sadly, in her dotage, Sophie's flatulence has become so frequent and so unpleasant that she's been banished to the car. It was putting the clients off and Bernard really had to do something. Woe betide anyone who accepts a lift from Bernard at the end of the day, after Sophie's been relaxing in the car for a full fruity eight hours. Sometimes the smell really does make your eyes water.

The office is quiet for the moment. Jez has been sent south of the river to pick up some Chinese lanterns for Saturday. They are quite the thing at the moment. You write people's names on them and light them and watch them float up into the sky. They are very romantic and unusually cheap, so they're increasingly popular at our weddings. I usually suggest them when there's a lull in the conversation. It's a bit of a game I play with myself, to see how long the bride thinks about it before saying what a great idea. I think the longest is about five seconds. It always gets them going. Tea lights, fairy lights, Chinese lanterns – brides are like magpies, anything that is shiny or twinkly goes down a treat.

So Camilla and I are holding the fort. Well, more precisely, I am. Camilla is surfing net-a-porter.com while talking to a girlfriend, who I presume is doing the same thing, as they are discussing which outfits to buy for the party of some bloke called 'Weed'. What his claim to fame and subsequent hilarious moniker is all about is anyone's guess.

My phone goes. 'Hello, Penrose,' I say, taking a final sip of my coffee.

'You weren't in the office yesterday,' says the by now extremely familiar voice of Caroline.

'I was at a dress-fitting.'

'Not for you, I hope!' She laughs uproariously.

'No.'

'A bride?'

'A bride.'

'Did she look pretty?'

'Very.'

There's a pause. 'Good for her,' replies Caroline. 'Anyway, I am coming your way later today. I thought I might pop in and discuss the party.'

'What party?'

'My birthday party, of course. I shall be thirty-three. That's definitely worth celebrating.'

And before I can suggest that it might not be convenient for me, she's hung up. Goddamn it – what am I going to do about this woman?

'I've got Alice on line one,' says Camilla.

'Put her through,' I say. 'Hi.'

'Hi,' she replies briskly.

'What's wrong?'

'It's the placements,' she says. 'They arrived last night at the house and they're terrible. The writing is horrible, the yellow card won't go with the flowers and the tablecloths will clash.'

'Oh, I am sorry, I—'

'Yes, well, sorry is not really good enough,' she interrupts. 'I have spoken to Bernard already and he has asked one of your top calligraphers to come in and I want you to supervise. I want the whole lot redone ASAP.'

She goes on to explain in exact detail how they should be done and where she wants everyone to sit. Such are the tensions, hatreds and feuds within her and the groom's extended families, she and Richard are going to be more like some UN buffer zone than the happy couple. Honestly, the closer this wedding gets, the more anxious I am becoming. I can sense there's going to be trouble. Richard is a northern boy made good and Alice is a southern middle-class girl whose parents paid through the nose for her education. There is certainly going to be a culture clash. I just had no idea that there were inter-family problems as well.

I have seen some tensions in my time, but there is nothing that divides a wedding like class. Weirdly, the really very posh don't seem to mind or notice at all. If the bride's father turns up in a brown suit, or her mother is sporting a pair of white plastic shoes, they don't really care. Everything is simply 'marvellous', 'jolly' or 'rharely good fun'. It is the middle-class parents who find a working-class element to a party difficult to handle. I remember one wedding we did where a posh girl was marrying a not-so-posh boy, and the father had worked himself up into such a fury that he had a heart attack as his daughter came down the aisle. The ambulance was called and the father was taken away. There was a terrible moment as they turned off the siren as they left the churchyard. The man had died – there was no longer any point in hurrying.

'It gives a whole new meaning to the words "over my dead body",' said Bernard, as the hysterical bride and rather shocked groom left the church. Despite her father keeling over, they did marry a few months later and I hear are still together.

But death at a wedding is not uncommon. We had a granny pass away a few months back in one of the pews. No one noticed until the church was virtually empty, and fortunately even then nearly everyone thought she was having an afternoon snooze. Bernard sorted out the removal of the body, while I had to explain away her absence from the group shots. We did have another granny keel over last year, but it turned out that she was just paralytic with alcohol and could no longer stand. She was carted away by a couple of burly ushers to sleep it off.

Alcohol obviously plays a huge part in inciting incidents, although nothing can really explain or justify the father of the bride stabbing the groom in the leg with his skean dhu at a Scottish wedding we did back in September. Fortunately the two of them had had too much whisky to be able to inflict real pain on each other – most of the punches missed as they flailed around the dance-floor. Bernard and I never quite got to the bottom of who started it. It seemed to flare up out of nothing and for some reason the DJ kept playing 'The Eye Of The Tiger' throughout the fight, which somehow rendered it all the more comic. But when the ceremonial dagger came out, Bernard almost squealed with delight. For a fastidious gay man who can't abide the touch of a paper napkin, his fondness for violence is bizarre. The father lunged and got the groom in the leg. Bernard couldn't stop himself from applauding. Sadly, the groom was too drunk to get his sword out of his scabbard in order for there to be a proper fight. But the poor bride screamed as her dress got spattered in blood. However, it clearly wasn't a serious argument because five minutes later the two of them were found slapping each other's backs at the bar. It was all forgiven and resolved over another dram.

Bernard's favourite fight he's witnessed, which was sadly before I joined him, happened at a class-divide wedding. A posh bloke was marrying a girl from the other side of the tracks and the wedding was very much split into two camps – those who drank port with their cheese and those who drank lemonade with their port. One half of the wedding was gritting their teeth and getting through it, thankful that they would never see the other half again, while the others were necking as much free alcohol as possible.

The bride and groom were leaving the reception in an open-topped Rolls Royce, and the wedding party was following them down the drive, when one of the groom's relatives offered to push the bride's great-aunt along in her wheelchair. He managed it fine until he reached a cattle grid, where he lost control of the wheelchair and both great-aunt and the chair ended up in a ditch. Someone shouted, 'They've put Auntie in the ditch!' To which someone else added, 'Let's get the bastards!' The bride and groom drove off, waving goodbye to their party, as all hell broke loose. Bernard always loves to add that four people ended up in hospital.

But more often than not, the tension is not so

overt. It normally manifests itself with bitching and little acerbic asides: the bride's dress is cheap; the bride's mother is wearing pistachio; the groom is wearing a white suit. One of Bernard's little tricks is that he always tries to find out what the groom is wearing. He is always saying, what is the point of the bride spending £3,000 on a dress if the groom turns up in a pink suit? The whole effect is ruined. I remember last summer we did a wedding where all the ushers turned up in shiny suits and ten-inch-wide ties. Bernard spent the whole ceremony chain-smoking in the graveyard because he couldn't bear to look.

However, there is nothing that sends Bernard into the stratosphere more than people being invited to the later part of the celebrations, like a second wave of also-ran guests who weren't good enough for the first half. 'It makes the guests feel bad about themselves,' he says. 'And you don't invite people to feel bad. Also what are they supposed to do until ten o'clock? Sit at home and wait until it is time to go out? It is not a good dynamic for a party.' And the thing that sends Bernard kicking and screaming to hell and back is a pay bar. 'Britney Spears had one at her wedding,' he always says. 'That is all you need to know. Don't invite people and ask them to pay. It is the rudest thing you can do. Just don't have so many people.' But the rudest thing either of us have ever witnessed was a father who was supplying wine for the wedding, who decided he was going to charge his guests at a pay bar after dinner in order to recoup the cost of the wine *and* food. Bernard was so shocked that he didn't know what to do with the information. Needless to say, after a couple of weeks of working on the wedding we decided to pass it on to someone else.

Sadly, it is a little late to be able to do the same with Alice and Richard. One can only hope that everyone behaves themselves on the day.

Camilla is still comparing Matthew Williamson and Stella McCartney down the line and online with her mate when Desmond arrives. Desmond is our calligrapher – or scribe, as he likes to describe himself. Six foot four of dreadlocked Jamaican, he is the coolest dude to ever walk the planet. Handsome, laid-back and with a sharp sense of humour, he looks like he should be DJ-ing on a beach in Ibiza instead of being one of the finest handwriting experts around. A member of the Worshipful Company of Scriveners, his fair hand is responsible for some of the most exquisite invitations, placements and lettering imaginable. His clients range from captains of industry to high-fashion luxury brands. He is a very good friend of Bernard's and one of our big-gun suppliers, but as he is so goddamn expensive (between £1,000 and £2,000 for a morning's work), we only call on him in an emergency, or if we have an oligarch we want to impress. His Arabic calligraphy goes down particularly well with our Middle Eastern clients. He is also so handsome that Camilla immediately drops her call.

'Hi Desmond,' she purrs as he saunters in with his case of quills under his arm.

'Good morning.' He nods his head. 'How are you on this beautiful day?'

'All the better for seeing you,' she giggles, winding her hair around her fingers and licking her lips. My toes actually curl for her.

'Desmond! Good to see you!' I shake his hand, trying to help the man out of there. 'Thanks for coming in at such short notice.'

'No problem, man,' he says, looking around the office for somewhere to work. 'Shall I use Bernard's desk?'

'Good idea,' I reply, watching him stride across the office, his long legs in drainpipe jeans. His bright-orange shirt and collection of gold and leather-thong necklaces would look ridiculous on anyone else, yet somehow Desmond manages to carry off his whole look with enviable aplomb. Camilla sighs unconsciously as he walks past.

He moves Bernard's Mont Blanc pens and blotting pad to one side. Out of his case he produces a selection of goose-feather quills (with the feather still attached), as well as various pots of different-coloured ink.

'Bernard said that the card is already here?' he asks.

'That's right,' says Camilla, bringing over a pile of stiff cream card. 'This came about half an hour ago.'

'Excellent. Thanks babe,' smiles Desmond. 'The bride wants black for the wedding and green for the rehearsal dinner? Is that right? And one large seating plan for each night?'

'That's right, I think. I'll just go and check my notes,' I say.

'And what was wrong with the last lot?' he asks.

'Card was too yellow, apparently,' I say. 'And apparently the writing wasn't right. She wanted ornate and she got italic.'

'OK then, dude. And what sort of green – apple or lime?'

'I would say apple,' I reply.

'Cool.'

'Would you like a cup of coffee?' asks Camilla.

'No caffeine for me, darling, it gives me the shakes and I need a steady hand in my job.'

'Oh God, of course, silly me.'

'Although a glass of water would be perfect.'

Camilla busies herself pouring Evian into a glass while I hand Desmond over the list of names and places where they are sitting, for him to start on the large seating plan for the Friday-night dinner. His work is meticulous and apparently effortless. Each curl and swirl and curve seems to flow from his squeaking nib. And he is fast.

'Honestly,' he says as he writes Louise's name on top table. 'Whatever happened to a quiet dinner and a few drinks for a wedding? Or even a bit of cake and a drink, like in the olden days? Why are they now doing the three-day things? When I get married I'm going to do it over a pub in Brixton with some mates, a few beers and my aunt's jerk chicken.'

'I totally agree,' lies Camilla, for whom a knees-up in Brixton is about as far away from her perfect big day as you can get. 'I think we should all chill out more about weddings.'

'Oh?' grins Desmond. 'Now you shock me there, Camilla. I had you down as more of a church-and-big-reception kind of girl.'

'Oh God, no,' she scoffs. 'Why would I do that? I'd like a chillaxed day.'

Camilla has suddenly developed what she supposes to be a 'hip' voice while talking to Desmond. Much like the plummiest of Sloanes always sniff and say 'mate' as soon as they speak to a cab-driver, she must think this new patois is more engaging than her usual RP. I am afraid I find it rather hard to keep a straight face. Fortunately Bernard's arrival puts Camilla out of her hip-hop misery.

'Darling!' he declares rather flamboyantly to Desmond.

'Darling!' Desmond declares right back.

'You look fabulous! I'm loving the orange shirt.' Bernard holds Desmond's shoulders and steps back to admire the look.

'Ozwald Boateng,' he smiles.

'Sadly, I am nowhere near tall enough or black enough for his stuff.' Bernard rolls his eyes with disappointment. 'Have you been working out, you bastard?' he asks, squeezing Desmond's sturdy biceps.

'No.'

Bernard raises his eyebrows. 'Oh no, don't tell me!' He clutches his purple-rinsed head in dramatic despair. 'You've got a new girlfriend. I can't bear it. The tragedy of it. You are far too handsome to be straight.'

'You win some and you lose some,' shrugs Desmond. He is used to Bernard's lame advances and I think would be disappointed if Bernard didn't launch himself at him with all the enthusiasm of a Labrador on heat.

'I know, but with you I am not even in with a fighting chance!'

'Jesus,' says Desmond. 'What the hell is that smell?'

'Oh Christ,' says Bernard, looking down. 'Sophie! Fuck me, that's disgusting! Camilla! By the way, you've got Sophie this morning. We've got to go to a tasting in Stockwell.' He points to himself and me. 'And I've got nearly two grand's worth of cake on the back seat of the car and we can't leave Sophie with the cake because she'll eat the bloody thing. So she's coming into the office – only until lunchtime, when I am taking the cake to Alice's sister's house for her to transport it down to Sussex.'

'Great,' says Camilla sarcastically. 'That'll be fun.'

'Any more cheek and you can take her for a walk as well,' says Bernard. 'We've got no clients coming in, so she can sit on the sofa next to Jez's desk – and I'll shut the door for you, darling,' he smiles at Desmond. 'So you can work in peace. Sophie – shoo!' he says. 'In your bed!' He points to the sofa. The dog trots over to the other side of the office. She may be flatulent but at least she is a little more obedient than she used to be. Those evening classes are beginning to pay off. 'Now,' says Bernard, 'let's have a look at what you've been doing.'

Bernard and Desmond close the doors to his office, then they have a ten-minute conversation that try as

I might I can't quite hear. It seems to involve much laughter and the mention of Elton John twice, his partner David Furniss once, Prada three times and Kylie Minogue. Desmond has clearly been spreading himself around quite a lot of late.

'Excellent,' says Bernard, suddenly appearing through the door. 'Shall we go?'

Twenty-five minutes later, we pull up outside Nigel's warehouse on an industrial estate in Stockwell. I get out of the car with a sheet-white face, just about ready to puke on my shoes. My hangover has not been helped by the horrendous stop-start driving that I have just experienced. It would have been more comfortable to have been shoved head-first into a kangaroo's pouch and bounced over the river. Bernard is also one of those deeply scary drivers who look you in the eye all the time while driving. And all the time you are smiling and talking you are secretly begging for the mad bastard to look back at the road.

'Who are we meeting?' he asks, turning to me and stretching out his clearly exhausted brake leg.

'Ian and Catriona,' I say, opening my file on the roof of the car. 'Their wedding's on September the sixth in Hampstead and this is the final tasting.'

'Righty-ho,' says Bernard. 'Let's go and eat some of Nigel's lovely grub.'

Walking into the offices of The Lilac Olive is like entering an Aladdin's cave full of delights. It's a huge set-up. There are three or four industrial kitchens with twenty-two full-time chefs, sous chefs and pastry chefs preparing the food, which ranges from the simple asparagus-tip-wrapped-in-Parma-ham canapé, to spun-sugar castles with caramel hazelnut batons. Adjoining the kitchens is a large warehouse storeroom of linen, glassware and silver. Hundreds of different-coloured tablecloths – oatmeal, lime, sage, white, toile de joie – are piled to the ceiling, along with matching napkins and chair covers. In one corner there's a collection of sample dining chairs attached to the wall. Gold, silver, perspex, wicker, mahogany or lime-washed – they are all on offer for you to choose from. Through a glass door off to the right there's another room with twenty-five sample dinner services arranged neatly on the shelves. Some are simple Limogues white plates, and there are square black sushi plates for a more contemporary look, but there is also a collection of bespoke dinner services that were made especially for The Lilac Olive by Royal Doulton. In the middle of the room are three sample tables, which have been laid out in various ways in order to help the client choose, using a selection of candelabra. Each table has a totally different look. In the far corner, there are also piles of different uniforms for the staff, to complement and match their surroundings. With so much choice available, it is a wonder that anyone can reach any decision in here at all.

'Good morning! Good morning!' Nigel's nasal voice echoes around his cavernous warehouse, as does the click-clack of his shiny shoes. 'How are we today?' He appears from between the linens.

'Fine and dandy,' replies Bernard. 'How are the haemorrhoids?'

'Ha bloody ha,' says Nigel, giving Bernard a weak handshake. 'The clients are upstairs in the tasting room, so curb your tongue.'

We follow Nigel upstairs, past his office and a group of busy-looking staff, through their rather nice dining room, where they get fed a chef's two-course lunch every day, and into the tasting room. A small sunny room in the corner of the building, it boasts two tables. One is laid like a show table, as it would be for a wedding, with a tablecloth, two chairs, a candelabra and two full place settings; the other is a long trestle where the actual tasting takes place, groaning with food. A tasting can cost a couple a thousand pounds if Nigel doesn't perceive them as serious, otherwise the cost is factored in to his quote.

Ian and Catriona are quite serious, so this delicious early lunch won't set them back anything. They already each have a glass of champagne on the go, and are clearly ready to enjoy themselves.

'I have been looking forward to this all week,' smiles Catriona as she comes over and kisses me on both cheeks. 'I haven't eaten for days.'

'Cheers,' grins Ian from the other side of the table. 'Very nice to see you both.'

Judging by the spread that is on offer, it looks as if they have chosen to sample a mid-range menu. The Lilac Olive's prices range from £8 to £15 per head for canapés and between £47 and £95 per head for a three-course dinner including coffee and petit fours, but excluding the cost of staff, wine, soft drinks, cutlery, glasses, table and chair hire, the marquee – the lot. And the extras are expensive. The chefs come from places like Spencer House and other private homes. The butlers who serve at the table have been trained at Buckingham Palace, Clarence House and the executive fine dining rooms at Shell and BP. They are usually Spanish or Italian and get paid £18 an hour. With a dinner for two hundred you would need two butlers per table of ten, as well as another five or six wine butlers who circulate between the tables, who are also joined by two head barmen and a couple of others – including the back-stage staff there would be about seventy in total. Or if you're the Beckhams you have two hundred and fifty guests and the same number of staff. So despite the fact that you are spending between £11,000 and £21,000 on food alone, you can more or less triple that once you have added in staff and other costs.

At which point one might be tempted to go for a buffet option instead, thinking it might be cheaper. But in fact it is not. With a dinner there are two courses and a pudding to cater for, so, for example, smoked salmon, lamb and then a cake. However, with a buffet you have to offer lamb and beef and fish and prawns – it is almost twice as much work and food, and therefore money.

Ian and Catriona look like they're spending £65 to £70 a head and they have gone for a very modern, fashionable menu, opening with a ceviche of three types of fish. Asian and ethnic is big at the moment, as is having three little options on a plate. So you can have three small starters, followed by three small mains and an assiette of desserts. It used to be terribly frowned upon to serve chicken, as it was considered the stuff of corporate events, but these days so few women eat red meat that chicken is often ordered by the bride. Having said that, there is nothing that gets up Nigel's rather large nose more than vegetarians.

I remember him late one night, having had a few too many chardonnays and a terrible service, shouting on about vegetarians.

'I mean, what is a vegetarian?' he slurred. 'They are usually people who don't eat red meat but who will suddenly eat bacon or ham or sausages. They will say they are vegetarian, but then ask for a nice piece of chicken if the person next to them is tucking in to some. "But you're a veggie!"' he shouted. '"I just don't eat red meat,"' he mimicked. ' "No! You're just a bloody fussy girl."'

Nigel is always in the habit of doubling the veggie order and insists that it is not printed on the menu. Otherwise he ends up in the same situation as he was on the night of the rant. Because it was printed on the menu, everyone presumed it was an option and his six vegetarians suddenly became thirty-two.

'Allergies' are his other bête noire. 'What the fuck is wrong with everyone?' he once asked me. 'We've got vegans, the lactose intolerant, coeliacs, macro-biotics. Christ, nuts were booted out last century! Why is everyone so ill? Maybe it is just fashionable to be sensitive.'

However, despite his moaning, Nigel is truly brilliant at accommodating the unexpected. Two weeks ago, he managed to find a nice piece of fish for the groom's mother, who suddenly announced, as they were sitting down, that she couldn't eat venison. She had already had a separate starter because she couldn't stomach the pasta first course. 'What the client wants, the client gets' is his motto and he always pulls it off with great aplomb. He knows to double the bread order if it is a Jewish wedding, and to bring in the prawns if the rabbi is not staying to dinner. He knows the Russians love their cured fish. And everyone loves a pudding. Pudding is, according to Nigel, the one dish that everyone remembers, which is why it must be spectacular. I beg to differ, as I am always far too drunk to remember what the pudding was, but he is insistent. A croque en bouche – a profiterole pyramid with crème anglaise covered in chocolate or spun sugar – is his favourite.

Ian and Catriona seem delighted with their starter, which sits on the plate for barely a minute. While Nigel talks them through the various ways of serving it – on square plates or with charger plates – they crunch and munch away. They sip at their champagne and pronounce everything to be delicious. I have to say, I agree. The salmon has the edge on the red mullet, I think. But Bernard is a fan of the sea bass.

The main course is again three different types of meat; this time each has been seared and seasoned and placed around a medley of small veg. The lamb and beef are particularly melt-in-the-mouth perfect. I am a little less keen on the venison.

'You can have this with a jus of some sort if you

want,' suggests Nigel, flaring his nostrils and inhaling over the plate. 'But personally I am over jus and emulsions; I prefer a quality meat, perfectly seared. I think it shows confidence.'

'It won't be dry?' asks Catriona, chewing away on her piece of beef.

'No,' says Nigel.

'And I am wondering if we need some mash,' adds Ian. 'To soak up the drink.'

Nigel shoots him a look that could turn milk at twenty paces. His food is not there to soak up alcohol, it is there to be savoured and enjoyed. His silence speaks volumes.

'Then again,' says Ian, 'maybe not.'

'The vegetables are amazing,' declares Catriona by way of warming the sudden chill in the air.

'Thanks,' smiles Nigel.

While two members of staff clear away the main course, a trolley with a small mountain of profiteroles arrives, along with a plate of three desserts, which consist of a small summer pudding, an apricot-compote-topped cheesecake, and a tiny champagne jelly with fruit.

'Now I know you wanted the assiette,' says Nigel. 'But I just wanted you to have a look at the croque en bouche to imagine what it might look like on the day and to see just how attractive it is.'

'Oh my God!' exclaims Catriona, her hands on her cheeks. 'That looks amazing!'

'But aren't we having a wedding cake?' asks Ian.

'Do you want one?' she asks.

'I am not sure,' he replies.

'Do you want to eat it or cut it?' asks Bernard. 'The one we have in the car is really a cutting cake. It won't taste nice and it's cost the best part of £2,000.'

'You've got a cake in the car?' asks Nigel.

'Yes,' says Bernard.

'In this heat?'

'What do you mean, "in this heat"?' snaps Bernard.

'It'll melt.'

'Don't be so bloody stupid.' Bernard rolls his eyes. 'And anyway, we're parked in the shade.'

'Are you sure?'

I have never seen Bernard walk off at such a pace while pretending to be nonchalant. I can hear him sprint down the stairs and then we all turn to watch him as he dashes across the car park to his old Mercedes, which is parked in the full sun. The 'Fuck!' that he shouts is audible through the glass window and the following display of hair-pulling, jumping up and down and general kicking of the car verges on the Basil Fawlty. It is so insane and out of control that Catriona starts to laugh.

'I know it's mean,' she sniggers. 'But I just can't help myself.'

'No,' I smile. 'I agree.'

Bernard slams the boot of his car and comes bounding back up the stairs. His face is pink with rage and yet drained with terror.

'Nigel,' he croaks, 'I am fucked. The cake is fucked. I am terribly sorry,' he apologizes to Ian. 'I never swear in front of clients. Please forgive me!'

'No, don't worry,' dismisses Ian. 'You are well fucked, mate.'

'Shit!' Bernard stares at Nigel, his hands limp by his side. 'The layers have collapsed!'

'Badly?' asks Nigel.

'They're fucked.' Bernard shakes his head. 'Sorry,' he says quickly to Catriona, who smiles back.

'Listen,' says Nigel. 'Get it out of the car, and I'll get our chefs to fix it for you. There's nothing they can't do.'

'Really?' Bernard looks like he is about to cry. 'But you guys didn't make it.'

'You're my friend,' says Nigel, patting Bernard on the back. 'And besides, it is always good to check out the competition.'

While Nigel goes off to save Bernard's bacon, Ian takes a swift slug of his drink and leans over to me.

'We're glad to get you on your own,' he says,

straightening his pale-blue silk tie and tugging at the double cuffs of his pink checked shirt. 'Cat and I were wondering if we could have some sort of snow storm after dinner?'

'A snow storm? In September? Well, there are machines that can do that. It shouldn't be a problem.' I shrug, making a note on my clipboard.

'No,' he laughs, patting me on the shoulder. 'Not that sort of snow.' He sniffs and then winks. 'You know, snow snow.' I am still a little confused, but am beginning to not enjoy where this is headed.

'What Ian means is could we halve the food budget and double the drugs budget?' Cat smiles sweetly. 'We'd like, I suppose, between fifteen and twenty grams of cocaine, to hand out to the guests?'

I have been asked for drugs before, but not quite this blatantly. It is usually the best man who comes up to me at the reception, breathing hot champagne breath down my ear and asking where he can score. I haven't actually been asked to mule a whole lot in for the bash. But I am not surprised, as drugs are increasingly common at weddings. In fact, I have lost count of the amount of times I have seen the happy couple drop an E just before or after dinner, only to become very happy indeed. I did have one couple take a pill just before they went down the aisle, which I thought was a little crass. But more often than not it is an after-dinner thing that results in Bernard and me trying extricate ourselves from the loved-up embraces of the bride and groom at four in the morning as they repeatedly tell us how much they love us, how that was the best day of their lives and haven't we both got the most beautiful hair? Which in Bernard's case is patently not true.

Coke is the drug of choice for the over-thirty bride. I think because it is more expensive and you can supposedly maintain some sort of control. It doesn't make you dance like an arse, hug a marquee pole, or repeatedly stroke the basket of fancies. You simply talk endlessly about yourself, which is permissible on your wedding day. It is supposedly more discreet, except for the constant trips to the toilet. However, if you talk to wedding photographers, they'll tell you it drives them nuts. You can tell in the photos exactly who's had a line by their rictus grins, their frosted nostrils and dead eyes. It doesn't make for very romantic snaps.

'I am afraid I can't supply anything illegal,' I reply, reaching for my po-face. Not strictly true – I did buy a huge amount of hash for the hubble-bubble pipes at a Moroccan-themed wedding a few years back. And I did once pimp a dancer for the father of the bride. He was keen for a private lap-dance after the go-go girls got down off their podiums, for which the randy old so-and-so gave me a fistful of cash. Other than that, I will hold the door for a bride while she has a line, I'll go and fetch her a nice clean mirror to chop out on, and I will make sure the lavatory is pleasant enough for her when she enters. But I won't do much else. Bernard told me about a wedding he did years ago where the loos got blocked up with used syringes because half the guests were on heroin. He said it was the dullest party he had ever been too.

'Fuck me!' declares Bernard as he walks back into the room, carrying a heavy melted morass of white sugar and sponge. His face is puce and covered in sweat. 'You had better bloody pray for a goddamn fucking miracle.'

Wednesday p.m.

Catriona and Ian stay in the tasting room, finalizing the details of their menu, which, if they get the snow storm they desire, now appears to be surplus to requirements. Meanwhile, Bernard and I follow Nigel into the kitchens to try and resolve Cakegate.

'Bloody 'ell,' exclaims the French head chef as Bernard arrives with the silver tray of melted cake. 'That is a super pig's ear.'

'You can say that again, Antoine,' agrees Nigel, looking down his flared nose at the mess. 'Can you rescue it?'

'Rescue!' snorts Antoine. 'I think it is better to start from the beginning, no?'

'Well, it needs to be in Fulham by half past four,' says Bernard.

''Alf four?'

'Yup.'

I don't think I have ever seen Bernard look embarrassed before. He is unflappable and indefatigable; he is always in the right and always knows best. It is fascinating to witness. He looks like a bespoke schoolboy, shuffling from one shiny handmade shoe to another, staring at the floor and mumbling slightly. That was clearly the last time he buggered anything up. And it was such an elementary mistake to make. I am convinced he was so obsessed about his dog not eating the cake that he forgot to guard against other catastrophes.

'What the fuck did you do to it?' Antoine asks, walking around the cake, picking off a couple of white sugar roses.

'I left it in the car and it melted,' explains Bernard, itching his ear and scratching his purple rinse.

'Very, very smart,' nods Antoine, still inspecting the exhibit. ''Alf four, you say?'

'That's right,' says Nigel. 'I said you could do it.'

'I will have to take Alfonse and Xavier off the silver wedding cake for the end of the week,' he says, frowning through a pair of thick black eyebrows.

'Fine,' agrees Nigel. 'Penrose here are one of our best clients.'

'You guys from Penrose?' asks Antoine.

'We *are* Penrose,' says Bernard, standing a little taller.

'Of course you are,' says Antoine, squinting slightly. 'I have done some of your weddings.'

'Really?' says Bernard.

'I do pastry. You would not meet me,' he shrugs. 'I never leave this shithole.'

'I thought we hadn't met,' smiles Bernard, offering his hand.

'OK, so fine,' he replies, giving Bernard's hand the briefest of shakes before turning around to bark at his team. 'Alfonse! Xavier! Come here, you bastards, and fix this fuck-up as soon as bloody possible. This is an emergency and I have told the bosses 'ere –' he indicates to Nigel, Bernard and I, 'that you can re-make this pile of shit into a thing of beauty by three o'clock.'

I look across at the large clock on the wall – it is quarter past twelve. That doesn't give them much time to resurrect this five-tier cake from its sugar-coated ashes.

'They can be a little later if they want – four would be fine,' I suggest.

'Don't be stupid,' quips Antoine, under his breath. 'Where is the challenge in that?'

Leaving Bernard and Nigel to chivvy on the French cavalry, I head back to the office as quickly as public transport will allow. I am supposed to be attending a registry office wedding this afternoon. They are a rather sweet couple – Nick and Esther – who have known each other since their early twenties and are celebrating with a small dinner for forty in an art gallery that we have taken over for the evening. It is not a big event. In fact, it is one of the smallest budgets we have ever dealt with at Penrose, but I think it will be one of the most stylish. Esther works in fashion and I think has managed to beg, borrow or steal most of her accessories. Her shoes, I know, have been given to her, and a friend has done the flowers for the dinner at cost price. I think the whole thing has only set them back about thirty grand and that includes her dress, which is couture. But before I head off to West London and then down to Chelsea registry, I have a couple of meetings in the office to deal with first.

Coming up the stairs to the first floor, I'm met by the pitiful sight of Sophie sitting on her own on the landing, her lead tied to the large white radiator. She looks at me with her doleful brown eyes, but just before my heart melts and I insist that she be allowed back into the office, I am buffeted by the thick stench of Winalot.

'Good girl, Sophie,' I say. Her tail beats the floor in reply. 'You sit there nicely. Camilla will take you for a walk in a minute.'

I am barely through the door before Camilla launches into tales of her 'dog-morning hell' and how it has been impossible to work and how Jez came and went, leaving her on her own to cope with everything. He went to the art gallery to help set up for this afternoon and then called and said he won't be back till tomorrow.

'That's good.' I nod, not really listening.

'Good! I have been here all morning on my own!' Her voice is so shrill it makes me wince.

'What's happened to Desmond?'

'Oh, well . . .' She blushes slightly. 'He asked me not to disturb him. I went in a few times—'

'How many?'

'I don't know,' she replies, looking a little defensive.

'How many?' I repeat.

'Five, six, I can't remember.' She smiles tightly. 'Anyway, he put his iPod on so he couldn't hear me.'

'Right.'

'So that was that.' She looks a little defeated. 'I got the hint.'

'It's very skilled work.'

'Not that skilled,' she snorts. 'A bit of curly writing. I can write and talk at the same time. Actually I can do anything and talk at the same time. Even sex.'

I follow her into Bernard's office, where Desmond has left an immaculate pile of place names on top of the desk and two large cards with the seating plan drawn in stunning ornate detail propped up against the side of the sofa.

'He left about twenty minutes ago.'

I pick up the pile of cards for the dinner and leaf through. They look incredible. The black curls and swirls are executed without fault. There is not a blot or a smudge or a spelling mistake. He really is a talented scribe. The whole thing appears so effortless. The seating plans are equally stunning. The bride and groom's names are illuminated in gold on each of the plans, with other important players such as the bridesmaids and the best man each given a little extra touch to make them stand out from the crowd. 'Not bad, I suppose,' says Camilla, looking at the green-penned cards for the rehearsal dinner.

'I think they're a work of art,' I reply. 'Can you get these all packaged up and ready to send?'

'Where to?'

'We're going to courier them to the house in Sussex today.'

'Really? Isn't that a bit expensive?'

'Anything to keep the bride happy,' I smile.

'Oh right, our mistake then.' She nods.

'I couldn't possibly comment.'

Camilla gets to work on packing up the placements and I get to work on the tin of biscuits in the office. I realize that a couple of mouthfuls of ceviche and a teaspoon of summer pudding is not going to keep anyone going beyond two o'clock. I am just tossing up the merits of a jammy dodger versus a pink wafer when Kathryn arrives. Dressed in an expensive-looking sheer silk summer dress, she looks like she's wafted through a meadow on her way.

'I am not too early?' she says, as she spots my hand in the tin.

'No, no.' I spit crumbs all over my desk. 'I was just—'

'The downstairs door was open and there was such a bad smell of drains in the stairwell I just couldn't hang around.'

'No, of course, sit down.'

'Thanks.' She smiles and perches neatly in the chair, crossing one slim thigh over the other.

'Biscuit?' I suggest, shoving the large tin towards her.

'No, thanks.' She looks as if she is about to retch at the mere idea.

'I suppose not.' I smile. I doubt she has kept down anything solid for at least a decade. She's got the haunted, bloodshot-eyed look of someone who 'purges' on a regular basis. Either that or she is about to cry again. 'Can I get you anything else?'

'No, I am fine, thanks,' she says. 'I had an apple on the way here.'

'So how are you?'

'Fine.' She smiles and makes an attempt at a breezy face.

'Good. I am pleased.' I open the file on my desk. 'I am not quite sure what we are supposed to be getting through today.'

'Well, last time we chose a green tablecloth and I am afraid I don't like it any more. I showed it to my mother and she said the only people who have green tablecloths are the elderly on their dinner trays in hospital.'

'It is not green,' I say. 'It's sage.'

'Well, it will clash with what everyone is wearing.' She smiles tightly, as if the matter is closed. I hate it when you think that something is sorted, only for a problem to surface once the mother or mother-in-law has shoved her great big fat middle-aged oar in.

'OK – what did your mother say that she wanted?'

'It's not my mother, it's me,' she replies, shaking her glossy blonde hair. 'It's all very well for you to sit and judge, but you don't know what it's like having to be in the middle of everyone's opinions and ideas.'

'No, I am sure—'

'It's hard, really hard being me.' She reaches into the pocket of her flowered dress and pulls out a snotty handkerchief. 'Especially when my fiancé is so unsupportive. I show him samples and ask him what he wants and he says, "Choose what you like" and so

I do, and then he turns round and says that it's crap. That I can't make choices, that I have bad taste, that things I choose are ugly. When he just can't be arsed to look himself. All I know is that everything I choose is shit.' Her head flops forward and she starts to cry. Her shoulders heave up and down and she sniffs into her hanky. 'So we are having the toile de joie.'

'OK,' I say. It's the mother's choice. Mothers love a toile de joie. It reminds them of stately homes in the 1970s, when all the sofas and chairs were covered in burgundy bucolic scenes from yesteryear.

'And we shall have it in the dark blue, and then have a dark-blue tablecloth over the top,' she says through her sniffs and sobs.

'Can I make suggestion?'

She looks up at me like I have just asked if I can sleep with her mother and if the whole family can watch. 'What?'

'That you have pale-cream linen over the top, not navy blue.'

'Why?'

'Because it will look very old-fashioned and a bit like some corporate event in 1978. And I also think if you want to have the toile de joie you might consider the burgundy. You are having an autumn wedding – the reds and russets are a theme, are they not?' Her newly purchased breasts begin to heave. I have overstepped the mark. 'It is only my professional opinion. You can do what you like.'

'But that's not true. I am so indecisive. I don't know what I like. I don't know what I want. My parents never loved me, you know . . .'

For the next fifteen minutes Kathryn goes on to tell me – and indeed Camilla, who is wandering back and forth, in and out of Bernard's office, packaging up the placement cards – all about her childhood. How she was sent away at the age of seven to boarding school, how no one ever came to see her at half term, how she was always farmed out to friends in the holidays. She goes on and on. As a result she is now so unsure of herself, so cowed, she can't even choose the table-cloths for her own wedding.

'I mean, it should be an easy thing, right?' she says, imploring me with her pink eyes as tears pour down her cheeks. 'It should be so easy, anyone can do it. But I can't. I've got no confidence. Do you know, I can't even see myself walking down the aisle? I look in my head and I see nothing.' She hits the side of her head with the palm of her hand. 'Nothing. Absolutely nothing. I have no idea what I am going to look like.' She stares at me, sniffing, waiting for me to say something.

'Um . . . you're going to look great.' I pause. This registers, but it is not enough. 'Beautiful. You are going to look beautiful. Truly beautiful,' I embellish. 'The most beautiful bride in the world.'

'Thank you,' she whispers.

'Pleasure,' I say. Jesus, I think, I wonder if Craig or Kurt or whoever she is marrying realizes that he's got a nutter on his hands.

'Only me!' comes a shout from the door.

I look across. Never have I been more delighted to see Caroline in my life. She may be a Tango-coloured stalker but at least she is positive and upbeat and not totally, utterly and unfathomably insane. She is just a little bit rich and a little bit bonkers and she fancies me. All the above is dealable with; the weeping bride is not.

'Caroline!' I declare effusively. 'How very lovely to see you.'

'I am so glad to find you in at last,' she replies, waving a very small black bag at me. 'You have no idea how many non-essential purchases I've made at Chanel this week as an excuse to come over to this part of town. The door was open so I came right up.'

'Honest as ever,' I smile.

'You know me, darling, I have the tact of a rattlesnake!' She hoots with laughter. 'Caroline,' she says, taking Kathryn's hand and shaking it. 'I am one of his ex-brides.'

'Ex-brides?' she asks, a little confused, still thinking about herself.

'Married for three years and four weeks, not that I am counting at all!' She laughs again. 'But they are brilliant here, they'll get you anything you need. Are you having the lanterns? Are you? Oh, you must, don't think that because everyone has the lanterns they're rubbish, because they're not. Everyone has them because they are just fabulous and so romantic. I mean people actually cried when we lit ours, and most of them were bankers, who we all know have no soul.'

'Sorry?' asks Kathryn, clearly wondering where all the attention went. 'Are we having the lanterns?'

'We haven't got that far yet,' I reply. 'We have yet to choose the tablecloths and the themed look for the wedding.'

'Keep it simple, simple, simple,' suggests Caroline. 'There is nothing more ghastly than anything over-complicated. God, like that . . .' She picks up the swatch of navy-blue toile de joie and looks at me. I round my eyes, willing her to stop, but she doesn't notice. 'I can't believe you're still offering this crap. This is the sort of stuff that women who think the annual golf-club dinner is the social highlight of the year force upon their daughters. You should get rid of it.' She chucks it in the bin. 'It's far too gin and Jag for you lot.'

'My father's got a Jag,' mumbles Kathryn.

'Darling! So's mine. Nearly all fat old men have Jags!' She laughs again. 'Sorry,' she says suddenly. 'Was I interrupting something?'

'No, no,' I insist. 'Kathryn was just winding up. I think maybe you should have one more think about it all. And let's chat on Friday morning, with a view to putting another meeting in the diary next week?'

Kathryn takes herself and her pockets of snotty tissues out of the office, while Caroline slips into the ready-warmed seat. Fortunately, Camilla is very much around, tearing off strips of Sellotape and sheets of brown paper, so Caroline's knee-touching, footsie and breasts-resting-on-my-desk as she pretends to rattle around in her bag for important things are curtailed. Camilla even perches half-buttocked on my desk for a good five minutes, grilling Caroline about her children, husband and latest foreign holiday.

Finally Caroline licks her finger and leafs through her pink croc diary.

'So I am thinking end of November for the party,' she says.

'When is your birthday?'

'December the eighteenth,' she says. 'But that is so close to Christmas, so I am going to bring the party forward. Who wants to be confused with Jesus?'

'Quite.'

'Honestly, everyone's livers are screaming by the time it gets to my birthday. So I'd like them fresh and pink at the end of November. Everyone will be desperate by then.'

'And it is your thirty-second?'

'I shall be thirty-three,' she says, flicking her striped hair and pouting her puffed collagen-filled lips. Without wishing to sound mean, she looks a hell of a lot older. There is something about rich women and grooming. A little bit is fine, but too much is ageing. The tan, the blow dry, the collagen, the botox, the fillers, the designer clothes, the padded black-and-gold Chanel handbag, all make her look more like she is knocking forty and less like she's just crossed the thirty threshold.

'And an intimate dinner for . . . ?'

'Forty,' she says. 'Or possibly fifty. It depends on how many of my friends I see in the South of France this summer.'

'OK.' I start making notes.

'And I want Nigel,' she says. 'He makes the best hazelnut meringue ever.'

We run through a few more details about the night. She is suggesting that we put up some sort of Bedouin tent in the garden, with real fires to keep the guests warm. But she holds back on some details, as she wants to secure another meeting on home turf.

'I know,' she says, like the idea has just occurred to her. 'Why don't we meet up at my house next Tuesday? Geoff is away and I'll cook you dinner.'

Before I can invent an excuse or worm out of the rendezvous my mobile goes and she chooses this as a great time to make her excuses.

'Hello?' I say, watching Caroline head for the door, waving and mouthing 'See you next week.'

'It's Alice.'

'Oh, hi, how are you? Your placements will be with you this evening; they've been redone and look great. They are on their way to you this afternoon.'

'Great. Thank you. Have you seen the cake yet?' she asks, her voice buzzing with excitement.

'Yes!'

'Is it fantastic?'

'I've never seen anything like it.'

'I can't wait!' she squeals. 'Um, one other thing, I heard from a mate who was at the wedding you did last weekend—'

'Right.'

'She was one of the bridesmaids.' Oh no, my heart starts racing. Please God let it not be the one I shagged. 'Josephine?'

Thank you, God. It's Matron.

'Oh well, anyway, she said that there was a great ice bar and how fantastic it was, and I want one.'

'It's a little short notice.'

'But I want one.' She clears her throat. 'If whatshername had one.'

'Sarah.'

'If Sarah had one then so can I.'

I get these kinds of calls all the time. It's a sort of wedding one-upmanship thing. If so and so's daughter had X, then our dear lovely daughter must have X *and* Y. It used to be businessmen in competition with their partners or associates, however it is increasingly happening between groups of friends or acquaintances. Bernard is always posing the question 'What is the wedding for?' Is it for the bride and groom? Then it should be kept simple and full of their friends. Is it a businessman showing off to his friends just how rich and successful he is, how far he has come, how he is a man of taste and distinction? Then you should pull out all the stops – and invariably they do.

Most people think that it's the WAGS and the celebs like Wayne and Colleen and Madonna and Guy who really shell out on their weddings – and I suppose £5 million is quite a lot of money for a weekend. But it is the businessmen who really spend the money. A couple of years ago Russian oligarch Andrei Melnichenko dropped a cool $35 million on his wedding to a former Miss Yugoslavia, Aleksandra Kokotovic, shelling out a rumoured $3.6 million for Christina Aguilera to sing just three songs. And the world's fifth-richest man, Indian steel baron Lakshmi Mittal, threw a $60 million extravaganza in honour of his daughter Vanisha's nuptials. The family sent out twenty-page invitations in silver boxes. Mittal put up a thousand guests in a five-star Paris hotel for the five-day affair. One night there was a party at Versailles; another event reportedly took place at a wooden castle temporarily erected in the Parc de Saint Cloud.

Mittal's event almost rivals what is considered to be the most extravagant wedding of modern times. The 1981 wedding of Sheikh Mohammed bin Rashid al Maktoum, who recently became the ruler of Dubai, to Princess Salama, earned that honour with its $44.5 million price tag ($100 million at today's rates). His family built a stadium big enough to hold twenty thousand people for the celebrations, which lasted an astounding seven days – hopefully long enough for the couple to greet all the guests. A quarter of a century later, it is still listed as the most expensive wedding in the *Guinness Book of World Records*.

That makes the wedding of Marie-Chantal Miller to Crown Prince Pavlos of Greece a relatively small knees-up for 1,300. Held at Wrotham Park near

Barnet in Hertfordshire, it was attended by 162 crowned heads of Europe, making it the largest congregation of crowned heads gathered together in the UK since the Coronation. They dined on foie gras, asparagus, lamb and a selection of veg, with a symphony of desserts. They danced until four a.m. and then enjoyed a champagne breakfast. There were Greek dancers and fireworks displays. They re-created the Parthenon using a giant marquee in the garden.

Really, when you are dealing with this level of money, the only thing that holds you back is your imagination. We have imported elephants from France for a party – for some reason we couldn't source any from the UK. We have had deer roaming free, as well as the odd zebra to enhance a black-and-white theme. Last year we re-created Venice for one client. There were revolving stages and huge palaces and performers and musclemen who shipped guests along canals in giant gondolas. In the middle of dinner we froze over one of the canals and then sent out some ice-skaters to perform. In the background we had re-created giant Canalettos that were five metres wide and three metres high. Hidden amongst the landscapes were cherubs whose faces had been replaced by those of some of the guests. And all this was realized in all its finery in Fulham Palace.

One of Bernard's phrases when asked how to spend big money at a wedding is, 'Do you want to melt it or burn it?' There is nothing he loves more than a few ice chandeliers slowly losing value above the host's head. Or a fabulous fireworks display that can burn through £60,000 in twenty minutes. Although his current favourite is a company called Aquatique who choreograph water to music, which is so spectacular he likens it to bringing Vegas to the English countryside.

I dash out of the office and leap into a cab while talking Alice though the pros, cons and prices of an ice bar. The bar itself is around £750 a metre, and she would need at least a couple of metres to create some sort of an impression. There is also an entertaining ice-shot-glass option at £25 for fifty glasses, or indeed ice plates for the ice cream. Nigel loves using ice plates for his puddings as it saves on breakages and washing up. As I come over the brow of Notting Hill, Alice finally comes to the conclusion that she wants all three – the bar, the plates and the shot glasses. That should get them talking in Sussex.

I pull up outside Esther's flat just as Simon is arriving with her wedding dress. It looks totally fantastic in a low-key glamorous sort of way: a slim-line fitted dress with a scooped neck and rosebuds all along the neckline.

'Simon!' I yell as I leap out of the cab.

'Mate!' he replies, keeping his foot in the door. 'You're cutting it fine!'

'Jez has been at the venue most of the day. I've just come from the office.' I run towards him. 'You look great!'

'Mykonos,' he says. 'Long weekend.'

'Weren't you doing last-minute adjustments? Slaving over some Swarovski crystals?'

'Fuck off,' he says, running his free hand over his tanned bald head. 'There is more to couture than bloody shiny shit.'

I have known Simon for about five years and he is one of the best couture wedding-dress designers around. He trained on Savile Row, so is famous for his sharp cuts and smooth lines. His great signature dress is held together using four seams, and each seam takes a day to complete, such is his precision. It appeals to the obsessive in all of us. The dress he loathes to make is the Jordan special, the meringue with a sweetheart bodice. But fortunately he has an amazing reputation and can pick and choose his clients; it is rare that a meringue ends up on the mannequin in his studio.

I have been to his studio just around the corner from here and watched him work a few times. It takes a certain type of bride to be able to work with him. They are usually quite well off, as his dresses range from £3,000 to £16,000 (though that particular one was hand-beaded by Locks of London, one of the finest beading companies in the world, who bead for the Queen). And the bride's other quality is that she has to be imaginative. Simon has complained to me before about how some girls can't actually visualize their dress. They need to see a dress and to touch it before they buy. Simon would normally spend the first of his three fittings talking to the bride and trying to work out her likes and dislikes. It usually only takes twenty minutes before he starts to sketch. But if they don't know what they like or want, it is impossible to make any headway. They also don't have any knowledge of silks and fabrics; they just repeat things they have heard, so he finds himself having to put them right.

'I've had girls actually asking me for Thai silk, like it was something to be aspired to,' I remember him telling me once. 'But it's shit. It has a nasty slug in it and it is no good to work with. It behaves very badly. The best silks are from Italy and France.'

The two of us march up the six flights of steps to the third-floor flat, to be met by Esther in her cream embroidered-silk dressing-gown. Her hair is up in a chignon, her make-up is pale and she has a small sprig of lily of the valley in the curls at the back of her head. She looks totally radiant and extremely happy.

'Come in,' she beams. 'Would you like a glass of champagne?'

We walk into her small but perfectly formed flat. The whole apartment has a 1920s feel to it, with art deco furniture and antique-glass mirrors that reflect the afternoon light about the sitting room. The girl has exquisite taste. She leans over a dusty-pink buttoned chaise longue and picks up a couple of antique glasses, before plucking a bottle of champagne out of the ice bucket.

'Who's joining me?' she asks.

'I am,' says Simon. 'But we'd better get a move on. Your cab is coming in half an hour.'

'I like cutting things fine,' she smiles, taking a sip from her flute. 'Anyway there's no great shakes at the registry, it is only Nick and two of our mates. The family are coming to the dinner.'

'That doesn't mean you are not going to be at your most fabulous best!' says Simon, flapping the dress out from underneath its cover.

'Oh, Simon,' she says. 'I mustn't cry, I've just done all my make-up. But that really is amazing. It is more beautiful than I could ever imagine.' She hands us both a glass of champagne.

'Let's get you into it, then,' he smiles.

'God,' she says, as she drops her dressing-gown in

the sitting room to reveal a very elegant set of underwear. 'It is stunning. What am I going to do with it afterwards?'

'Just don't ask me to dye it for you,' says Simon, undoing the zip. 'The last dress I dyed was a bloody disaster. It was supposed to be dyed burgundy and it took ages and ages to come back. Eventually I got a call saying there was a parcel in reception for me and this small bag was there. I felt nauseous. I opened the bag and inside was what looked like a piece of coat lining that had been boiled in beetroot for hours. All the dressing had gone in the material, and the zip hadn't dyed because it was plastic and the tread was a different colour. It was a disaster.'

'That sounds rubbish,' she says, stepping into the dress.

'Some girls take the bodice off and wear it with jeans,' he says.

'Really?'

'But just don't send it back to me in a plastic bag,' he says, coming around to the back of the dress. 'There is nothing more depressing than spending all this time and love on a dress, steaming it and pressing it and tweaking it, only for it to be returned in a plastic bag the next day, like used goods.'

'I promise to look after it,' she says, leaning forward for him to do the zip.

'For God's sake, what has happened to your breasts?' Simon steps back in mock horror and starts to laugh. 'Normally brides *lose* weight before their wedding.'

'Yes, well,' smiles Esther.

'I bank on at least a few pounds – I made the dress a bit smaller on purpose. Last week I had a girl who had huge knockers that I'd spent weeks working out how to cantilever into position, only for her to lose two stone at the last minute, and mostly off her boobs. There was nothing left. I had to remake the whole dress overnight and pad it out where the boobs had been. It was like having to rebuild a house from the very foundations.' He makes a heaving, straining noise as he tries to pull the seams together at the back. 'Christ, can you squeeze those boobs down? What the hell has happened to you? OK,' he says, putting his foot on the sofa for extra leverage. 'On the count of three, you squash the breasts and breathe in and I'll tug.'

'Is there anything I can do?' I ask.

'Come and help me at the back.' I come round and grab the top of the zip. 'OK – one – two – three! And push and heave and—' He pulls at the zip and it slides slowly to the top. His hands go scarlet with the strain. 'There!' Esther turns around. 'Oh,' he says. We both stare at her enormous chest, which through lack of room in the dress has subsequently poured over the top. Esther turns to look at herself in the mirror. She still looks stunning, if a little short of breath. 'Are you OK in that?' asks Simon.

'Yup,' she replies, trying hard to inhale. 'I think I might be a little bit pregnant.'

'Oh,' says Simon, running his hands over the top of his now very shiny head. 'Congratulations?'

'Thanks,' she says, smiling slightly.

'Huge congratulations,' I say, giving her a tight hug. Her bosoms practically cup my chin as I lean in to kiss her.

'You must be thrilled,' adds Simon, recovering slightly.

'I am shocked,' replies Esther. 'I didn't really want to spend my wedding sober.' She takes a sip of champagne with all the enthusiasm of a man in a desert. 'Oh well.'

'I have sewn in the little blue ribbon at the bottom there for luck,' he says, squatting down and turning up the hem. 'And I have finally put the label in as well. I didn't want to tempt providence before and have the thing sent back, now did I?'

Simon is full of couture superstitions. Never tack the dress in red or green thread, otherwise there will be a fight or someone will be jealous. He always spits on his dresses as they leave the studio so that they don't come back. He says if he drops his pins he'll be busy, and if he drops his scissors someone is out to stab him in the back. He is old school and as a result his clothes are beautifully made and fabulous to look at.

'OK then,' smiles Esther, slipping on her pale satin shoes and adjusting her shoulder-length veil. 'How do I look?'

Both Simon and I step back to admire her in the fading summer sun which pours though the large sash window in the sitting room. She looks stunning. Radiant, glowing, happy and absolutely gorgeous: just as a bride should. She picks up the small bunch of lily of the valley that's been sitting in a glass of water in the kitchen.

'Darling, where did you get that?' asks Simon, eyeing the flowers.

'Tash got them for me,' she smiles, giving the bouquet a large sniff. 'She's been nurturing them in her greenhouse for months. They are so out of season, I know, but I love them.'

'Clever her,' says Simon.

'So . . .' Esther pauses by her front door. 'Wish me luck.'

Thursday a.m.

Esther and Nick's wedding went without a hitch. Well, apart from the obvious. And I think it was probably one of the most moving weddings I have been to and indeed organized.

She was driven to Chelsea in one of those ridiculous Karma cabs – bejewelled Ambassador cars decked out in kitsch sequins and mirrors and models of Ganesh – which since she was travelling on her own was done entirely for her own entertainment. And when she arrived, there were only the chief bridesmaid, the best man and Nick and me there to meet her. The ceremony was short, sweet and totally devoid of any pomp or circumstance. Normally, I find a registry-office wedding depressing. The councillor seems more suited to signing planning-permission or skip certificates than engendering any feeling of romance into the proceedings. However, this one was endearing in its simplicity. I think maybe sometimes I get fed up with all the show and fuss about what is essentially just two people getting together. It was delightfully refreshing to have the whole thing over and done with in fifteen minutes. And then we were all in black cabs back up to West London for the party.

The small art gallery just off Kensal Rise looked fantastic. For a bloke who is usually only interested in gelling his hair and sex-texting girls, Jez seemed to have applied himself with remarkable conscientiousness. Not only had he followed Bernard's instructions to the letter, but he had also pulled it all together just in time. The look on Esther and Nick's faces as they pulled up outside the venue and took in the giant flares and the twists of rosemary and lavender all over the pavement said it all. They were so pleased and excited they couldn't stop smiling. Inside, the usually white room had been lined with midnight-blue velvet and the whole ceiling glittered with twinkling stars. There was one long dark table down the side of the room, out of which silver birch trees covered in tiny pink roses appeared to be growing. They too were covered in tiny lights and sparkles. Everyone had been told to wear white, which they had all done, and it looked fantastic. In fact, the only sods that stood out were Simon, Jez and I, but then we were working, not partying along with the rest of them. I was trying to keep an eye on Philippe, the extremely high-maintenance chef who was serving up black cod Nobu style using the facilities in the church hall next door. It was obviously not an ideal piece of organization on our part to have the waiters walking up and down the street outside carrying dishes, but there was no other way. At least they weren't having as terrible a time as Nigel had a few weeks ago when they fused the bride's father's entire house; every circuit tripped and no one could find the master switch. Eventually dinner for 250 was prepared by tapping the next-door neighbour's electricity. They were extremely generous about it, especially considering they hadn't been invited.

So I was on Philippe duty, making sure he had all that he needed. This wasn't a Lilac Olive gig, in fact it was done by one of Nigel's competitors, Perfect Parties, run by a right old sleazeball called Piers. Piers is fortunately too chic to attend any of the parties he caters and sometimes organizes – he usually sends along some Sloane sidekick with a diminutive chin and a tongue seemingly too big for his mouth. Neither Bernard nor I can abide Piers or anything he touches; the only problem is that he does have some of the most sublime chefs in town. Philippe was trained at Nobu, hence his black-cod special, and he has been a personal chef for a couple of high-maintenance movie stars. But he got bored of his food growing cold on the table, as they preferred a line of cocaine to a sliver of tuna sashimi. The last straw for him came when he made a tuna carpaccio with rocket leaves sprinkled on top for the couple he was looking after and the wife turned to the husband and said, 'Oh, that looks lovely. Shall we share?' And Philippe had another three courses prepared in the kitchen. So now he works for Piers and cooks food that hopefully gets eaten.

Jez was on drinks. He was looking after two barmen and four waiters who were handing around champagne-and-hibiscus-flower cocktails, as well as vodka mojitos, and apple fizz for the teetotal members of the party. Once the group sat down, these guys began to hand around the wine and champagne.

However, it was Simon's job that was the most tense. He was keeping an eye on Esther and the dress. He had a needle and thread at the ready should his stitching give way under the strain of keeping her bosoms in order. And all was fine for most of the evening. It survived the drinks, the dinner, the speeches and the first dance. But it was the moment when the bride really got cracking to some Beyoncé track that there was a scary ripping sound from one of the shoulders. Quick as a flash, Simon downed his glass of champagne in one gulp and had Esther in the toilets, sewing her back into her dress.

'One of the worst moments of my life was when a bride ripped her frock coming out of the car as she arrived at the church,' he said afterwards. 'It was shocking. She ripped it right the way down the back as she pulled herself out. The sound was terrible. And I had to rush over and stitch her up in the graveyard, while everyone sat there waiting in the church.'

Esther went back into the party, only for the whole thing to happen all over again about half an hour later. This time, despite Simon's protestations, she ditched the dress and borrowed Nick's white linen jacket, which she wore over nothing but her underwear, and went on to dance the night away. As did everyone else. A DJ mate of theirs had flown over from Pasha to play, and he kept everyone rocking until about four a.m., when we had to shut the place down, so it could return to gallery status by morning.

Having finally hit my mattress at about five thirty a.m., I am feeling a little ropy for my seven-thirty breakfast meeting with Giles's fiancée Heather at the Wolseley. I stumble through the door just after half past seven and can't believe how busy the place is. I have had numerous power breakfasts here, but never so goddamn early as this. I glance around the room, taking in the crisp tablecloths, the efficient service, the glossy atmosphere and equally glossy clientele. There's a table of men in suits going through pages and pages of figures. To the left is a tall, lean chap leafing through the pink pages of the *FT* while making short shrift of a full English breakfast. I ask at the desk for Heather and a waiter takes me over to the far corner, where a slim girl with cropped blonde hair, dressed entirely in black despite it being summer, is sitting. She is sporting red lipstick and drinking a glass of hot lemon and water while furiously typing away on her BlackBerry. In front of her rests a silver basket containing several warm, untouched croissants.

'Heather?' I hesitate to sit down.

'Yup, that's me,' she says briskly.

'I'm—'

'I know,' she says, glancing swiftly at the huge clock above my head. 'You're ten minutes late, so we've only got twenty minutes. So we should get going – right?'

'OK,' I say. 'Whatever you want.'

'So – winter wedding, right –' She is off like an express train. Telling me what she likes – red, candles, tea lights. What she doesn't like – anything twee that has silver bells on it. They were thinking Christmas

Eve, but my chat with Giles apparently put them off. 'I've got cash,' she says, her head wobbling from side to side. 'We don't both do eighteen-hour days in the City and go in on Saturdays for our health, now do we?' Her phone goes. 'Heather!' she barks. 'Are they floating? Count me in 2 per cent now. Bye.' She hangs up and draws breath. 'So now we are thinking of, you know, the week before, right? What do you think?'

'Do you mind if I order a cup of coffee?' I ask, rubbing the growing frown on my forehead as I try desperately to concentrate on what she is saying rather than the rapid movement of her red lips.

'Oh,' she says, slightly taken aback. She looks at me in a way that suggests coffee and indeed sleep are for wimps. She is clearly a Margaret Thatcher, four-hours-a-night girl and she is ready to grab the day and indeed anyone by the bollocks. As I sit opposite her I feel the testosterone seep out of my system and I can't help feeling that our roles should be reversed. She is wheeling, dealing, buying and selling million of pounds' worth of stock, while I am about to get my pretty file out and talk dresses and drinks and nice little canapés. 'Do you want a skinny or a full-fat latte?' she asks, looking me up and down, trying to work out how many calories a man of my girth is allowed.

'A double espresso,' I reply.

'Oh, you're a real addict,' she sniffs, going back to her BlackBerry.

'It comes with the job,' I say, joining in her very busy game.

'Really?' she replies, not the least bit interested. 'Now obviously both Giles and I are very busy, so this is where you come in. How many meetings do we have to do?' She has her diary up on her screen.

'We don't have to do any if you don't want to.'

'Really?' She smiles. 'Well then, let's not. What's the point of meeting in the flesh when we can do it all on email? You can just send me over all your ideas and I can just tick the boxes of whatever you do. Hello?' She picks up her phone again. I manage to catch the eye of a passing waiter and order a double shot. She hangs up. 'So where were we? Oh yes, no meetings – that's great. Just keep me in the loop, right? I want something stylish, you know, that people are going to be impressed by, that sort of thing, and I want to look good.'

'Have you thought about what sort of dress?' I ask.

'Sorry?' She looks up from her BlackBerry.

'The dress?'

'Oh, I was thinking white.' She nods.

'Good.' I nod too. 'From anywhere in particular?'

'Where do people get them from?' she asks.

'Vera Wang?'

'There then.' She taps away. 'Can you get them online?'

'You are normally required to do a couple of fittings.' She looks at me as if that is the most boring and annoying idea she has ever heard. 'I would offer to go myself, but you know . . .' I look at my body and then hers. She barely manages a smile. She gets up from the table, pops her BlackBerry in her pocket and holds on to her phone, like an addicted smoker might clutch a packet of cigarettes.

'So I'll be in touch, right,' she nods, holding out her hand. I shake her mobile and off she goes. She marches between the tables and before she is out into the street she is on another call. Jesus, I think as I tear one of her discarded croissants in half, I wonder if she will find the time to walk down the aisle.

'Your coffee, sir,' says the waiter, delivering my espresso.

'Thanks,' I reply, shovelling in the other half of the croissant.

I am in the office by eight thirty and I'm secretly hoping that I might be able to sneak in a quick snooze under my desk before anyone else comes in. But I'm surprised by Bernard whistling a merry tune while trying to order up bouquets of flowers.

'Morning!' He waves across the office. 'I'm on hold

for my credit card details. Do you think it is OK to give chefs flowers? All the other things like hampers, champagne and chocolates they get themselves. So flowers are OK?' I doubt that flowers are high on a chef's agenda when it comes to gifts, but he seems so delighted with his plan I don't want to put him off. 'I did think of Jo Malone smelly stuff,' he shares. 'But I didn't want them to think that I was coming on to them!'

'I'm sure Nigel's broken half of them in already.'

'You think?' Bernard holds that thought for longer than is decent and is fortunately interrupted by the florist on the line. 'Oh sorry, my number is—'

A few minutes later, Bernard is sitting at Camilla's desk, his feet on a pile of magazines, flashing a plaid scarlet knee-length Turnbull and Asser sock, holding forth on the marvellousness of Nigel and his chefs.

'They are artists,' he declares. 'I couldn't believe how they rescued that cake. They made pillars out of cardboard and iced them and sliced off all the melted sugar icing and re-iced the whole thing. It looks amazing. Like new. It took them three hours, which is about a third of the time the bastards took to make it in the first place. And they did it for nothing. So kind of them. So kind.'

'Who knew that Nigel had a decent bone in his body?'

'I know.' He nods in agreement. 'Usually the man's a total cunt. He is the most irritating fucking caterer we have to deal with.'

'He's not that bad.'

'Fucking is. I have been working with him for fifteen years. More. Oh fuck me, I am *old*,' he moans, running his hands through his hair. 'This is a young man's game, this job. Talking of which, how did Jez do last night?'

'Very well until about two a.m.'

'Yes?' Bernard's eyes narrow with suspicion.

'It wasn't really his fault. He'd done so well setting it all up, supervising one of Piers' sidekicks – Toby, I think his name was – and the whole party was rocking. It was about two in the morning when I found him round the back, finishing off a bottle of tequila with Esther's cousin, who is eighteen but still at school.'

'Oh. Not a good look.'

'It would have been fine if she hadn't projectile vomited all over Jez's shoulder while he was trying to snog her. Anyway, her mother got involved and Jez was accused of leading her astray, and the girl had to be escorted home by both her parents because she couldn't actually stand up.'

'OK,' says Bernard. 'Not a total disaster. At least he wasn't caught with his trousers round his ankles giving her one over the bins.'

'No – thank heavens for small mercies. And Esther told me the girl's been suspended a few times from school already, so she is hardly a Miss Goody Two Shoes.'

'Well then,' sighs Bernard. He's been around the block far too many times to let some snogging and sick interfere with his day. 'Apart from that?'

'Excellent,' I reply.

'Good, I am glad,' he says. 'They are a very nice couple, even if the bloke, Nick, is a little bit ginger.'

'I think he'd say he was strawberry blond.'

'They all do,' smiles Bernard. 'The footballer's fiancée is coming in again this morning. I hope you've made some notes about what she might want to do?'

'Yup,' I say, looking through the pile of paper on my desk. 'It is all here somewhere, right down to the price of five songs by Elton John.'

'Everyone knows he's a million a show and he does six a year. It is not so much the price of him, or indeed any of them – Lionel Richie, Donna Summer, Billy Joel, Rod Stewart – it is all their poxy demands that drive me mad. They want their own marquees, private jets, helicopter transport to and from the airport, and that's just to get them to the wedding. When they're there, they want their own food and drink and they get all grumpy and pissed off because the schedule has slipped a bit and the poor father of the bride is going on a bit, and they start getting all arsy backstage, saying they were contracted for forty-five minutes between seven and seven forty-five and if they don't hurry up they've got to go. Some of them will literally do their set and cut it short if the speeches have overrun. Don't you remember, the other day Rod Stewart didn't even get to 'I Am Sailing' before he pissed off.'

'Elton was nice.'

'Yeah, well, he flew over, performed and was back in his villa in the South of France by three p.m. with a million quid in the bank. What's not to be nice about?'

'That's true.'

'Oh, and fucking contracts,' he says, shaking his head. 'They drive me crackers as well. You can't video this. You can't photograph that. And then they come on stage and the whole wedding party lurches forward brandishing their mobile phones, and all the paperwork that you've spent weeks tweaking and negotiating back and forth with their expensive lawyers and our equally expensive legal team is null and bloody void. And then the bride and groom go backstage to say thank you and the star turns around and asks where the photographer is, having said we weren't allowed one anywhere near the private area, and I end up taking shit photos of Elton with the happy couple with my fucking snappy snap.'

'Anyway,' I say, 'when Camilla comes in I shall ask her to have a quick search to see who's on tour around the time of Keeley's wedding.'

'I thought she wanted Take That?' says Bernard.

'Oh yeah,' I nod.

'Lionel Richie is always one of the most popular, and he's not too bad at about £250,000 – she could always have him.'

'Either that or she'll ask for someone we've never heard of,' I say. 'How old is she?'

'Early twenties,' says Bernard. 'I hope we get Take That. A boy band.' He smiles. 'Now that would be fun.'

Bernard goes back to his office to put in a phone call to Nigel and shove his head up his backside and thank him profusely yet again for helping him out yesterday. I can hear his grovelling obsequiousness from here and it's enough to make you want to puke. Then again, I am feeling quite queasy anyway. Two hours' sleep tends to do that to me – it gives me a dry mouth, and makes me irritably disorientated. I am going to need more caffeine than a junkie fresh out of rehab just to get me through today.

My mobile goes.

'Penrose.'

'Good morning,' comes Kathryn's now familiar depressive voice.

'How are you?' My heart sinks; I am rather hoping she doesn't truthfully answer the question.

'Fine,' she replies, surprisingly. 'I just wanted to apologize for yesterday. That's twice I have done that to you now.' She laughs weakly.

'I know,' I agree, doing the same.

'Well, anyway, I don't normally sit and weep in front of people, so I am sorry. God knows what the other woman thought.'

'Oh, Caroline's fine, she wouldn't mind, she's been married herself.'

'So she knows.'

'Yes,' I agree to whatever the hell she means by that. Keeley is due in the office in about half an hour and I have still got to get some concepts and ideas together for her to have a look at. We also need to get a couple of photographers to come and pitch to her as well. So time is of the essence.

'She knows how stressful the whole thing can be,' she continues.

'Yes, I suppose.'

'And how difficult it is.'

'Mmm.' I am flicking through the ideas file we did for a rich Russian last year to see if there is anything that might tempt Keeley. The well-off always tend to want the same sort of stuff. There are various status boxes that usually get ticked – lobster, caviar, a pop star to sing. I remember going out with one rich client just before Christmas and ending up in Boujis nightclub of all places. We were drinking Grey Goose vodka cocktails, but the man still called the waiter over. 'Oi, garçon,' he yelled above the loud music. 'Bring me a bottle of that Cristal champagne. But keep the cork in it. We don't want to drink it,' he said, turning to me. 'We just want to look like everyone else.'

'But I don't suppose she had a father who was sleeping with the chief bridesmaid!' she declares, before bursting into tears again.

I am afraid at this point I put the phone down on my desk and press Loudspeaker. She carries on talking and crying and sharing all her family problems, while I flick through one of our marquee catalogues, wondering if Keeley would like a traditional cream silk-lined number or something a little more adventurous. Occasionally, when there is a pause in the sobbing, I pick up and mumble sympathetic noises down the phone. Finally the gasping and sobbing comes to an end with her apologizing once more.

'I am sorry,' she sighs. 'There I go again.'

'There you go again,' I agree.

'I don't know what's wrong with me.'

'Yes – well.'

'I promise it won't happen again.' She blows her nose down the receiver.

'OK then, speak soon,' I say, trying to bring it all to an end.

'Yes, yes,' she mumbles and hangs up.

'Not the snot monster again?' asks Camilla, dumping her handbag on her desk. 'That woman needs a full-time therapist, not a wedding planner.'

'I think she needs to find a few friends.'

'That dog's not here today, is it?' she asks, looking under her desk and towards Bernard's office. 'It stunk the place out yesterday. I can't tell you how pleased I was to drop it off at Bernard's last night. Did you hear about the cake?'

'I know, good as new.'

'Alice was over the moon. She rang the office last night on the verge of tears – good tears,' she adds. 'Saying how great it looks and how much she liked the placements.'

'Great. I like to hear about happy satisfied customers,' I smile, clicking my pen. Keeley is due in about ten minutes so I need to concentrate on my list. 'Oh, can you do me a favour, Camilla?'

'Yes.' She sounds dubious. 'What?'

'Can you find out if Take That or anyone else is

touring in Ireland next year at the beginning of July? You know, for possible acts for Keeley's wedding?'

'How do you expect me to find that out?' she asks, curling her top lip. 'I don't know where to begin.'

'This coming from a girl who can outbid everyone on eBay for a pair of Christian Louboutin shoes because you have put a programme on your computer,' I reply. 'If you can beat everyone to the Louboutins you can find out if the Pussycat Dolls are playing Dublin.'

'No bride wants the Pussycat Dolls at their wedding. "Don't You Wish Your Girlfriend Was Hot Like Me?" Hardly the song to do a first dance to.'

'Yeah well, just check who else is around. We want to look like we've made an effort when she arrives in six minutes' time.'

'All right,' she sighs, sitting down at her computer and logging on. 'Have you heard from Jez this morning?'

'Mmm?'

'I hear he made a total tit of himself at the wedding by trying to shag the fifteen-year-old bridesmaid.'

'She was eighteen and not a bridesmaid and he wasn't trying to shag her. Well, he might have been, but it didn't get that far – she puked all over him.'

'Oh,' she says, looking over her shoulder at me. 'I'm glad. There's nothing more pathetic than shagging the bridesmaid.' She stares at me. 'It is such an old cliché.'

'Really?' I say, suddenly feeling an urgent need to shuffle some important papers. 'Ah.' The door buzzer sounds at a delightfully opportune moment. 'That'll be Keeley.'

'That'll be Keeley,' shouts Bernard from his office. 'No one mention plumed horses and bloody baby's breath. Bring her straight in here and offer her whatever she wants to drink.'

A few minutes later Keeley floats into the room. The symphony of honey has been replaced by a bright box-white velour tracksuit with matching white Chanel padded pumps. This time, however, the tracksuit is undone to reveal a white cropped top, high round boobs and a toned bronzed flat stomach, complete with diamond belly piercing. Her honey blonde hair is scraped back into a high ponytail – a look that Bernard is prone to call the Croydon facelift.

'Hiya,' she says, smiling sweetly. 'I am on me own this time, so please be nice.'

'Lovely to see you,' I say, leaping out from behind my desk. 'Would you like anything?'

'Do you have any carrot juice?' she asks. 'I am on this detox diet and I am supposed to have three a day.

It tastes disgusting – I have to hold my nose to get the stuff down.'

'I am sure Camilla can pop out and get you one,' I say, as Camilla flicks me the V behind Keeley's back.

'Would you?' asks Keeley, spinning round.

'Sure,' squeaks Camilla, suddenly feeling the need to scratch her head.

'Shall we go through?' I say, putting my hand in the small of her perfectly formed back.

'Sorry about the clothes,' she says, looking down. 'I have just been on the Stairmaster.' Lucky Stairmaster is all I can think, as I guide her into Bernard's room.

'Keeley!' says Bernard, rushing over to shake her hand. 'Lovely to see you again. How have you been? Has that great fiancé of yours been scoring goals?'

'They're not playing at the moment, it's out of season.'

'So he is hanging around the house annoying you, getting under your feet,' Bernard jokes.

'Well, we've got four and a half thousand square feet so that would be difficult,' she replies. 'Anyway he's out most days playing golf with the lads.'

'Is that what footballers do on their days off?' I ask.

'They still have to train,' she replies. 'But he likes golf, and test-driving cars is his other thing.'

'Sounds great.' I smile, thinking the opposite.

'So,' says Bernard, indicating towards the green leather sofa. 'Any more thoughts on the wedding?'

'Well, yes,' she says. 'We definitely want the same castle as Victoria and David, if we can, but the week after, so as no one thinks we're copying.'

'Right.' Bernard nods. 'Anything else?'

'And the food – maybe just a steak? If you can't do Christmas dinner with the trimmings, then steak and chips is our next favourite.'

'OK. Maybe I should put you in touch with Nigel, one of our best caterers, and you should have a meeting with him so you can see what sort of fantastic stuff he does. I can also put you in touch with Piers, who is very good at a slightly more esoteric menu – a bit of Asian fusion. A few of his chefs have trained at Nobu.'

'Oh, I've been there,' she says. 'Ever so nice. They do a fantastic chocolate pudding dish. Not that I had any of it, but it looked great.'

'That's all a good idea then,' says Bernard. 'Now one thing we need to organize for you is security.'

'OK,' she nods.

'I would say about £40,000 should cover it, which should include about £20,000 for police outriders. How has your agent got on with a magazine deal? Because whoever you sell it to, if you are selling it, should pay for the security, or else it will come out of your fee, I think.'

'We are considering offers at the moment.'

'Oh,' says Bernard, sounding a little disappointed. After his conversation earlier in the week, he was obviously hoping that he had managed to persuade her otherwise.

'They are only offering £500,000 each at the moment, which I think is a little tight, don't you? Bearing in mind that Keith was one of the top goal-scorers in the league last year and I was runner up in Rear of the Year?'

'Yes, I see,' nods Bernard.

'And I was Specsavers' Specs Wearer of the Year last year,' she adds, waving a white-tipped finger.

'I didn't know you wore glasses,' I say.

'I don't. I wore them for a shoot once, that's all.'

'Right then, we'll need to sort out the security and then let's work out later who is going to pick up the tab, if indeed anyone is. Do you have any preferences about who you have?' he asks.

'Sorry? Like a firm we like?'

'Well, not so much that, but I once had a Russian oligarch who announced that he didn't want any black security guards.'

'Really?' says Keeley, looking shocked. 'But that's racist.'

'It is,' agrees Bernard.

'I despise racists.'

'So do I,' says Bernard. 'So you don't mind who we get?'

'No, just so long as they are proper.' She crosses her legs. 'And good looking! That bloke Whitney Houston had in the film *The Bodyguard*, he'd be nice.'

'I'll see what Kevin Costner is doing these days,' I laugh.

'Who?' she says, looking a little puzzled.

'The bloke from the film.' She smiles confusedly, giving me the benefit of her bleaching treatment. 'Never mind.'

'We also need to check to see if there is any public right of way through the castle,' says Bernard. 'After last time . . .'

Bernard and I had a bizarre experience once with the police when we were doing another celebrity wedding a few years ago now. I was on site the week beforehand, sitting with the head of security, when a senior police officer came up and asked to see whoever was dealing with the party. We went into the catering tent together to have a chat and he said he wanted to help. He mentioned that there were a couple of footpaths going through this wedding and the public had a right of way and could legally walk into the marquee. I suggested that perhaps we didn't want ramblers at the party and he said he could shut it for us, by putting a few police here and there. I said, 'Give me some costs and I will clear it with my client.' So they came back a couple of hours later and asked for £16,000 for eight policemen, but said that they still couldn't get the footpath closed. So I said, 'No, thank you.' To which he replied, 'It is going to be looked upon pretty dimly by the press if you end up with hordes of people trying to get in and no proper security to deal with this.' He then walked off. My head of security then turned to me and said, 'Did he just threaten a riot? That's blackmail.' So we paid him in the end, just to stay off our backs.

But before we can try and get any further decisions out of Keeley, one of the photographers arrives. Tall, slim, good-looking, with dark curly hair and a twinkle in his eye, Mike is the sort of guy that girls always fancy and he knows it. Keeley's face brightens up no end as soon as he walks into the room. He charms everyone, which is why he is such a good photographer, and why he is Bernard's number-one choice.

'Good morning,' he says, leaning over and planting a very wet kiss on Keeley's cheek. 'May I just say you are so much more gorgeous in the flesh.'

'Oh, thank you,' she giggles.

'So what's the story?' He parks his black-jeaned backside in the middle of Bernard's desk, right between Bernard and Keeley. Bernard looks furious, but Mike is too busy engaging to notice. 'You, your fiancé, Keith – is that his name?' He says it like he doesn't know which wedding he is pitching for. 'And four hundred of your closest friends?'

'That's about right.' Keeley grins away on the sofa.

'My portfolio is next door, if you would like to have a look. But before you see the most beautiful bridal photos of your life, let me tell you a bit about me. I normally do all the big weddings – not always glamorous celebrities like you. I do civilians as well.' He laughs. 'So if you are having finger food and champagne, you probably don't need me! But if you're spending two million and you are literally covering the whole of the front of the church in flowers then I am your man. Which I have seen, by the way – it looked amazing. I can do three weddings in a weekend. Or I can spend three days with just you. I have a team of assistants who come with. Not all of them are as good-looking as me, but we can't have everything, can we, Keeley?'

'No,' she giggles.

'With a fabulous wedding like yours, for example, I would normally have two guys at the church, two with the bride and two at the reception. We do all the before shots – you, the dress, you getting in the dress, you in the dress. Just the other day I was doing a naked bride, getting ready – stunning, she was – and her dad walked in and started taking all sorts of snaps. It was very odd. I felt a little uncomfortable being there, actually. Anyway, we also do the marquee in all its splendour and the food and the drink, all that. We cover all eventualities. Should the camera break, we have a spare each. Should one of the guys accidentally put his camera in the holy water, which they did the other day, we have another. If the lights break, we have back-up. And I am insured should I drive off the road on my way to you!'

'Oh,' says Keeley, her hands clutching her cheeks.

'My guys shoot about fifty rolls of film each. We use film, not digital, because it is much better. And we are about £600 a hour, or around £5,000 a wedding, and that is excluding the prints. So about £10,000 in all. It sounds a lot, I know, but if your marquee is £50,000 and your flowers are £50,000, at the end of the day what do you have left? Just memories.'

'I see,' says Keeley.

'Now shots-wise – you want the getting-ready shots, the arriving at the church, the back down the aisle with the husband, the cake-cutting, the first dance and the family. That more or less covers it all, and then you've got the extras – the fun things, the reaction shots. But the others are your basics – Oh, hello there, Lucien.' We all turn in the direction of the door. Standing in the frame, lit by the bright sunshine, is Lucien. Slim, blond, quietly spoken and very posh, he is the second photographer Keeley is supposed to meet. Except that he has arrived, portfolio tucked under his arm, half an hour early. 'I didn't know you were pitching for this too.'

'I didn't know *you* were pitching either,' he says in his clipped soft tones. 'I am terribly sorry. Have I made a mistake?'

The whole room turns to look at Bernard.

'Christ!' I say. 'Is that the time? I've got a marquee man to meet!' I leave the room, pick up my bag and Alice's wedding dress from the hat stand, and make a very sharp exit.

Thursday p.m.

I manage to get as far as the M23 before Bernard calls me.

'You shit!' he shouts down the telephone. 'What sort of fucking wing man are you, leaving at the first sign of trouble?'

'I don't know what you mean.'

'Don't come over all innocent with me. You know as well as I do you shouldn't have two pitching photographers anywhere near each other. It was a total unmitigated fuck-up.'

'I didn't book them,' I venture.

'I know you didn't book them, but at least you could have stayed around and helped me clean up the mess, or have been some sort of buffer zone between the two of them.'

'Why, what happened?'

'What do you think happened? They started to show off, that's what bloody happened!'

'Oh dear – did Mike tell his—?'

'Yes, of course he did!'

Mike has a story that he likes to tell about a posh wedding he did a couple of years ago now. It was a very glamorous occasion with some very smart people drinking lots of delicious wine and champagne. He says that he put down one of his cameras somewhere, only for it to go missing and then turn up somewhere totally different half an hour later. A week later, when he came to develop the film, instead of a roll of pretty bridesmaids all he got was a collection of cock close-ups. He didn't know what to do, so he called the bride and told her what had happened and she asked to see the evidence. A few days later he turned up at her house with the penis pics and jokingly asked if she could identify any of them. She managed to name two out of the five, which he didn't think was bad going.

'And he told the one about the bride's mother,' says Bernard, sounding somewhat exasperated.

Mike's other story, about the mother of the bride coming out of a wedding car with her knickers around her ankles, is a little less problematic. Apparently, she smiled at him as he spotted the pants on the floor, but instead of hastily bending down to pick them up, blushing with mortification, she gave them a flick with her shoe and caught them in mid-air. She popped them in her handbag, gave a little mince in her dress and said, 'Oh, that's a lot cooler now.'

'I don't think Keeley minded any of it really, until he started to show her the photos he has of naked brides.'

'What?' I say, swerving to avoid a car.

'He's got a whole collection at the back of his book. Full-on bush shots. The lot. You should have seen the look on her face.' Bernard sounds like he's beginning to laugh a bit. Either that or he is becoming hysterical. 'She was so shocked, and at the same time she was trying to flatter his artistic integrity. I tell you, it was painful to watch.'

'And how about Lucien?'

'He played the posh card and told her about a wedding he did in Ireland where Ronan Keating played to 1,200 guests, where they had a three-tier marquee with fountains and flowing Mouton Rothschild '95 at £220 a bottle. And about another wedding where he had to photograph the Queen in a family shoot and they put Post-its on all the chairs with things like HRH and DOE, only for the Post-its to disappear after they'd got up. So the Queen had a

Post-it on her arse telling everyone she was HRH.'

'And she laughed?'

'Yup.'

'I think he's got the job.'

'Well, I wouldn't be surprised if she went for her local snapper after that,' says Bernard. 'There may be a little too much soft focus and the pictures might all come in an album Photoshopped to hell and covered in silver bells, but at least they're not a bunch of freaks.'

'Maybe.'

'Having said that, half the provincial wedding photographers and video directors do porn on the side.'

'Bollocks,' I laugh.

'They do. I heard a great story the other day about a bride turning up to check on wedding rushes, only to find a large double-penetration shot on the screen when she walked into the room and three hairy old men watching.'

'What did she do?'

'Went red and asked where her tapes were. The man was extremely apologetic and the hairy accomplices left soon after.'

'At least the family weren't caught bitching on the tape, which is what happened to my cousin. My aunt was filmed and the audio picked up her complaining about the cost of the wedding, about the groom and how she gave the whole thing six months. Quite hard to deny when it is there in glorious Technicolor.'

Bernard goes on to fill me in on the key decisions Keely came to after I left. She quite liked the look of the Aquatique water displays and fancied having little fountains all the way along the main path to the reception. She obviously wants a fireworks display, but a big proper one, not something that looks like it's been picked up at the garage. Boyzone, according to Camilla, are available and on tour in early July, which she liked the idea of. But she would apparently really love James Blunt. 'You're Beautiful' is her favourite song and the one that she wants for her first dance, so if he could be there to sing it in person, then that would be great. Bernard then suggested that they try for Take That as well, and as they are her favourite group she suddenly got very excited indeed. At this rate over half the budget is going to go on bands, leaving us very little left for all the other frills like secret gardens, animals, dancers, magicians and tumblers. I'm about to tell Bernard to be a little bit more abstemious when it comes to booking acts, but I nearly miss my motorway exit and end up shouting that I'll call him back.

I only find Alice's parents' house by mistake. Or more accurately, by wilfully ignoring the sat nav that sent me around the village three times, dogmatically ordering me to turn right and then left, ignoring the fact that the route finished in Brook End Drive, a cul de sac by the church. Turning around yet again, I remember a conversation we had about a stream running through the garden and whether we should put a security guard nearby to stop drunken revellers from falling in the water. So with a combination of common sense and luck, I finally pull up at the end of the long gravel drive, forty minutes late.

The house is a pretty red-brick Georgian rectory at the end of a long narrow lane, which I know is going to cause us problems later. The amount of times I have seen the bride blocked in at her house when she's trying to get to church by the convoy of staff minibuses arriving to set up the reception doesn't bear thinking about.

The slam of my car door is the cue for two over-weight elderly Labradors to lollop towards me and take it in turns to sniff my crotch. Both my hands are occupied in keeping the wedding dress above ground, so I am somewhat defenceless when it comes to heading off their interest. I am eventually saved by Alice's mother, Louise, who comes crunching over the gravel towards me with a headscarf on her head and a pair of secateurs in her hand.

'Casper! Titus! Stop it!' she yells. 'You dirty

animals. I am sorry,' she says to me. 'They have an obsession with male genitals, most especially after a long car journey. Is that the dress?' She points with her secateurs.

'Yup.'

'Have they fixed it properly? Taken the button off and shortened it all?'

'Absolutely. There are only twelve buttons down the back of the dress, just as you asked.' I smile, hoping that the two women are right and that hawk-eye here won't notice a thing.

'Well, you'd better bring it in with you. Alice will be thrilled. She was beginning to get worried that it was never turning up. Anyway, I am glad you are here. The marquee people have called and they are on their way. They should be here within half an hour or so. Come with me.'

I manage to knee both dogs in the face before following Louise back up the drive. Dressed in a pale floral dress with short sleeves, her bare freckled legs glow bright English white in the sunshine.

'I hope this weather holds,' she says as we walk into the house. 'The last thing I need is people traipsing around the house looking for cardigans and umbrellas.'

'I think it is going to be fine,' I smile. Truthfully, I haven't checked. And in fact I always think that it is best to plan for rain at an English wedding, and then you are pleasantly surprised if it doesn't. All my out-door weddings have wet-weather contingency plans, right down to where the photographer can place the family for the group shots.

The inside of the house is not quite as chic as the outside suggests. There's stuff everywhere. The shelves are loaded down with objects, the walls are covered in paintings and mirrors and framed curios; each room is stuffed with crumpled, gently biodegrading furniture. Even the cloakroom is full of coats and scarves and hats, half of which look as if they haven't moved off their pegs since 1976. Minimalism is clearly not a word that anyone understands here.

'Alice!' shouts Louise. 'The dress is here!'

There's a squeal of excitement from the top of the house and the sound of two pairs of running feet.

'Hi!' shouts Alice. 'Can I see? Can I see? Have they fixed it?'

'Hi there.' I smile, standing at the bottom of the stairs. 'Here it is.'

She dances down the stairs and practically falls into my arms at the bottom. 'How are you?' She grins at me excitedly.

'Fine.'

'Good journey?' she asks, kissing me distractedly on the cheek as she picks up the dress.

'Not too bad,' I say.

'How long did it take?'

'About an hour and a half.'

'See,' she says to her mother. 'I told you it doesn't take two hours from London. It's going to be fine. No one is going to be late.'

'Well, let's hope your father and his dolly bird turn up on time to take you to the church.'

'Trisha is not taking me to the church,' Alice replies.

'Well, don't expect me to sit anywhere near the woman,' spits Louise. 'She can sit with Richard's family. They are much more her speed, anyway. Oh, by the way,' she continues, 'this is my other daughter, Grace. This is—'

'I know who you are,' says Grace, flicking her long blonde hair. 'And you're not as good-looking as Alice says.'

'I am sorry about that,' I reply.

'Ignore her,' says Alice. 'She hasn't had a boyfriend for nearly a year.'

'You're single, aren't you?' asks Louise. I shrug slightly. 'Well, there you go, Grace, you've got a friend.'

'Whoopeedo,' says Grace, her head shaking with sarcasm as she looks me up and down. 'What fun.'

'Do you want to see the cake?' asks Alice, suddenly realizing the attention is not on her.

'Love to,' I reply. Anything to get away from Louise's lame matchmaking.

Alice lays her dress carefully on the sofa in the sitting room and indicates for me to follow her into the kitchen. She takes me past the Aga and a long pine dining-room table, into the pantry. The marble-topped sideboards and old slate floor make the room significantly cooler than the cosy kitchen.

'There,' she says, removing a couple of tea-towels that have been placed over the top.

'It looks great,' I reply. The chefs at The Lilac Olive have surpassed themselves. Each of the five tiers has been re-iced and re-piped. The white pillars have been put back and anything that might have looked a little botched or bollocksed has been covered with very beautiful handmade icing roses. To the untrained eye it looks incredible.

'I didn't ask for the roses. But I think they make the cake, don't you? It looks incredible. Thank you,' she says, hugging me and kissing me on the cheek. It takes me all the will in the world not to kiss her right back.

'What are you two doing in here?' Grace asks, her head poking around the door.

'Looking at the cake,' we both say at exactly the same time.

'The marquee people are coming up the road.' She smiles tightly. 'Shouldn't you be helping them? Seeing as you are the planner?'

'Thank you for telling me,' I smile right back.

Just as I walk through the front door, I hear a high-pitched squeal behind me.

'Mum! Your fucking dog is lying on my wedding dress! Titus, get off!' Alice is shouting and slapping the dog at the same time.

'Well, it's your fault for leaving it there,' declares Louise, running into the room. 'You know he likes this sofa in the afternoon, it gets all the sun.'

The shouting continues as I walk across the gravel back down the drive. Over the wall, I can see three trucks moving slowly along the lane. There's the loud squeaking of brakes and some equally loud swearing coming across the fields as the lorries try and avoid the overhead branches of the oak trees that line the lane. These boys are cutting it fine bringing the marquee in so late. Normally I'd like to see them rolling in on Wednesday morning for a Saturday wedding, but it is high season and I suppose they can't afford to have them sitting on lawns not earning money. Although the marquee business is a nice little earner once you've got your money back on your initial outlay. A good tent will set you back between £30,000 and £50,000, so once you have rented it out about ten times, from then on you are making about 80 per cent profit.

Finally the convoy turns up the drive. I wave at Steve in his cabin; he's a nice bloke and we have used his company a few times now.

'You haven't left yourself much time,' I yell as he parks up the truck.

'Oh man,' he says as he climbs down, wiping the sweat off his brow with his bronzed muscled forearm. 'We were hoping to get here earlier, but the tent was in such a state. Some army bloke had a party in it yesterday and there was food all over the ceiling from a food fight, there were broken chairs everywhere after they had put them all in the middle and made a pyramid and raced each other up to the top, and the black-and-white panelled dance-floor was covered in blood after a fist fight. And there were puddles of puke all over the floor and the walls. We have just spent all morning hosing the thing down and trying to dry it off.'

'That's disgusting.'

'At least there wasn't a frost last night. Just before Christmas my guys had to chip the frozen vomit off the sides of the tent.' He sniffs, exhales and raises his eyebrows. 'Don't tell the bride, obviously. This tent is brand-new, of course.'

Behind him a handsome selection of butch and buff

youths jump out of the lorries and stretch in the sun. Students, out-of-work actors and a couple of resting models seem to make up most of the crew. The ex-Mrs Oxford is going to have an enjoyable afternoon watching them all heave and sweat, putting the marquee up.

'So can you remind me where we're putting this?' He scratches his thick black hair. 'We made a site visit a couple of months ago now and I can't remember.'

'It's through this gate and on to the main lawn,' I say, pointing to a small garden gate.

'Shit,' he says. 'That's a long way to carry all the poles and stuff. Can we take the truck into the field just here and chuck it all over the fence?'

'I don't see why not,' I say. 'Anything to save time.'

'Too true, mate, too true.'

'Let me just go and clear that with Mrs Oxford.'

He obviously doesn't hear me, or else he is one of those people who only retains information that is useful or pertinent to him, because by the time I return with Louise, Steve is in the field and has already started to unload the poles and footplates over the side of the fence.

'What the hell do you think you are doing?' booms Louise. Steve and about six other young men in vests and jeans turn to look at her. 'I have got a thousand pounds' worth of wildflower seed planted in that field and there you are churning the whole thing up. Take your vehicle out of there immediately and carry the things through the gate by hand as we agreed. We discussed using the field back in March and in March I said no.'

'I am very sorry,' says Steve, using his most charming wide smile. 'But we are short for time and I was just trying to get this up as quickly as possible for you and your husband.'

'I am divorced,' she replies stiffly.

'Well, you and your daughter,' he tries again.

'Yes, well,' says Louise, warming slightly. 'The answer is still no.'

'Right you are then,' he nods. 'Through the small gate it is then, lads.' Six pairs of eyes roll.

Steve and I walk round to the back of the house just to make sure that he has the correct measurements and is going to erect it in the right place. Alice and Richard have gone for a minimalist marquee with an ivory interior, having been advised against the white by Steve. 'It looks a bit naff, if I am being honest,' he said at his site visit. 'And I'd have the flat wall linings and not the pleated. Although a bit more traditional, the pleats are only there to disguise the fact that the tent isn't straight.' There was much agonizing about what to put on the floor – white carpet was too wintry, the level wooden floor was too expensive and probably too noisy. So in the end we've gone for the sea-grass look, which is neutral, not noisy and not hugely expensive.

'So one foot plate here,' I say, standing right at the bottom of the stone stairs that lead off the back terrace and into the garden. 'And the other one on the other side.'

'Hi there,' says Alice, appearing on the terrace. 'Do your guys want anything?'

'Not yet,' says Steve. 'Wait till they've got going a bit.' She shrugs and goes back inside. 'That's pleasant,' he adds. 'Normally no one gives us the time of day, and if we ask to go to the lav, they point us in the direction of the nearest field.'

'Talking of which, where are we going to put the lavs?' I ask.

'I seem to remember they were towards the stream, no?' He looks down the garden. 'At the back of the tent, and we're building a tunnel to them, so they are not anywhere near the guests while they're eating. There's nothing worse than a back draught.' He laughs and scans the garden, looking a little confused. 'Where are the facilities, mate?'

'Sorry?'

'The toilets? Where are they?'

'Haven't you got them?'

'No. D'you see any lavs on our trucks? We've got tents, cables, poles and flooring. We don't have any loos.'

'Really?' My heart is racing now.

'She went for the minimum package,' he says. 'I've not got tables and chairs either.'

'No, I know about them. But you haven't got loos?'

'Nope.'

'But you can get them?'

'Nope – we are fully booked. It is wedding season, mate. Things are so fucking tight we're marrying a girl on a Tuesday next week.'

'Fuck,' I say. The panic is really rising. My hands are sweating and my mouth is dry as a bone. 'Fuck. I am fucked.'

'You told me you didn't want our £300 Portaloo thing, you were going to go for the bespoke one—'

'What, the five-grand loo?' I squeak. 'I would never have gone for the five-grand loo at this wedding. That's more than the bride's dress cost.'

'But I remember you talking about having them handmade with a seating area and a mock Damien Hirst print or plasma screen on the wall.'

'No, that can't be right. Maybe I was just telling you about them?'

'Whatever,' says Steve, walking off to join his crew. 'I've got no lavs and now neither have you.'

With my heart pounding in my ears, I leg it to my car and close the door. I riffle through all my papers just to check and double-check that I am the one who's buggered it up. And Steve's right – Alice and Richard went for the cheapest option, thinking that they could get a deal on loos somewhere else. Or maybe I suggested I could. Fuck knows. I do so many of these a week, I can't remember what I have said to whom. I take a deep breath and call Bernard. I am braced for his reaction, but because of my earlier hasty exit he uses my incompetence as an opportunity to swear more violently than a ho on crack. It is a relentless tirade that gives me tinnitus halfway through.

'Have you finished?' I sigh, getting out my pen. 'Do you have any numbers that might be any good?'

Eventually, after some more grovelling, he shouts a few numbers down the phone.

'And don't pay more than three grand,' he barks.

'Three grand?' I exclaim.

'Yeah well, we've got to swallow this one, haven't we? It's your fuck-up. And they have us over a barrel. This is one of the busiest wedding weekends of the year, and they've got lavs so they are going to see you coming and charge you a lot of money, aren't they?'

'Oh.'

'I know Nigel paid five grand for emergency

loos last year when he did something quite similar.'

'Five grand?'

Bernard hangs up. He is furious with me and I can't really blame him. The thing now is to rectify my error with as little loss to the company as possible. It takes me six phone calls and four people laughing at me before I manage to track down a nice bloke called Peter who is in his second season hiring out event lavatories and has got a few left over. Initially he offers me a couple of the single workmen loos that you get at building sites, but then he manages to find a three-plus-one loo, which is three ladies' toilets and one blokes' toilet, plus three urinals, in one unit with basins, oak flooring and coordinating carpets, which according to the purple guide (health and safety at events) is supposed to cater for about 275 guests. I could kiss the guy. I sound so pathetically grateful down the phone that I think for a minute he might screw me on the price. But in the end he charges me a simple £2,000 – twice as much as I should pay, but not as much as Bernard predicted. He has himself a deal and my arse is saved.

I walk on to the back lawn with a wide grin on my face to share the good news with Steve, only to find him getting the full Louise Oxford hairdryer. She is yelling so loudly that he is actually wincing.

'No! No! No! How many more times do we have

to discuss this? The entrance to the marquee is off to the right so that the guests can see Granny's cherry tree when they drink their aperitifs on the terrace. I went over this very carefully with you when you came.'

'Back in March,' says Steve.

'Yes!' she shouts. 'Back in March. Can't you remember anything?'

'God, if I had fifty quid for every time I've had to move the marquee for bloody Granny's tree, I'd be a rich man,' he mutters to me, and he pulls up the foot plates and moves them half a metre to the right.

'Thank you!' shouts Louise, as if she's been totally worn out by the whole experience.

Fortunately, Richard's arrival proves to be enough of a distraction for her to leave the boys alone to erect the tent.

'Everything going all right?' he asks as he comes out on to the terrace. 'Richard,' he says, shaking my hand rather firmly.

'We have met before, I'm planning the wedding.'

'Course!' he says, snapping his fingers in my face. 'I am a little distracted. Lot on my plate.' I smile through my irritation. 'Shouldn't the entrance be a little over this way?'

'Not if you want to see Granny's cherry tree,' replies Steve, looking up and wiping his sweaty brow.

'Oh,' says Richard. 'Perhaps I shouldn't get involved.'

'Not if you know what's good for you,' I reply.

'I worked that out a while back,' he laughs. 'Why do you think I've been with Dad and his girlfriend and my sister and my mum all day, keeping a "low profile"?' he says, putting quotation marks around the words. Shorter and stockier than I remember, Richard has become so assimilated down South that he has lost most of his Manchester accent. In fact, as he chats away about the adjoining cottages in the next-door village where his parents are staying, it is hard to discern where he is from at all. 'Anyway,' he adds, 'keep up the good work. I'm off to find out when the best man is getting here.'

Steve and his crew are hammering in the stakes when the hire vans arrive with all the catering and kitchen equipment. As well as marquee hire, Alice and Richard have rented everything from butter knives to dessert forks, from sugar bowls to coat-rails and hangers. Although The Lilac Olive does provide a selection to choose from, Alice wanted something a little different and has opted for one of the numerous catering hire companies. Perhaps the best-known one, with the largest amount of choice, is Jones Hire Services. They can provide anything from dinner plates to soup tureens to sauce boats, and from ramekin dishes to mother-of-pearl canapé forks and spoons – anything that you could possibly want when it comes to catering for your guests. Obviously it all comes at a price, and woe betide anyone who fails to wash up, as they charge another 25 per cent of the hire charge to clean the stuff afterwards.

Bernard always says that out of all the wedding-industry services, furniture and catering-equipment hire is the best business to be in. You'd be amazed how often we shell out between £10,000 and £15,000 a wedding on banal things like coffee cups and teaspoons. You might think that each item doesn't sound expensive, but in the end it all adds up. Even at the simplest wedding for your average 160 guests there's at least £880 on tablecloths, £190 on napkins, £1,000 for the chairs, £150 for the white wine glasses, £150 for the red wine glasses and £250 for the felt underlay on the tables. Even the pepper pots can be up to £25 a pop and that's before you've hired the ovens and the grills for the kitchens. And it is such a simple business. You buy the equipment, deliver it and charge a third of the price to rent it. Breakages are all paid for and sometimes you can charge triple the price. So if a glass costs £2 to purchase, it will cost the hirer £6 to replace. And they rent this stuff out three times a week in low season, and almost every day of the week in the summer. It is no wonder that the partners of Jones are said to be driving around in Bentleys.

I have to say, the look on the faces of the Oakes & Co staff as they arrive to find the marquee not completely erected and lined is derisory. Only after assurances from both Steve and I that their stuff won't be left out overnight and that it will be properly stored do they actually agree to deliver. Steve, the rest of the crew and I form a line and unload the vans. It is a hot, sweaty job and not something I should strictly be doing. As my shirt sticks to my back and my leather-soled shoes start to rub, I begin to wish we had employed a gang from Gallowglass to help, but due to budget constraints they were the first luxury to be culled. By the time we have finished the kitchen is packed with boxes, tables, chairs and stacks and stacks of linen.

'I am glad to see we've got nice long tablecloths to the floor,' I say, picking up a large white linen cloth off the pile. 'All the better for shagging under.'

'What is it about sex at weddings?' says Steve. 'Everyone always thinks that they are the first to do it. Honestly, these days it is kind of rude not to shag the bridesmaid.'

'I hope that's not true,' says Alice, walking into the kitchen. 'One of my bridesmaids is my sister and the other one is twelve. Anyway, no one's having sex at this wedding. My mother would be furious.'

'I am not sure you can stop them,' says Steve.

'You don't know my mother,' says Alice.

'I think he does,' I laugh. She shoots me a look. 'I am sure you're right.'

'I did a wedding last week,' Steve continues, oblivious to Alice's growing annoyance. 'And we had lit the garden really nicely with big historic lights around the place, and anyway this couple went off into the bushes and started having sex and they were illuminated and writ large on the side of the marquee. The whole wedding ground to a halt to watch them. The marquee emptied, the band stopped playing and when they finished, the whole place erupted in a round of applause.' Alice stares at him, looking worried. 'Oh my God!' he says, tapping me on the shoulder. 'Do you remember Eltham Palace?'

'Oh, that was awful.' I shake my head, willing him not to carry on.

'You'll love this.' He grins at Alice. 'So actually, it was a bit like here with your stream, but it was a moat and it was quite a deep moat. But anyway, this girl was wandering around the wedding looking for her boyfriend, and she asked the security guards if they had seen him. She was in a bit of a state, slightly frantic. After all, he might have got pissed and fallen in the water. Then a security guard found a pile of clothes by the moat. Could he have been that drunk that he wanted to have a swim? The drag nets were radioed for. This was serious. Then a bit further around the bushes they heard the sound of laughter. They went to investigate and there was the bloke, stark-bollock naked, having sex with one of the bridesmaids. The guard coughed to give the bloke a chance to get himself together before the girlfriend turned up, but it was too late. The girlfriend shouted, and then the bridesmaid slapped him for not telling her that he was with someone, and all the time he was starkers with this fight going on around him. Brilliant stuff.' He laughs. 'I do love a good wedding.'

'Yes,' I say, rubbing my sweaty hands together, attempting to move Steve out of the kitchen.

'Oh, my favourite,' he says on the threshold, 'was a wedding by the sea. There was a group of guys on the balcony drinking champagne as the sun came up, when one of them said to the group, "Oh, look over there, look at that romantic couple, I bet they've just had sex in those bushes." "Definitely," agreed one bloke. Then another one said, "Dave, isn't that your wife?" They all went to the edge of the balcony to have a stare into the early-morning light. And sure enough it was.'

'That marquee is not going to erect itself,' I say,

shoving Steve out of the door. 'What the hell do you think you're doing?' I hiss as we get through the door.

'What? What are you talking about?'

'Couldn't you see that she was getting all uncomfortable while you were talking?'

'No,' he says as we walk towards the marquee. 'You're paranoid.'

'Brides are super-sensitive around this stage, they're just terrified of things going wrong.'

'Well at least I didn't tell the one about the bride who was caught shagging the best man the night before the wedding,' he smiles.

'Thank heavens for small mercies.'

'There's still time,' he says. 'Have you seen the groom? He's got no fucking hair. Who'd marry him?'

'Obviously Alice is.'

'She needs rescuing, mate. Let me tell you, that one is not going to last.'

'Steve!' comes a shout from the other side of the marquee. 'Steve!'

'What?'

'We've hit water!'

Friday a.m.

Steve, his crew and I were up till four in the morning trying to sort out the leak. One of his out-of-work actors had managed to hammer a stake into an irrigation pipe. It wasn't entirely his fault, seeing as the ex-Mrs Oxford had insisted that the marquee be moved a metre to the right, so the original survey that Steve had done for pipes and cables was now null and void. Obviously this minor detail was conveniently forgotten when it came to Louise's wrath, and even when the matter was explained for the third or fourth time, she continued to take none of the blame.

Steve insisted that it wasn't too bad a problem. Nothing he couldn't handle. In fact, it was nothing compared to the main drain that he'd hit only a few weeks previously in a university quad. The grass had rumbled and then ballooned, the explosion of water and effluent went everywhere and managed to put the whole place under at least a foot of stinking water within twenty minutes. But this little leak would be fixed in no time. And it was – well, just before midnight. There will just be a slightly squishy area towards the back of the marquee, which should be avoided.

However, the leak put the mounting of the marquee back even later and it was about one a.m. before the sides started to go up. Poled tents that look like a big top with guide ropes are no longer de rigueur; these days tents are plastic, with frames that are not so pretty from the outside but are much more useful inside. They come with Georgian orangery, Gothic or clear panel windows, and can be stacked storey upon storey, with balconies and lifts and escalators and viewing platforms for the fireworks. The highest marquee we have had was three storeys and it towered over most of the surrounding trees. It was for 1,500 of the bride's nearest and dearest, and the interior was entirely bespoke, with lavatories like the ones at the Dorchester, with powder-puff girls to give you a manicure during the wedding, should you so wish. The marquee itself was £250,000 and the same again was spent on the 'icing'. The icing is what you see in the marquee – the lining, the carpet, the flowers, the chandeliers. The non-icing parts are the generators, the scaffolding and the staff loos.

It was about two a.m. when Steve started to work on the icing. And I am afraid come four a.m. I left him to it. He seemed to have it all under control; the only thing he was fretting about was the wind direction.

'You've got to be careful with these things,' he said, stifling a yawn. 'One puff and they go. I had one go last year; it blew off in one gust and left everything else behind intact. So there was the hardwood floor, and all the tables and chairs. There was even a waiter still laying the tables, and in the trees behind was the marquee, wrapped around the branches. It was extraordinary.'

I promised to check on the wind direction and the weather forecast in the morning before I finally managed to crawl into the tiny bed in the attic that Louise had made up for me. It was obviously once one of the children's bedrooms because it still had a few fluorescent stars stuck to the ceiling. They did their best to twinkle in the growing light. I closed my eyes and prayed for more than three hours' sleep.

Alice wakes me at nine a.m. with a cup of very milky tea. It is not how I take it, but who is complaining? I am a little embarrassed to have slept so late, but she doesn't appear to mind.

'The marquee looks amazing,' she beams, sitting on the edge of my bed. 'Steve's done a great job. The lining looks fantastic. This is all so exciting!' She squeezes my leg through the duvet.

I pull the covers a little higher to cover my bare chest. 'That's great news,' I say, thinking that Steve must have pulled off the mother of all cleaning jobs. Either that or none of them have inspected the lining too carefully.

'Also Daisy's just called. Apparently she can't make it after all!' Alice beams and gives my leg another squeeze.

'Great news,' I say again. 'The florist should be turning up any minute,' I add, shifting uncomfortably in my bed. I have no underwear on and I haven't even washed my face or brushed my teeth. This is all a little intimate for my liking.

'Alice!' comes Richard's booming voice.

'Up here!' she yells. Oh Jesus no, I wince. This can't be happening. I can hear Richard's steps bounding up the stairs, followed by someone else.

'There you are,' he huffs as he reaches the top of the stairs. 'Morning,' he nods at me. 'I have been looking for you all over. You need to talk to your mother. She keeps making noises about us cutting the cake on the terrace, and both of us know that we are doing it in the marquee before the first dance, right?

Oh, have you met the best man, Andrew?' he suddenly asks me. A slim neat blond bloke walks towards the bed. His hair is brushed over with a side parting; his handshake is soft and he looks straight at my chest.

'Yes, yes,' I say. 'At the pub. Our first meeting.'

'Sorry to catch you in flagrante,' he smiles.

'I was up till four sorting out the marquee,' I say defensively, as I try and pull more duvet towards me.

'I am sure you were. It looks wonderful,' he says, still staring. 'We were all just saying.'

'Good, I'm glad,' I say, sounding anything but.

'I can't believe they actually managed to hit the only bit of drain in the area, though,' laughs Richard.

'There was a reason for that,' I retort.

'Yeah, well anyway, Alice, can you have a word with your mother? She is only throwing her weight around because your father is coming over this morning with his latest squeeze and she wants to make sure there is nothing for him to do.'

'And your lot are such happy families,' snipes Alice.

'Temper, temper, you two,' says Andrew, putting a hand on Richard's shoulder. 'You're getting married in the morning.'

My mobile goes and all three of them look at me, somewhat surprised.

'Sorry,' I say. 'This is a business call.'

'Let's leave the boy alone,' Alice declares, springing off the bed and ushering the two men out of my room. 'Give the man some space. See you in a minute,' she adds, turning to me and giving me one of her sweet smiles.

Never have I been so delighted to receive a call in my life. The fact that it is from the blubbering bride is immaterial. I pick up with great enthusiasm.

'Good morning, Kathryn. How are you?'

'Is it?' she replies.

'For some people,' I try and joke.

'Do you mind if I talk to you about something?'

'No, no – go ahead.' I lie back in bed, stretch and take a sip of Alice's lukewarm milky tea.

Kathryn then launches into a ten-minute diatribe about how her fiancé is possibly having an affair. She has been through his emails, even the deleted ones because she knows how to get into his server, and she thinks that he might be shagging some girl called Claire who he works with. She has no concrete evidence for this other than that the emails are a little bit flirty, and that if they work together, why would they bother to email when they could easily go and have a chat? About halfway through the conversation the tears somewhat inevitably start to flow. And I am afraid this time I am unmoved.

Actually, I am moved, I am bloody furious. The woman is an attention-seeking crackpot and now she has me down as her speed-dial shrink. I listen for as short a time as is polite and then make my excuses: I am at another wedding and I have the florist arriving any minute.

Finally she lets me go and I immediately call Bernard. Would he mind if I fired a client? He is a little unsympathetic at first, but after I explain my week and the total lack of decisions that I have been able to make, we both conclude that it makes bad business sense to carry on working with her. Her cost per minute is far too high. It makes me hanker after Heather, the Wolesley bride. She might have to pop her BlackBerry on the altar, just in case she gets an important email, or demand that the church gets wired for wi-fi, but at least she's straightforward and not annoyingly high maintenance. I sit up in bed and compose a very diplomatic email explaining that I can't spend the first hour of each meeting discussing her personal life, especially as the meetings only last an hour. So it is with 'great regret' that we have to cancel the contract, as we don't appear to have made any decisions at the last three meetings.

By the time I have doused myself briefly under the pressureless shower that dribbles tepid water, she has replied, 'You are just like all the others.' Which I have to say I am very happy to accept, just so long as she never calls me again.

Suited, booted and showered, I come downstairs to be slapped full in the face by chaos. The kitchen is heaving with people, leaning against every chair, table and unit, drinking coffee and shouting. Alice introduces me to everyone. Her father, Alistair, is a tanned, not-so-toned sixtysomething with wandering eyes and a lascivious smile. His hair is swept back and his shirt is undone to his man-boobs – he looks like he's just stepped out of a nightclub. Trish, his current squeeze cum secretary, is all tits, teeth and tan. Her T-shirt is low-cut, her skirt skims her buttocks and she is cock-struck by Alistair. She laughs at his every move and gesture and clings on to his forearm like it's a life raft. Next to surly Grace is Katie, Richard's younger sister, who looks a lot older than him and hasn't lost her baby weight despite the fact that her daughter is twelve years old. There is no mention of the father, so I am presuming he ran for the hills at the earliest opportunity. They all say they are here to help set up, but they clearly all need a good sit-down before they start.

I walk out of the back of the house, down the stone steps and into the marquee. Some of Steve's guys are still hard at work, playing around with the lights and the wooden dance-floor. Towards the back of the tent, the ground is still a little soft, but it's nothing that twenty-four hours of drying out won't cure. There's a tunnel for the toilets, which have yet to arrive, and a couple of smaller marquees where Nigel and his gang will set up the industrial fan cookers.

'Excuse me,' asks a young freckle-faced chap, waving a cable and a plug at me. 'Where are we taking the power from?'

'Some is coming from the house and the other lot is coming from the barn.' I nod towards the old stable block in the corner of the wildflower field.

'OK,' he says. 'Just so long as everyone knows which one is which. You can't run the fan cookers off the barn. It won't cope.'

I am distracted by the arrival of the florist, a pretty and efficient girl called Alex. We were forced to use her once by some historical venue because she was on their recommended list, and Bernard was so impressed that he put her on our own.

'Hi there,' she says as she lugs a huge plastic bucket packed full of pale lilac stocks towards the marquee. 'That's my assistant, Trudi.'

'Hello,' says a lanky twentysomething blonde following on behind with an equally heavy-looking load.

'Do you need any help?' I ask.

'There are plenty more buckets of hydrangeas and delphiniums in the van,' Alex says, nodding over her shoulder.

The van is much larger than I expected and the smell of flowers is overpowering. There's bucket after bucket of lilac, pink and purple blooms. Some I recognize, like the sweet peas at the front, others I have no idea about.

'Oh God,' comes Louise's voice over my shoulder. 'I knew I should have insisted on coming to the meeting.' I turn around to see her standing behind me, sporting a pair of yellow Marigolds, her fists punched firmly into her waist. 'I can't abide the country look. I'd much rather the whole thing was done with white roses – so much more sophisticated.'

'Carol chose those,' I say. 'Richard's mother.'

'I am perfectly aware who Carol is,' spits Louise. 'I have met the woman once and that was enough. However, I do find it irritating that her suburban taste has been transported to the Sussex countryside.'

'Well, she did pay for them.'

'And don't I know it? And don't I know how much? And do I get my arch of flowers that I wanted round the entrance to the marquee? No. It was going to add another £7,000 to the bill and Carol didn't want to pay. So my daughter doesn't get what I want! Quite why Richard didn't pay for the flowers like he is supposed to, I don't know. Too busy trying to please all the people all the time. I don't think I have ever met such a spineless man.' She exhales in disgust and takes herself back off to the kitchen.

I have to say, these days it is more usual for the mother of the bride or the bride to choose the flowers, although traditionally it is the role of the groom and/or his mother. But most brides know what they want, or if they don't, they bring something that has 'the look' of the wedding, like the invitation or a picture of the wedding venue, to give the florist some pointers. However, a florist mate of mine had two photos of sofas and a Munch painting brought to a meeting once by way of inspiration. He did manage to conjure up something which seemed to please the bride. But such maverick requests are unusual as most brides go for the wedding staples – roses, orchids, hydrangeas, stocks and lily of the valley. Of these, lily of the valley is usually the most expensive as it is only in season in winter, and in order to have it at any other time it has to be forced or retarded in greenhouses in Holland.

Flower fashions are dictated as much by clothing fashion as they are by big celebrity weddings, and they swing from the super floral to the minimal depending on the current trends. The hedgerow look that demanded copious amounts of greenery is not quite so fashionable as it was. And there is supposed to be a move to all things seasonal and organic and indeed British. Much like our food, local flowers, grown by local people for locally sourced brides, are very much in vogue. Which is all well and good when you are popping down the aisle in May or June; however, later in the year when the first frosts have done their damage, there is bugger all for a bride to choose from apart from some tired old roses and a couple of carnations.

For very chic, very expensive weddings, the flowers are ordered and grown specifically in advance. The bride puts her order in six months ahead and the supplier, usually in Holland or the UK, sets a whole load of bulbs or plants aside. Last year we had a bride who wanted hyacinths in the middle of July, which is quite some ask for a spring-flowering plant. Anyway, the supplier held them back and when they arrived they were incredible. White flowering hyacinths in the middle of July. We had an arbour built especially for the photographs and in the ground we planted our sixty flowering hyacinths. It looked stunning. Like spring had just come to a small part of the garden. However, on the day, everyone forgot about the arbour, the photographs were taken elsewhere and no one even visited the woodland glade. It was £6,000 and six months' work totally down the drain.

'These are all in great condition,' I say, lifting up a bucket of pink roses.

'Well, Alex and I have been prepping them for twenty-four hours,' says Trudi. 'Taking the leaves off, giving them a good long drink so they don't collapse halfway through the service.'

'Giving them food,' I smile, joining in.

'Plant food?' She takes a step back from me like I have said the most offensive thing in the world. 'You only feed a plant if it needs it! Otherwise we leave that stuff well alone.'

'I have just spotted a huge stain in the marquee,' Alex declares, as she leans into the van to grab another bucket. 'So one of the plinth displays should move a bit to cover it.'

'Really?' I say. 'I couldn't see anything yesterday.'

'It is only when the sun shines on it,' she says. 'Looks like vomit to me.'

'That would figure.'

'Luckily I brought some extra flowers.'

A clever florist will always bring a few extra buckets of blooms along just in case. Not that they ever get thanked for it. On the day most brides ask for extra flowers, extra vases and extra displays, and they somehow never expect to see them on the bill. Most florists get the happy couple to part with 60 per cent of the cost when the budget is agreed, and then the balance a week before the wedding, otherwise they can suddenly find themselves chasing the couple while they are on honeymoon or calling for months afterwards. It is much better to get everything paid for before everyone forgets.

And of course flowers are so expensive. The average national spend for a wedding bouquet is just under £500, and it is hard to get one for less than £150, which still seems a lot to spend on a bunch of white roses. Talk to florists and they explain that their wedding mark-up – which is anything from five times the cost of the flowers to simply adding zero on to the end – is because of the time and effort that goes into preparing for a wedding. Quite apart from the three or four meetings that they have with the bride, it will take an experienced florist the best part of two hours to make a wedding bouquet. And they can only be made on the morning of the wedding. So if the wedding is at ten a.m. then the florist can be up at three making the bouquet. Also, for a simple dome of twenty white roses, twice the number of roses will be ordered, only for half of them to be rejected in order to create the perfect bunch. With so many rejects and so much time and planning required, it is easy to see how some of the really big florists, like Rob Van Helden and John Carter, end up regularly charging over £100,000 for a big wedding. You can obviously do a wedding for much less, but as soon as you start having guests sitting down to lunch or dinner and you want displays in the middle of the table, the costs start mounting up. You have 150 guests, which is fifteen tables at £40 a table, and that is before you have paid for the staff to deliver the flowers, and the people to take them away late at night. Or for a more formal wedding you may have a vase of twenty orchids on each table at £12 a stem, which comes to £240 a table, for maybe twenty tables, so you can see why any bride or groom would be only too happy to farm out the cost.

Alex's budget for Alice and Richard's wedding is £30,000 and that includes the marquee, the pews and the church, as well as the buttonholes and bouquets for the bridesmaids and the bride. It is hard to believe that the contents of this Ford Transit van are so valuable.

'I have a whole lot of vases at the front that you could carry out for me,' adds Alex. 'Is there anyone else who might lend a hand?'

I venture back into the kitchen and tentatively ask if anyone might want to help the florist girls out. Grace looks at me as if I have just asked her to dig a trench with her fingernails, and Alice is equally dumbstruck. Louise quickly intervenes on her behalf, saying that as the bride her job is simply to look beautiful and hard work is not on the menu. The only person to ditch their coffee is Alice's father, Alistair. I have a feeling it was the use of the word 'girls' that swung it.

'Good morning, ladies!' He announces his arrival with a loud smoker's cough and an enthusiastic rub of his hands. 'How exactly can I be of service to you?'

I follow Alistair, who follows Trudi with his eyes firmly trained on her buttocks; we go back and forth from the van to the marquee. It takes us about half an hour to carry all the buckets over and no sooner is the job complete than Alistair plonks himself down at one of the circular dining tables and sparks up a cigarette.

'So, girls,' he puffs, running his hand though his slicked-back hair. 'How long have you two been in the business?'

The girls respond politely to his questioning and advances. It is the pretty Alex rather than the younger Trudi who has caught his eye.

'So, Alex,' he asks, stubbing out his cigarette in the matting and placing himself indecently close to her. 'Will we have the delight of your company tomorrow?'

'Um,' she says, suddenly feeling the need to walk around the other side of her display oasis. 'Well, I shall come and deliver the bouquet, buttons and bridesmaids' flowers in the morning, and check on the flowers in here and the church. But I won't be coming to the wedding.'

'Oh?' he replies, following her around the plinth. 'I was rather hoping we could have a little boogie.' He raises his hands and swings his hips from side to side by way of a suggestion.

'Alice and Richard did invite me,' she says, moving further round and stabbing a pale-lilac stock into the wet oasis. 'But I tend not to go to weddings that I have done flowers for. I am staff. I don't know any of the guests. What am I going to talk to people about? Even I can't talk about flowers all evening.'

'I bet you can,' says Alistair, smiling and curling up his short nose in a bizarre attempt to look cute. 'I bet you can talk about flowers all night.'

'Coo-ee! Darling!' Trisha waves from across the lawn. 'You're needed! Alice wants to go through the order of service with you!'

'Coming, cupcake!' he shouts back with a little wave. 'I'll see you ladies in a minute.' He grins before sloping back up to the house.

'Christ,' mutters Alex as he goes. 'He's a bit of a one.'

But before Alex, Trudi and I can discuss the oleaginous advances of Mr Oxford, there is a high-pitched scream and sprinting out of the house comes a rather plump-looking child.

'Liberty! *Liberty!* Get your arse back here now!' Richard's sister, Katie, comes storming out on to the terrace, waving what looks like a bridesmaid's dress in the air. 'Get yourself back here now!'

'No!' shouts the tearful Liberty from behind a rhododendron bush down by the stream. 'I hate it. I don't want to wear it.'

'I don't care what you want! You asked to be a bloody bridesmaid and I've coughed up 120 quid for the privilege, so get back here. Now!'

Sobs emanate from behind the leaves, which are joined by great long sniffs as I approach.

'Are you OK?' I ask.

'No!' she says, turning to glare at me with red tear-stained eyes. Her pale-brown hair hangs lankly by the sides of her large flushed cheeks, and a column of snot shoots in and out of her nose each time she sniffs. It is not a pretty sight.

'Can I help?'

'Not unless you can help me lose a stone overnight,' she cries.

'Oh,' I say. 'Is the dress too small?'

'Yes,' she says, her face crumpling. 'They measured me six months ago and I've grown. It's not my fault. I am twelve.'

'It's your job to grow at twelve,' I say.

'But now I am a laughing stock. I can't be a

bridesmaid. I am too fat for the dress and that's that.'

'I think I know a man who can fix it.'

'Really? You're just saying that.' She shoves her hair behind her ears and wipes her nose on the sleeve of her tight pink T-shirt.

'No, I am not,' I say. 'It will involve a bit of time and money, but I am sure we can sort it out. I'll have to make a phone call first.'

Simon is charm itself when I call him. As a clinically obese teenager himself who still has eating issues as an adult, he is only too happy to help a pubescent girl who has porked out of her dress. He promises, if I manage to bike him the dress, that he will get it to Bernard, who is coming down to oversee the wedding early tomorrow morning. He says he won't charge, as it is such a small quick job and he clearly feels a certain sense of solidarity with the pubescent overweight.

So by the time the furious Katie comes marching towards us both at the bottom of the garden, the situation is solved. This earns me a grudging 'thank you' from her, but a very fabulous warm hug from Alice. Even her mother manages a stiff smile, although I can't help thinking she was rather hoping that Liberty might not make her aesthetically challenged appearance down the aisle after all.

Back in the marquee, Alex and Trudi are getting along nicely, filling the tables with stunning lilac and pink flowers and pinning small bunched twists of lavender to the back of every white chair cover. It is amazing how a marquee comes alive once the flowers are in place. Alex is gossiping about a friend of hers who has just come back from doing a wedding in the Middle East.

'There were twelve of them out there for nearly two weeks doing the flowers,' she says, picking up twists of lavender. 'They worked from six a.m. through to two a.m. every day for twelve days, prepping five thousand vases at a time. They had sixty thousand roses that needed cutting and dunking in water.'

'Imagine the rubbish,' says Trudi.

'I know,' agrees Alex. 'It was huge. They had ten thousand white orchids flown in from Malaysia and eighteen thousand lilies from Holland, all for this incredible display where they were just dripping off the balcony. They had urns that took ten men to lift at one time.'

'What was the budget?' I ask.

'Well, there wasn't one, but the flowers cost £400,000. But that was without the vintage crystal and silver bowls for the roses or the bespoke vases for the orchids. It sounded incredible. There was a dinner for eight hundred women in the evening in a marble marquee that was made for the event, with marble floors and water features. There was no drink, no men and an awful lot of couture.'

'How dull,' says Trudi.

'It was all over in an hour and a half.'

'Where were the blokes?' I ask.

'They were having some sword-fighting dinner in tents in the desert.'

'That sounds much more exciting,' sighs Trudi. 'I think I'd much prefer to be a bloke if I lived in the Middle East.'

'But there were so many dinners and lunches,' continues Alex. 'Each had new flowers and there were new venues for each – there was a garden party where the place was decked out with white spray roses and white urns and white furniture and white umbrellas that had all been shipped in. And the clothes they all wore! Valentino for breakfast, Chanel for lunch, Lacroix for the garden party and Dior for dinner. He said he had never seen so many frocks in his entire life, and the queue of Bentleys lined up outside the party was extraordinary. Apparently they asked him to sign a contract saying that he would never re-create any of the floral designs ever again.'

'But everyone puts roses in a crystal bowl,' says Trudi.

'I know,' agrees Alex. 'There are some things I would be very happy never to repeat again.'

'Like the orange and yellow arum lilies with orange beads in red vases?' laughs Trudi. 'That is the only time I have ever seen you cry.'

'Well, it was so disgusting, and the vases the bride insisted on using kept falling over because they were so goddamn cheap, and the caterer minced over and said, "Oh, this *is* different." That was enough to make me lose it. Never again am I doing something I hate because the bride wants it. I think I'd rather lose the job than go through that humiliation again.'

Alex and Trudi continue discussing the various hideous floral displays they have witnessed, while I am distracted by the sound of a horn in the drive. To my relief it is a truck pulling a luxury-lavatory trailer. A rosy-cheeked chap with thick straw hair sticking out at all angles leaps out of the driving seat. There are two other blokes sitting next to him in the front.

'Hi there!' he says, smiling, with a broad hand out-stretched.

'Peter?'

'That's right,' he nods.

'Am I glad to see you.'

'So I gather,' he says, pulling his jeans up over his flat stomach. 'Nice place.'

'I know.'

'How many people are you expecting?'

'Two hundred and fifty.'

'This should do it,' he says, nodding over his shoulder. 'But it will probably take quite a battering.'

'I shouldn't think so,' I say, looking a little confused.

'Are you kidding?' he says, grinning broadly, looking for signs of jest on my face. 'A posh wedding? They're the worst. The sick, the sex, the knickers we find in the system, the foot marks on the ceiling. They only ever happen at the posh weddings. They kick the doors down, use every flat surface available for cocaine. There are always wraps of the stuff everywhere the next day – that and a bloke fast asleep in the cubicle.'

'Yes, well,' I agree. 'Now you put it like that.'

'I tell you, mate,' he says, walking round to the back of the truck. 'The worst are those polo matches. We did one the other day where a girl called up to ask if we could get her wallet out of the loo. What did she have that out for, I wonder? The wealthier they are, the filthier. They just don't care. Where do you want it?'

'The other side of the marquee. We have built a tunnel for it.' I point down the garden.

'Right,' he says, pushing his thick fringe off his forehead. 'Can we go through the field? If not, you should tell the lady of the house we risk buggering up her lawn.'

After some swift negotiating, Louise finally agrees that 'just this once' the truck can take the loo trailer through the field. Peter cranks the engine into gear and to the accompaniment of Louise's yells, sighs, winces and instructions he eventually manages to get the lavatories somewhere approaching the back of the marquee.

'Pavel! Andrei!' shouts Peter at his two Polish assistants. 'Here.' He mimes lugging the trailer the final ten yards to the back of the tent. 'We'll need to tap power from somewhere,' says Peter. 'And you need to ask the bride what sort of music she wants in the lavs. Also,' he adds, 'I think you should suggest to her that she not use these on the day. The amount of times brides have got the blue stuff on their dresses – it's bad, and it doesn't come out.'

'I had suggested that she use the lavatories in the house already,' I nod. 'Also we all know what's in that stuff.'

'Yeah,' he nods and laughs.

The blue loo systems are sealed units, so whatever chemicals are put into the system are then pumped around and around. So the more people use the lavatories, the more potent the concoction that gets pumped around. The blue liquid that is used to flush the lavatory is not water, or blue liquid and water, but the contents of the previous occupant's bowl. Knowing that, quite why anyone would want to spend any time in a cubicle involved in drug-taking or romantic pursuits is beyond me. It is effectively one big churning cesspit that gets more full of cess the longer the party goes on.

'The other day,' continues Peter, while guiding the trailer, 'someone made a huge mistake, and it wasn't me, because I was called in to fix it, but they put the vacuum system in the wrong way round, so when you pushed the button to flush, the thing just blasted back at you.'

'No shit!' I say.

'Well, actually, plenty of shit,' he replies. 'What I found weird was that after it happened to two or three people you would have thought everyone else would stop using them. But no. About eight or nine people were covered in blue crap before someone suggested that perhaps no one should use the loos.'

About half an hour later everything is connected up. The spotlighting works inside, there is hot and cold running water in the taps and some Chris de Burgh on the stereo.

'Is this the bride's choice?' I ask, wincing slightly.

'No, it is the standard testing CD,' says Peter, fiddling with the soap dispenser. 'She is looking for some music in the house. You've got no attendant in these toilets,' he continues, screwing up the dispenser, 'so can you make sure that someone keeps an eye on this stuff?'

'What?'

'I have had it up to here,' he says, tapping his forehead, 'with people nicking my Molton Brown. Every time I do a wedding like this it happens. Do you know, a mate of mine did a posh do at the Tate the other day and they had Jo Malone in the lavs, and they were all cleaned out before the main course! This same bloke did these really smart loos with Aynsley china door handles and hand plates, and someone pinched everything, unscrewing the lot with a nail file. It's not that they really want the stuff, I think they just have a few drinks and think, why not?'

'Well,' I say, brushing down the front of my suit and puffing myself up with indignation, 'I can assure you, this is not that sort of wedding.'

Friday p.m.

Walking back up to the house, I am beginning to regret my sweeping assurances that this is going to be a perfectly run and well-behaved wedding; I can hear Louise swearing from here. She is ordering Alistair and Trisha out of the kitchen and shouting at Richard and Andrew to go and do something useful. I knock tentatively on the kitchen door, only to hear her yell, 'You are ALL ruining what is supposed to be the best FUCKING weekend of my life!'

'I'll be off then,' says Peter, who, much to my surprise, has followed me up the garden.

'Oh!' I say, turning around.

'Oh!' Louise reiterates, desperately trying to regain her composure. 'And will we be seeing you again?'

'You probably won't.' He smiles over my shoulder. 'We are coming very early on Sunday morning, before any of you are awake. We need the toilets back for a corporate do on Monday morning, and they take twenty-four hours to turn around.'

'That's nice,' smiles Louise.

'Who knew there was that much money in shit,' laughs Alistair. 'Quite literally, where there's muck, there's brass.'

'Alistair!' hisses Louise, her lips all pursed and affronted.

'Absolutely,' laughs Peter, as if he has never heard that joke before. But then he's pocketing a cool £2,000 for a weekend for a loo that costs just £220 to clean up and turn around, so the joke is clearly on us. 'See you guys around!' he smiles. 'Or perhaps not.'

As Peter leaves the drive, the courier arrives to take Liberty's dress back to London. Katie comes ambling out of the house, as if moving faster might actually kill her.

'Make sure it's back by tomorrow,' she says, holding the pink frilled dress aloft.

'Of course,' I say, taking it from her dimpled hand. 'I was actually thinking Monday,' I mumble, trying hard not to kick the woman in the shins.

'You what?' she asks.

'Nothing. Of course, tomorrow morning, as soon as we can.'

One of the problems of being a wedding planner when it comes close to the actual big day is that the family can start to treat you like a servant. I have had some real cheeky bitches asking me to go and get them fags from the pub, or a drink from downstairs, or top-up cards for the bridesmaids' mobile phones. Which is why I mostly try and keep out of the family's way. My duties are to make sure the marquee is looking good, the caterers are behaving, that everything is arriving on time and that what has arrived is correct.

Talking of which, I had better quickly run through the order-of-service sheets with Richard that I have just walked past in the hall.

I find Richard smoking on the terrace with his feet up on one of the cream brushed-wood dining chairs that he appears to have taken from the marquee. He is on the phone, apparently talking to an usher.

'Yeah, right, yeah,' he laughs. 'There's a lunch at the Fox and Rabbit in the village before the wedding, for the ushers, at about twelve. Yeah – too right!' He roars with laughter and throws his fag into the flowerbed. 'Dutch courage! Catch you later.' He hangs up.

'Not too much Dutch courage, I hope,' I say.

'What?' He looks at me like I have interrupted a deep and profound thought.

'Not too much of the old shandy.' I make a drinking gesture. 'I had a vicar who refused to marry a couple once because the groom was too drunk. He didn't think he was of a right and sentient mind, or whatever the expression is, to understand what he was saying, so they had to call the whole thing off and wait until a week later.'

'Shit,' says Richard.

'Absolutely,' I agree. 'Can I talk to you about the order of service? I just want to check a few things with you.'

'Hi, babe,' says Alice, arriving on the terrace in a denim miniskirt and white T-shirt. She sits herself down on a deckchair next to Richard. 'What are you doing?'

'I just want to go through the order of service,' I say, handing them both a copy.

'Haven't we been through this a hundred times?' sighs Richard, stretching into a yawn.

'We'll have a chance to go through it again at the rehearsal this afternoon, but I just want to look at the printed copy to make sure it is all OK with you guys.' I pause. They are both looking at the sheets, one more enthusiastically than the other. I opt to carry on while I have any semblance of attention. 'So you are coming down the aisle to the Queen of Sheba?'

'That's right.' Alice nods.

'And the hymns are "Dear Lord and Father of Mankind", "Praise My Soul the King of Heaven" and "I Vow to Thee, My Country"?'

'That's right – I think,' says Richard.

'And the readings are 1 Corinthians 13 and *The Prophet*,' I say, looking down at the sheet. 'And 1 Corinthians is being read by your dad, Alice?'

'That's right.' She nods. 'He was practising this morning at the cottage, apparently.'

'And *The Prophet* is Andrew? And he's OK with that?' I ask.

'Er, well, I haven't asked him yet,' admits Richard, scratching his crotch with embarrassment.

'What?' yells Alice, leaping out of her chair and suddenly sounding worryingly like her mother. 'You were supposed to ask him two months ago!'

'Yeah, well, some of us have jobs,' he snipes back.

'What's that supposed to mean?' Her hands go straight on to her hips and her teeth clench. This is clearly an old argument.

'You know what that means. You've been getting married for at least the last six months and everything else has taken a back seat, including your work,' he says, staring back at her equally defiantly.

'What are you now, my boss?' Her shoulders shake with anger.

'No, it's just that every single one of your mates has had it with the bride thing,' he says. '"How can she say that? Doesn't she know I am getting married?"' he mimics. '"I can't do that – I am getting married. I don't have time – I am getting married." You've got a fucking planner!' He points at me. 'How goddamn difficult can it be?'

'Yes, well, some of us like to do things properly, which is more than can be said for you, because you can't even remember to ask the best man to do a reading when you see the bastard every goddamn day of your life. In fact, I think you spend more time with Andrew than you do with me!'

'That's because he doesn't nag!'

'I don't nag!'

Just as I am wondering quite how to extricate myself from this domestic, my phone goes. It is the vicar, asking if someone will collect him from the station. He has been in the neighbouring diocese all morning and the taxi company said there was a forty-five-minute wait. I pass on the message to Richard and Alice and they both look at me, extremely irritated by the interruption.

'OK, then,' I say, looking at their tense faces. 'I'll go.'

'Thank you,' replies Alice. I turn to walk away. 'And another thing,' she barks. 'Take your fucking feet off the fucking dining chair. We have spent thousands of pounds hiring this shit – the last thing we need is for you to bugger it up and lose us our deposit.'

After such a fraught atmosphere in the house, I am quite looking forward to getting out of the place and going for a relaxing drive to the next village to pick up the vicar, David Clinton. We have spoken a few times on the phone already when I was booking him and the local St Mary's Church. He seems like a nice enough chap, helpful and not quite as mad as the snake pit I'm leaving.

As I reverse the car around, I spot Alistair slinking his way back out into the garden and down to the marquee. He is off to sex-pest the poor florists again. Although I have to say, both girls looked like they could handle him quite easily.

Pulling up outside the station I spot Reverend Dave leaning against the wall, taking in the sun. He is wearing a white shirt, soft brown shoes and the sort of baggy high-waisted jeans that only ever seem to appear on priests or geography teachers. He is also sporting a dodgy pair of purple-tinted sunglasses that only a paedophile would find groovy.

'Good afternoon.' He smiles, revealing a set of very English teeth, like a partly bulldozed graveyard.

'Very kind of you to pick me up. I am extremely sorry to bother you, but by the time the cab came to collect me and drop me at the house, we would all be a good fifteen minutes late for the rehearsal, and I hate to keep people waiting and I hate to let them down.'

'It's fine,' I reply, opening the car door. 'In fact I am quite pleased to be able to get out of the house.'

'That bad?' he asks, plonking himself next to me and smoothing down his very thin mousy hair. 'I haven't met this couple yet, actually, which is a bit bad. Normally I'd like to meet them a few times to discuss a few things, like how many children they want, and if they've been married before.'

'I imagine that's quite a conversation.' I smile, turning the car around.

'Normally it is fairly straightforward.' He shrugs. 'Although the other day I had someone who forgot.'

'What? That they had been married?'

'Yup,' he says, looking out of the window. 'It's a big thing, bigamy. I had to stop a wedding once because the groom was still married. I made them both come to the vestry to explain themselves. He'd apparently just made a mistake. He'd forgotten that he'd forgotten to get a divorce. A bride I married also forgot to say 'yes' to the 'Have you been married?' question on the form. She'd ticked the 'no' box because it was so long ago and she thought it didn't matter any more. It was a green-card marriage, so apparently she thought it didn't count. It wasn't until someone told me at the reception that this husband was so much nicer than the last one that I realized we had a situation. So I had to go back to the house the next day and ask her what she was playing at. Fortunately, she was divorced; otherwise it would have been a police matter. And you can see why – lots of scam artists make lots of money out of bigamy. It's a lucrative business.'

'And yet it is so expensive getting married,' I laugh.

'Especially if you have a planner,' he says, turning to look at me. 'What is the world coming to, when a couple are too busy to organize the most important day of their lives?'

'Maybe it is just that we do it better,' I reply.

'But what's better?' He sighs. 'The average cost of a wedding is £21,000 and only £250 is spent on the church. Don't you think we've got something wrong? That the emphasis is a little skewed? Most people think of the church bit as something to get through before the party. But in my experience, if people put a bit of effort into the service it tends to be a much better wedding.'

'I can see that, I suppose.'

'I tell you,' he laughs, 'if I had a pound for every time the bride has come down the aisle to that wretched Queen of Sheba and I've had to sit through 1 Corinthians 13 and the awful *Prophet*, which is Corinthians for those who think they are trendy, then I'd be a very rich man. I can't believe couples are so dull and unimaginative. I don't know of a single vicar who doesn't loathe the whole lot. I personally can't read Corinthians without thinking of Tony Blair. "Love is patient, love is kind . . ." I just hear his voice all the way through. Still,' he grins, 'mustn't groan. There are some churches that do more funerals than weddings. Thankfully, mine is not one of them.'

'So are you busy at the moment?' I say, trying to sound breezy and all the time thinking about the order of service sitting on the back seat of my car. What will he do when he sees it? Will Reverend Dave pretend it is fine, or will he just remain mute?

'I've done four weddings this week,' he says, smoothing down the front of his jeans.

'God!' I say, and then immediately apologize. Is that swearing? I'm not sure. 'Goodness,' I continue. 'How can you write an address for all of those?'

'I don't. I have six addresses on my computer at home and cut and paste them accordingly,' he explains, rolling down his window and looking back out of it. 'Oh! Afternoon, Mrs James!' he shouts suddenly at a large middle-aged woman in gardening gloves at her garden gate. 'See you Sunday! Sorry,' he adds, turning to me. 'She does the flowers for the church. No,' he continues. 'I have the six and I try to add a few bits and bobs. About how brilliant it is that Susie and Roger met at school, how great that they have been together since the office party. You don't want a dry theology lesson. You know, "A marriage is . . ." thing. Otherwise you've lost them. You do want to try to capture the moment a bit. I think seven minutes is the perfect length. Any shorter and they feel cheated, and any longer and they get all fidgety. But it is desperate if you are clutching at straws, trying to think of interesting things to say.'

'I can imagine,' I say.

'That's part of the reason for the forms, so I can try to find out something about the couple, to see if they're suited. I had a couple in last year who only had sex in common. They were from different walks of life and wanted different things. It was lust that held them together. It was obvious that it wasn't going to last, and it didn't. I do try to get couples to think a bit about what they are doing. Ask themselves some questions. Most people prepare more for a holiday than they do for a lifetime together.' I turn left up the lane that leads to the house. 'Oh, this is nice,' he says, poking his head out of the window. 'I have been up here before, but it was a long time ago. Is the father a bit of a Lothario?'

'Sorry?' Is that the sort of question a vicar should ask?

'Is the mother a bit ginger?' he tries again.

'That's right,' I say.

'I have definitely been here before, but it was years ago. I think I might have had tea here when I first joined the parish about ten years ago.'

We pull up in the drive and Alice comes out to meet us. Her face looks swollen and her pretty turned-up nose looks a little red. She has very obviously been crying, but judging by her over-effusive smile, it is clearly something she doesn't want us to mention.

'Good afternoon,' says Reverend Dave, grasping her hand with both of his. 'I am the other one in the white dress.'

'I am so sorry we didn't collect you,' Alice says.

'Don't worry.' He pats the back of her hand. 'I am sure you had better things to do. How is everything coming on? Are you on time? On schedule? How are the flowers?'

'It is all OK, I think – I hope. At least the loos arrived this morning. We didn't have any of those until an hour ago,' she says, trying to raise a smile.

'But the matter was very much in hand,' I add.

'Ah! Vicar!' booms Louise from the hall. 'Are we ready for the rehearsal?' She walks towards us in a new floral wrap-dress that is clearly intended to show off her curves, but instead rather sadly just shows off her underwear, which is clearly visible in the bright sunshine.

'We have met before,' he says, holding out his hand.

'Have we?' queries Louise.

'It was a while ago, I think.'

'Not when I was married?' she snorts.

'Probably.'

'God save us!' she replies. 'Are we all ready to go to the rehearsal? Because I want you home and in the bath before the dinner tonight,' she adds, looking at Alice. 'We have taken over Othello's.' She smiles at Reverend Dave.

'Oh, very nice, I am sure,' he replies.

'Well, it is the best restaurant for miles around,' she adds, just in case the man has forgotten.

'Only the best,' he says. 'Actually, if you don't mind, I would rather the couple just come on their own, along with those directly involved in the service.'

'Oh,' says Louise, sounding extremely put out. 'Well, I would rather be there to see what is going on.'

'Are you reading a lesson?' asks Dave.

'No,' she says, her eyes narrowing at the realization that her ex-husband is. 'But . . .'

'I think it is for the best,' he continues. 'You must have so much you need to do here at the house. Although, looking about, you do seem to have it all under control.'

'Thank you.' She smiles, her lips tighter than ever. 'Now you say that, I can see my role is here – where all the important things need doing.'

'Quite,' nods the vicar. 'Who is doing the readings? And let's take a look at that order of service, just to see what we are in for tomorrow.' He rubs his hands with enthusiasm and looks around for someone to hand him a booklet.

'Here you are,' says Alice. 'Fresh off the press.'

'Excellent,' he replies, sniffing the freshly printed paper before opening it. 'Sheba,' he mumbles as his finger goes down the pages. 'Corinthians, *The Prophet* and – Oh!' He smiles. 'And "I Vow to Thee, My Country". A full house! Great! What can I say?' And for a moment I think I see him struggle to fight the huge wave of boredom that's just enveloped him. 'Very traditional.' He grins. 'Very traditional indeed.'

'Oh, I am glad you like it,' says Alice, her nose wrinkling as she smiles. 'We really thought about it.'

'It must have taken hours,' agrees Reverend Dave.

St Mary's Church is about ten minutes away by car. Perched at the top of a small incline, it is about four hundred years old and is short and fat and utterly charming. With a skinny path leading to the door, it is surrounded by a cluttered, tumbling graveyard that appears to be home to about twenty grazing sheep.

'That brings a whole new meaning to the word recycling,' says Andrew, the best man, getting out of the car and spotting a large ram on a particularly grassy grave.

'Don't,' says Alice. 'You have now totally put me off my main course tomorrow.'

'OK then,' says Dave, pulling the large metal key out of his bag. 'Let's crack on, shall we? Just to say to you that obviously the church will look very different tomorrow. The florist will have done her stuff and the place will be packed.' He opens the heavy wooden door and a rush of cold air blasts out.

Inside, the church is a good solid traditional venue. There's a stone font to the right as you enter, a reasonable-length aisle and rows of wooden pews. The pulpit sports a large lectern with a bronze eagle. The altar is small, with a large ornate gold cross, with three relatively simple stained-glass windows above it.

'Welcome to St Mary's,' says Reverend Dave. 'It will be a bit warmer tomorrow, with the doors left open.'

'Nice church,' says Andrew. 'Do you think everyone will fit in?'

'The church has capacity for 150,' I say. 'So there will be standing room only at the back. If possible, it would be good to have the elderly sitting and the younger guests standing.'

'Well then, I am at the back,' announces Alistair, shoving his shades to the back of his head as he ambles up and down the aisle.

'Actually, you are with your daughter,' I correct him. 'And then you are in the front pew on the left. Bride to the left and groom to the right.'

'Oh yes,' says Dave. 'Though I like to encourage the families to mix, just in case there is too much segregation, particularly when it is a mixed marriage. The last thing you want is a black side and a white side. Or one side in morning suits and the other one not. But this one is probably well mixed anyway, isn't it?' He looks from Alice to Richard.

'You might think that,' mumbles Andrew, walking towards the altar.

'Right then,' smiles Dave, breezing on. 'So imagine the place is full, there are flowers everywhere—'

'On the side of the pews?' Alice checks with me.

I nod. 'Sweet peas and lilacs.'

'So the ushers have done their ushering, your parents are over here on the right, Richard—'

'Not together,' Richard corrects. 'Mum is on her own and Dad and Bev are in the row behind.'

314

'OK,' nods Dave. 'And your family, Alice – your mum and dad are there on the left.'

'On their own?' asks Alice.

'No, with Trish,' says Alistair.

'Trish is not in the front row,' insists Alice. 'She is not family.'

Her father stares at her and then smiles. 'Whatever you want, baby, it's your big day. Trish won't mind, she'll sit where I tell her.'

'OK then – you take your father's arm. The left one. You are on his left. He's on the right, and then . . . the bridesmaids?' Dave looks around and spots the surly Grace and the chubby Liberty. He seems relieved. 'No tots then?'

'Sadly, no,' says Alice, looking round at the motley crew about to follow her down the aisle.

'Thank goodness for that,' smiles Dave. 'I can't bear a tot at a wedding. They run loose and you can't control them. These days they usually belong to the bride and groom, so no one wants to discipline them. No one is in charge. People don't know how to behave in church any more and they think it is fine for a three-year-old to run up and down the aisle and rock the flower arrangements until the stems come tumbling down. But anything that distracts the couple is a bad idea. Having said that, I had a big bride poured into a small dress the other day and that

315

proved to be more distracting than a whole nursery of small children!' He laughs.

'I know what you mean!' chuckles Alistair.

Liberty's cheeks blush the same unfortunate colour as her tight T-shirt.

'So, music,' picks up Dave. 'The Queen of Sheba – is it a CD, or have you hired the organist? I would say her repertoire is small, but I think even she can stretch to Sheba. The CD player is a bit dodgy, that's all.'

'We have a string quartet and a soprano,' I say.

'Singing "Ave Maria" during the signing of the register?' he asks. I want to say no. But he is right. That's exactly what the clients have asked for. You can come up with suggestions until you are blue in the face, but what the client wants the client gets. So I just smile. 'Excellent,' he nods. 'All very traditional. I had a wedding the other day, not in this church but in St Peter's up the road, where the bride said that she wanted to come up the aisle to the Robin Hood music—'

'"Everything I Do" by Bryan Adams,' says Alice.

'That's the one,' he nods. 'But sadly the organist didn't understand that, and when the bride came down the aisle, she pressed Play and out came "Robin Hood, Robin Hood, riding through the glen. Robin Hood, Robin Hood, with his band of men!"'

Richard bursts out laughing. 'I'd pay to see that,' he says.

'Right then,' says Dave. 'So you come down the aisle. Nice and slowly. I can't tell you how many brides have bolted to the altar and have been left standing there for five minutes waiting for the music to finish. It is not a race. The slower the better, and you two –' he nods towards Grace and Liberty, 'you take your cue from the bride. So the slower she walks, the slower you do. Now Richard, do you want me to nod when Alice is near? I have had quite a few grooms burst into tears when the bride comes down the aisle.'

'Have you?' Andrew looks confused. 'How bizarre.'

'They can't cope with her in all her finery. Do you want to look? It is strange not to. Although I know a Scottish vicar who was so overcome with the sound of the bagpipes that he forgot to nod at the groom. And the bride was furious that he didn't look at her. So I would suggest halfway down, and then you can compose yourself should you want to cry.'

'I don't think that will be necessary,' laughs Andrew, slapping Richard on the back. 'You're not the crying type.'

'You'd be surprised what happens on the day,' says Dave. 'I had one groom stammer so much while saying his vows he wet himself at the altar.'

'Christ,' mutters Alistair, shaking his head like a man who has recently had to get in touch with his prostate.

'Fingers crossed that doesn't happen to you, Rich!' laughs Grace.

'OK, we are all here.' Reverend Dave spreads his arms out in front of him. 'Alistair, you hand over Alice to me, and then I hand her to Richard . . .'

'Like chattels,' says Grace.

'Well, not exactly,' says Dave.

'Don't you think marriage is an outdated institution propagated by the male patriarchy, whose only intention is to keep women in their place?' she asks, shaking her head slightly.

'Or indeed a coming together of two people who love each other,' replies Dave in a jaded voice. 'So Alistair, you are there . . . and then I make my welcome address. I hate telling people not to throw confetti and take photos in church, so could you all spread the word beforehand—'

'But we have organic biodegradable rose petals,' I interrupt.

'Oh,' he sighs. 'I am sure those are fine. But no photos inside the church, because once they start . . . I had some bloke with a perm, medallion and open-neck shirt walking backwards down the aisle last week, snapping the bride like she was J-Lo on the red

318

carpet. And then he plonked himself between her and me and I nearly punched his lights out. Anyway, the photos are very boring. You don't move for ages. So then we do the vows. With or without "obey"?' he asks Alice.

'Oh,' she says, looking at Richard. 'With?'

'Without,' he says.

'Without,' she repeats.

'Oh, I almost forgot. When it comes to the "due impediment" it is not funny to hear the whole church cough,' he says. 'So if you have a group of rugby mates who think it's hilarious to cough, then tell them not to.'

'And that includes you.' Richard smiles at Andrew.

'Oh no, the end of another cunning plan,' he replies.

'Then I pronounce you man and wife,' continues Dave.

'And you can kiss the bride?' asks Alice.

'That's an American thing,' says Dave. 'I can put it in if you want. Like you haven't already!' He laughs.

'Yes, please,' says Alice. 'That's the best bit.'

'OK, and then we go and sign the register in the vestry out the back there.' He points to a small door off to the right. 'You are married in the eyes of the Lord when you say your vows, and you are married in the eyes of the Law when you sign the register. All

I ask is that you don't spill ink down the front of your lovely dress. I had someone do that not so long ago and she had to have a bridesmaid stand in front of her in every single photo.'

Dave finishes the rehearsal with a little pep talk about how this is a joyous occasion and that everyone should have fun. Weddings are to be relished and enjoyed and every moment is to be savoured. He tells Alice that everyone is on her side, the whole congregation is rooting for her, so she must keep her head up and smile. He runs through a few more timings, telling Richard to get his ushers there at least half an hour before kick-off. The elderly like to arrive early to get a good pew and there should be someone there to seat them.

On the way back, with just the two of us in the car, Reverend Dave is a little quieter than before.

'That went well,' I enthuse, trying to make some form of conversation.

'Mmm,' he says.

'You're coming to the reception?'

'Would I miss sitting next to the village atheist? Or the aunt who loves church architecture? Or the bloke whose Uncle Barry is a vicar?'

'I suppose you must have a list of twenty questions that you trot out all the time!'

'Just getting one out would be nice sometimes. You need the patience of a saint to sit next to these people – which is why you are put there, of course.'

'Yes, I can see that might not be great,' I say.

'It is not the nicest way for me to spend my Saturday night. I would, quite frankly, rather be with my wife and children.' He sighs, puffing out his cheeks. 'Is there a good spread?'

'Oh, excellent,' I reply, trying to cheer him up.

'Thank goodness,' he says. 'I always find the richer the people, the meaner the spread. With a working-class wedding you always get good food, they make an effort. Some posh weddings I have been to, you're lucky to get a sausage roll. The bride looks great, the flowers are amazing, but the champagne runs out and you end up with a cup of tea and a sandwich. There really is a limit to how many terrible canapés you can eat.'

'You won't stay late?' I suggest.

'No, I'll slip off at the speeches,' he says. 'Don't you think that best man is a bit odd?' he asks suddenly. 'He seems furious.'

Sadly, I don't have time to contemplate Dave's theory about Andrew because all the way back to the house I field calls from Bernard, checking up on the flowers and the loos and the Oakes & Co rental. Then Nigel calls to find out if his ovens are ready, and if he has a special tent for mise en place and laying out all the canapés. Simon calls and tells me the dress has arrived and he's let it out as far as he can. Then the band – the Taylor Six – call to ask what time their sound check is tomorrow. They also ask what the first song is. Bearing in mind they sing everything from Snow Patrol to James Blunt, I say I'll check with the happy couple.

By the time I have dropped Dave off and reached the house, Alex and Trudi are just finishing up and the marquee looks fantastic. There are lilac displays on every table and huge plinths with cascading flowers at various focal points in the marquee – by the entrance, the stage and top table.

'We are in the church tomorrow morning,' says Alex, looking exhausted. 'I shall pop by later tonight and early tomorrow to give the flowers a spray, but unless it is extremely hot tomorrow they should last, no problem. What is the forecast for tomorrow?'

'Good,' I say, not having checked yet. 'Good, that's what I have heard.'

'Oh Mum, don't you think it looks fantastic?' Alice declares, standing behind me.

Dressed in a stunning low-cut red frock which knots at her cleavage and stops just above the knee, she is clearly ready for the rehearsal dinner. As is

Louise, who is wearing something equally revealing, but in black. Except she has rather overdone the make-up, painting two dark-blue circles over her eyes and splashing a shiny burgundy on her lips. She looks like a seven-year-old who has been playing dressing-up. Next to her is a heavy-looking woman with a tight grey perm, dressed in a pair of beige keep-the-crease slacks and a purple satin shirt. She is clutching a glass of champagne to her chest with both hands, as if fearful that someone might take it away from her.

'Thank you, Carol,' says Alice, giving the woman a kiss.

'Pleasure, love,' she smiles. 'Just so long as you are happy.'

'Carol,' I say. 'Very lovely to meet you.' I go over to shake her hand.

'Oh, sorry,' says Louise, her voice distinctly more plummy than before. 'This is the planner. This is Carol.' She moves her maroon-painted fingertips from me to Carol.

'My mother-in-law.' Alice shrugs her shoulders.

'Not yet, darling, not yet,' says Louise, moving away; her nostrils flare like she has just inhaled something unpleasant.

'Only twenty-four more hours,' adds Carol, tapping Alice on the back of the hand. Louise winces.

323

'Paul and Bev should be along in a minute,' she adds, taking a gulp of champagne.

'Things just get better and better,' says Louise.

'How many are we for the dinner tonight?' asks Carol.

'Seventy,' I reply. 'It is as many as the restaurant can hold.'

It takes about another forty-five minutes for the party to disappear off to the restaurant, and although I have organized it, arranged the menu and some extra flowers and got Desmond to draw a seating plan, it is much better that I don't go.

Steve is coming back tonight to make sure that the lighting is working in the marquee and the garden. We have to sound-check the equipment, and make sure the mikes and speakers are working and that no one is going to electrocute themselves during the speeches.

Steve and I have been going up and down ladders for the last three hours when people start coming back from the dinner. Katie is one of the first to fall out of a minicab and stagger up the drive, helped along by her twelve-year-old daughter. There is one point when she looks like she might retch into the flowerbed. But she mumbles, 'No, no, you're all right,' to Liberty, which the girl takes as an instruction to move on.

Next are Grace and Andrew, who seem to be perfectly perpendicular as they disappear off inside the house. They are rapidly followed by Alice, Louise and Richard, who all scream up the drive, with Louise at the wheel.

'You have got to start being nicer to Richard's family!' shouts Alice as she marches out of the car.

'I don't have to do anything!' replies Louise, shaking her finger. 'My house, my party—'

'My wedding!' shouts Alice. 'And you!' She turns her attention to Richard. 'You aren't supposed to be here! It is the night before our wedding. It is bad luck for you to see me. You are supposed to be with Andrew in the B&B down the road.'

'I can't help it if we forgot our suits,' he says.

'Well think!' she yells. 'I am off to bed.'

Richard is left standing by Louise's car. 'Don't look at me, sunshine,' says Louise. 'I am off to bed too, and anyway I am far too drunk to drive.'

Steve and I look at each other, smile and crack on. We have a few more technical dry runs to sort out before we can hit the sack. And anyway, my small child's bed in the rafters doesn't exactly exude comfort.

In a corner of the marquee we find an open bottle of champagne and start to knock it back. We're both exhausted and need a lift. Steve starts checking the sound system again and tweaking the lights.

'How about the pink?' he shouts.

'Perfect!' I shout back. 'Great with this track.' I get up and with the bottle in hand start swaying around to 'She's The One' by Robbie Williams.

'Is this the first-dance song?' he shouts.

'No,' says Richard, suddenly standing right next to me, also with a bottle in his hand. 'It's "Have I Told You Lately" by Nat King Cole.'

'It's "Have I Told You!" ' I shout.

'We've got that,' he yells back. 'Shall I put it on?'

'Yes, please,' says Richard. 'Can you dance?' he asks me suddenly.

'Yeah,' I say.

'You know, properly, like the waltz?'

'Yeah.' He is really quite drunk because he is swaying and standing, which takes some doing.

'Can you teach me?' he slurs. 'Before tomorrow? Like now?'

'Sure,' I say. Bizarre as this may sound, I am quite used to dancing with grooms on or just before their wedding day. I have often been asked for a quick reminder of how it's done by those so nervous they don't know their left foot from their right. I take hold of his hand and place it in the small of my back and put my hand on his shoulder.

'Make sure your hand doesn't slip down to my

arse,' I laugh as I take a step backwards. 'Remember, don't push her around too much. Whatever Fred Astaire did, Ginger Rogers did backwards in high heels.'

'OK,' he mumbles, lurching somewhat.

'So it is basically one-two-three. A waltz is a three-four. So forward step, and then side and feet together and back, and then to the side, and then feet together. It's not hard; it's like stepping around a box. So forward step, side, together and then backwards step, side, together. One-two-three, one-two-three. You can move it around if you want. Shall I lead?'

'Yes,' he says, a little more floppy.

'One-two-three, one-two-three—'

'What the fuck is going on?'

Richard and I turn and, squinting through the pink light, manage to make out Andrew standing in the dark, holding a bottle in his hand. Nat King Cole keeps on playing.

'It's not what it looks like,' says Richard, releasing my hand and taking a step back. 'It's not what it looks like at all.'

Saturday a.m.

Quite what Andrew thought was going down last night is anyone's guess. But neither of them stayed around long enough to discuss it. Andrew chucked his bottle of champagne on the floor in disgust and stormed off, leaving Richard to run after him. They both wandered off into the night, leaving their morning suits in the hall.

However, by the time I wake at seven thirty to greet Nigel and his team of caterers, the suits have gone. I am hoping one of them crept back in the night to retrieve them, rather than anything untoward happening. But to be honest, there is too much going on for anyone to think about anything except the problem that is immediately in front of them.

Bernard drives through the gates at eight fifteen. Suited, showered, powdered and puffed, he looks immaculate and very much in charge. He decided a long time ago that he was never going to stay down at a wedding if he could possibly avoid it. Last weekend, however, the hotel was too far away for him to drive there and back in a day, and anyway he managed to get himself a proper room. It's just B&Bs he can't bear, and he'd rather eat his own dog than stay in the bride's house.

'Morning,' he says, looking me up and down. 'Who did you sleep with?'

'No one. I just haven't had as much time in the shower as you, or indeed as much water.'

'Here's the bridesmaid's dress,' he says, handing me a pressed pink ruffled dress, wrapped in a transparent sheath. 'Let's hope she hasn't popped on a few more pounds in the last twenty-four hours.' He walks towards the marquee, expecting me to follow behind, briefing him as we go like some American president. 'So the flowers?'

'Great,' I say. 'Not the mother's thing, apparently.'

'She didn't pay for them, if I remember?'

'Correct,' I nod. 'She wanted Claridge's in the country, and instead—'

'We have Fulham,' he interrupts. 'Very pretty, very young girl. Remind me, how old is the bride?'

'Twenty-seven.'

'Very appropriate – just. How are the lavatories?'

'Excellent,' I reply, trotting on after him. 'A three-plus-one with music, Molton Brown and oak flooring.'

'Well done,' he says, poking his nose into the ladies'. 'Make sure the girls put flowers in there and some petals on the floor. Pretty it up a bit.'

'Of course.'

'And Oakes & Co. have got the kitchens and oven and fridges,' he checks, poking his head into the catering tent. 'Nigel! My darling! How are you?'

'Bernard!' Nigel smiles, coming over to press cheeks, stooping slightly as he comes. A lifetime of compensating for his height means he always hunches in doors. 'We're a couple of men short, which is a bugger,' he says. 'We were all there waiting for them to load canapés at three o'clock this morning and I ended up putting half of them in the van myself.'

'They're looking good,' says Nigel, lifting up a layer of greaseproof paper and looking at the rows of neatly arranged Parma-ham-wrapped asparagus tips in a brown plastic container. There are hundreds of containers, each with a different amuse bouche, all piled high in the tent, and they keep on coming as a line of white-shirted waiters with black trousers files back and forth from the large vans in the drive to the tent. 'We're laying up in the tent at the moment,' adds Nigel. 'I don't like the Oakes stuff as much as mine,' he sniffs. 'God knows what the bride thinks she is doing with square plates for the starter and then round for the main, but there we go. You start with square and keep square all the way through.' He shrugs. 'Everyone knows that. And have you seen the cruets?' He picks up a bog-standard salt and pepper mill. 'Well, at least they won't go walkabout, unlike my mother-of-pearl ones. No one is taking this lot home. Do you remember that wedding?'

'What, the one where they grabbed all the table centres?' says Bernard.

'Yes,' he snorts. 'Bunch of fucking kleptomaniacs.'

'Do you have enough power?' checks Bernard, looking at the row of plugs and leads and extension cables on the floor. 'Do you need a generator?'

'Well, we haven't got one, so we'll have to make do,' Nigel smiles. 'Oh, there was one thing that we were all wondering – where is the wine?'

'Wine?' I ask.

'Wine?' Bernard looks at me.

'Because it says on the invoice – and I have just checked, if you want to have a look – that the client is to supply the wine and the champagne,' he says, licking his finger and leafing through the stack of papers on the cooker.

'Have you seen any wine about?' Bernard asks me.

'I have seen some champagne – a bit, but not enough for a wedding,' I reply.

'Shit!' he says.

'Shit,' I agree. 'Shall I ask the bride?'

'No, absolutely not. That breaks every rule in the book – no stress for the bride on the day. Call the groom.'

I finally get through on the third attempt. Richard sounds dehydrated and hungover, his voice is rasping.

'Oh, right . . .' I can hear him scratch his head. 'I spoke to Majestic and asked them about the price and everything.'

'Good,' I encourage. 'But did you actually order any?'

'Oh.' He coughs. 'Um, I am not sure. I don't think so.'

'Can you remember giving them your credit card number?'

'No.'

'In which case you didn't. He didn't,' I say to Bernard, who immediately reaches for his phone and the company credit card.

'Shit,' says Richard, panic rising in his voice. 'What shall I do? I have ruined the wedding!'

'Don't worry. The matter is in hand. We'll sort it out. Just eat some breakfast and we'll speak later.' I hang up. Bernard is already on the phone to one of our many suppliers, ordering up champagne, white and red wine and buckets and buckets of ice. The big problem is not getting the wine here in time, it is getting it cold enough to drink. I leave Bernard to his negotiating and go up to the house to deliver the bridesmaid's dress.

Alex and Trudi are in the marquee, spraying the flowers and checking that none of the lavender twists have come off the backs of the chairs. I pass on Bernard's suggestion about the lavatories, and they both seem to think they have enough blooms left in the van to sort that out. I am just heading off to the house when Alice comes storming towards the marquee. Her wet hair is stuck to her head and she is somewhat precariously wrapped in her dressing gown.

'MOVE YOUR VAN NOW!' she yells, her cheeks flushing pink with fury. 'My hair and make-up girl has been honking her horn for the last ten minutes because she can't get in the drive.'

'Oh, I am sorry,' says Alex, rather flustered at being shouted at so loudly. 'We had no idea.'

'And what the fuck are THOSE!' Alice shouts again, pointing to two planters full of flowers on either side of the entrance to the marquee.

'Planters?' stammers Alex.

'What the FUCK are they doing there? They are supposed to be at the corners of the dance-floor.'

'Your mother asked us to move them,' says Trudi.

'My MOTHER?' Alice's head is spinning around like something out of a Chuckie movie. 'I'm the BRIDE!'

'I know you are,' I smile soothingly.

'And you can fuck off!' she shouts at me. 'Richard's called me and there's no wine and it's your fault. You couldn't even organize a piss-up in a fucking brewery.'

'So would you like me to move the planters?' asks Alex quietly.

'Of course I fucking would,' she shouts, turning to walk back to the house. 'And move your fucking car! This is the worst day of my fucking life and it is all your fault.'

She marches back up to the house, sobbing loudly.

I look at Alex and then Trudi. 'You two OK?'

'Fine,' smiles Alex. 'As Bridezilla moments go, that was fairly tame. I remember one bride standing in the reception of the hotel in her underwear, waving a bridesmaid's dress in some poor bloke's face and shouting at him, "Do I look like a fucking seven-year-old?" They had lost her wedding dress, but they kept on insisting that it was hanging up in her cupboard. They found it eventually, but she was so angry. I have never heard screaming like it.'

'Oh God,' laughs Trudi, clicking her fingers. 'Do

you remember that woman who went mad?' Alex looks puzzled. 'The short one?'

'Oh, yes!' says Alex. 'She had the most beautiful wedding, with a pale-grey silk-lined marquee with a thousand handmade hurricane lamps hanging off the ceiling. The floor was a hand-laid whitewash and there were tea lights everywhere and everything was bespoke. She walked in wearing her curlers to check everything out. And she sat down at the top table – and she is quite short, just knocking five foot – and when she sat down she couldn't see over the top of the table and the flower displays that we had put there. She went nuts and started shouting and screaming, and then I made the mistake of offering her a cushion. That was it. She hit the ceiling.'

'Short people can be very sensitive,' I say.

'I know,' she nods. 'Anyway, I took the flowers away and she apologized the next day.'

'I hope Alice calms down soon,' says Trudi.

'We've got a long way to go yet,' I say.

'Sometimes I find it amazing that these women get married at all. I can't believe they manage to get a man in the first place, let alone hang on to him and get him to propose. They are so spoilt and un-pleasant, they make me want to run a mile,' says Trudi, walking over to pick up a planter. 'Then they make themselves over so much for the wedding it's ridiculous. The tan, the nails, the Botox, the weight loss – they end up looking nothing like the woman the poor bloke fell in love with at the beginning.'

She is right, of course, weddings can bring out the worst in a girl. I think perhaps I am so used to the stamping feet, the shouting, the ridiculous demands – the high drama of it all – that I actually find women who aren't having tantrums like sugar-high toddlers rather unengaging. No wonder my mother finds my inability to find a girlfriend so frustrating.

I walk up to the house with the bridesmaid's dress over my arm, and meet the hair and make-up girl in the hall. I introduce myself and she tells me her name is Victoria, or Vicky, and she is from a local salon near Haywards Heath. We offered Alice any number of girls, and indeed blokes, who we have on our list, but she opted to go local. Judging by Vicky's scraped-back, buttock-length white-blonde hair and white, square-tipped acrylic nails, I can't help but think Alice might have made a mistake. This is a girl who clearly knows the pleasure of running a nail extension through a hair extension – I just hope her bridal beauty regime is a little more organic. The number of extremely pretty girls I have seen done up like Polish prostitutes on their wedding day does not bear thinking about. No matter how many times you impress upon the bride that she shouldn't have a tan for her wedding, and that her hair and make-up should not be too dramatic or different from usual, they all still make the mistake of shoving on the slap and crimping their hair, teasing it into curls so they end up looking like some Best in Breed at Crufts.

Looking for either Katie or Liberty, I wander into the kitchen, only to come across Alistair helping himself to a large and rather powerful-looking Bloody Mary. In fact, his drink appears to have so much poke he's turned the tomato juice pale pink in the process.

'Jesus!' he says, his eyes watering post-glug. 'That's got some kick. Have you seen Trish anywhere?'

'No.'

'Oh,' he shrugs. 'She came over with me from the B&B this morning, but I seem to have lost her.'

'How was the dinner last night?'

'Fine,' he sniffs. 'Louise was on fine form, taking little snipes at Richard's mother all night.'

'Really?'

'She can't resist it,' he continues, taking another large sip. 'Oh God! I think I might have made that a bit strong.' He looks at the drink briefly, before deciding that it is fine to continue. 'She has always been the same. I found it attractive at first, her sharp comments, but now I realize she is just a cow. She drove me to drink.' He raises his glass. 'Cheers!'

It is on the tip of my tongue to suggest he ease back on the stiffeners before the wedding, but it seems rather rude. I am reminded of a father and daughter who stopped off for a shot or two of whisky in the graveyard before she went down the aisle. The only thing was they finished the hip flask. They weaved down the aisle together in a cloud of whisky fumes and when the groom lifted her veil he visibly recoiled. It wasn't the most auspicious of starts. At least Alistair is on vodka – the fumes aren't anywhere near so bad.

'Have you seen Katie or Liberty?' I ask, motioning towards the bridesmaid's dress.

'I think you'll find them upstairs,' he says, looking above him. 'There's been a lot of northern shouting going on this morning. Quite why those two got to stay in the house I shall never know, when real family have to sleep elsewhere.'

I leave Alistair to his extraordinarily strong hair of the dog and follow the sound of hairdryers upstairs. On the first-floor landing I can hear Katie berating Liberty for something or other, so before it reaches a crescendo I knock on the door.

'Delivery!' I say.

'What?' comes Katie's screeching voice.

'Bridesmaid's dress.'

'Oh right, come in—'

I enter the room to find Katie half-dressed in a turquoise frock with huge sleeves, and frills down the front. It looks like something you might put over a toilet roll. It flares out from below the bosom and does nothing but add to her 'baby weight'. She is barefoot, with slightly streaked legs that she must have fake-tanned when drunk last night, and she has a black-feathered fascinator on her head that makes her look like she has been mugged by a passing murder of crows. As looks go, it is not the most successful I have seen.

'Can we fix it? Yes, we can!' I enthuse, waving the dress. They both look at me like I'm a twat and barely mumble a thank-you. Liberty disappears off into the en suite bathroom to see if Simon really has managed to save the day.

'Mum!' she shouts. 'Can you come and zip me up?' Katie huffs into the room, as if it is the most annoying thing she has ever been asked.

'Breathe in, for God's sake,' she orders. 'Hold your bloody breath!'

After much puffing and squeezing, Liberty appears in the doorway.

'Great! It fits!' I say. I can't believe you got it on, I think.

'I hate it,' she says, looking at herself in the dressing-table mirror. 'I look like a Teletubby.'

Actually, she looks like a big fat pink blancmange. The dress is stretched tight across her stomach and gathers in a tight fan under each armpit. 'You look great!' I enthuse. 'Bridesmaids always hate their dresses, that's their job.'

There's a knock on the door. 'Can I come in?'

'If you have to,' says Katie. 'It's like Piccadilly Circus in here.'

Grace comes in, sporting a grown-up, floor-length version of Liberty's dress. If Alice's desire was to make her younger sister look like a big summer pudding coming down the aisle behind her by dressing her in dusty pink frills, then I am afraid the plan misfired. She looks fabulous. It is extraordinary for a girl to pull off a full-length pink dress with frills at the bottom and around the neck, but somehow it looks hip and vintage on her and her surly attitude steeps the whole thing in irony.

'You look great,' I say.

'Yeah, right.' Grace shrugs. 'Come on, Liberty.' She goes over and gives the girl a hug. 'We can be pink together. What was Alice thinking?' she asks, pulling at the frills around her bosom. 'I actually think this is a form of bullying. What do you think, Liberty?'

'I look like a Teletubby.'

'Which one?' asks Grace.

340

'The gay one,' she replies.

'Then you'll fit very happily with all the boys downstairs,' I smile. 'Half of them would give their eye teeth for that dress.'

Who knows why brides put their bridesmaids in such hideous frocks? I am not sure if it really is because they want to make themselves appear better looking, if it really is as conscious as that. Bridal shops will tell you that it is difficult to find one dress to suit all shapes, so inevitably you end up with one that suits none of them. Although these days there are some post-*Sex and the City* brides who dress their bridesmaids in different styles and strong colours to suit the people wearing them. A few months ago I organized a wedding where the bridesmaids were very glamorous and their outfits were stunning. The bride was American, and in the US the bridesmaids go down the aisle ahead of the bride. The aisle was narrow and the chairs had been placed opposite each other, so when the girls came down the aisle, one after the other, it was like a catwalk. The first girl got a ripple of applause. But by the time the fourth came down the whole congregation was whooping and whistling their appreciation.

'Anyone home? Anyone here?' Mike has turned up and is roaming around downstairs.

'Mike!' I come to the top of the stairs. 'Good to see you.'

'Mate!' he grins as he comes bounding up the stairs in a grey suit and white shirt, his dark curls smoothed back with product. 'So did I get it?'

'Get what?' I reply, knowing exactly what he is asking.

'The Keith and Keeley job.' He presses his long thin hands together in prayer and closes his eyes. 'Say yes, say yes!'

'I don't know. I haven't been to the office since I saw you.'

'Bernard here?'

'Of course. But I don't think he knows any more than I do.'

'Of course he does, the wily old fox knows everything. Where is he?'

'In the marquee.'

'Releasing his inner OCD?'

'I'm not sure it is that inner,' I reply.

'True,' he smiles. 'Hardly in the closet, is he?'

'Have you seen the bride yet?'

'Just got here, mate. It's raining in London,' he says. 'Have you got a wet-weather set-up for the photos or do you want me to see if I can find one?'

'Do you think?' I ask, looking out of the landing window.

'Can't you see the clouds?'

'It won't rain,' declares Louise, arriving on the landing with Carmen rollers in her copper hair, wearing a short red kimono that reveals rather a lot of her hefty white legs.

'You sound like a woman who can command the weather,' says Mike, approaching in full-charm mode. 'I'm Mike McCabe, photographer, at your service.'

'Hello,' says Louise, licking her bottom lip. 'Louise Oxford, mother of the bride.'

'No!' exclaims Mike, taking a step back. 'I thought you were the sister!'

'Oh no, please!' she replies. My thoughts exactly.

'But look at you!' continues Mike, seemingly unembarrassable. 'Do you work out?' I am almost on the point of puking on his shiny shoes.

'Shall I show you to the bride?' I interrupt the oil slick of compliments.

'Mrs Oxford,' he says, taking her by the hand and kissing it.

'Louise!' she blushes.

'For fuck's sake,' I mutter.

'Keep in with the mother,' he mumbles. 'Works wonders if you are caught doing something later.'

Alice's room stinks of hairspray and hot tongs. She is sitting in the bay window, at a huge triple-aspect dressing table, wearing her bridal underwear and a fluffy white dressing gown. The table itself is covered in brushes, pots, lipsticks, rollers and trays of different colours of blusher and eyeshadow. Vicky seems to have brought a whole department store with her. Alice herself appears to be very much a work in progress. Half her hair is up in rollers and the front section is being curled into ringlets. Her face is a shade darker than her neck and her fingernails have been painted a pearlized pink.

'Hi there, Mike,' she says, removing her chin from Vicky's grasp. 'How are you?'

'Not as gorgeous as you!' he exclaims, coming over to squeeze both her shoulders. 'You have to be one of the prettiest brides I have ever come across.'

'You're just saying that,' she says. You're right, I think.

'Now that I have found you here in all your glory, I should get going,' he says. 'My bag's down in the hall. I won't be a minute.' He rushes off downstairs.

'How are you doing?' I ask. 'Can I get you anything? Glass of champagne?'

'Do you think?' she asks, turning two blue eyelids towards me.

'It might help you relax.'

'Go on then. Oh, by the way,' she adds as I approach the door. 'I had a chat with Mum this morning and I think we should have the speeches before the food.'

'Before?' My heart sinks.

'Yeah.' She nods. 'Both Dad and Andrew like a drink, and I think it would be so much better than after.'

'Whatever you say.'

I pass Mike on the stairs, but am too preoccupied to engage with any of his quips. Nigel is going to hit the roof. There is nothing that pisses him off more than serving dinner after the speeches, and you can see why. Backstage he has sixteen chefs trying to keep the food warm, chomping at the bit, waiting to get their lamb out. They are all speed-snorting, pill-popping nutcases, so to try and keep them still and quiet while Daddy goes on and on about his little Princess Poppet at nursery school is nigh on impossible. Then, as well as the chefs, you have all the butlers messing about with nothing to do. Nigel once likened it to trying to keep sixty-five people quiet behind the bike sheds. And then there is the logistics of it all. When do you put the lamb on? You don't want to burn it, or let it get cold. They always say the speeches will be fifteen minutes, but what happens if the best man goes on a bit? We once did a wedding where the best man had a slide projector and talked for forty-five minutes about what he and the groom got up to at university. I tell you, dull was not the word. People's ears were practically bleeding with boredom – I think about five or six people actually fell asleep. We also did a wedding where the bride was French, so all the speeches were repeated twice in both languages. It was worse than the Eurovision song contest.

The kitchen is full of men in white coats chopping and seasoning and laying things out on plates. Nigel is not in the best of humours when I arrive because there are no staff toilets and his chefs are pissing in the garden rather than using the Portaloos and he is worried that none of them are washing their hands. So his reaction to my news is pretty predictable.

'Oh fucking cunt!' he shouts, and cuffs a nearby sous chef. 'I fucking hate it when they do this.'

'I am sorry, I am just the messenger.'

'Did everyone get that?' he moans, his nasal voice drawling across the marquee.

'Yes, sir,' reply a number of chefs.

'Did everyone get that!' he yells.

'Yes, sir!' they all yell back.

'Can you smell burning?' I ask.

'No,' yawns Nigel.

'No – really.'

'It's the first sign of a stroke,' he says, wandering out of the tent.

'What is?'

'Smelling burning.' He inhales through his huge nostrils. 'Come to think of it . . .'

'It's worse outside,' I say. 'Bernard!'

Bernard pokes his head out of the marquee. 'What?'

'Can you smell anything?' I ask.

'Burning?' he suggests. 'Is it electrical?'

'Hang on a sec. What power are you running the fridges on?'

'The cable from the house,' says Nigel.

'And your six ovens?'

'The cable from the barn.' He shrugs.

'Jesus Christ!'

I have never seen two middle-aged men in suits and leather-soled shoes run so fast through a field in my life. The smell grows more intense the closer we get to the barn. All the electrical cable in the place is quite literally melting. It is smoking and burning red hot, as bits of melted plastic coating drip to the floor.

'Fuck!' says Bernard.

'Fuck!' agrees Nigel.

'This whole place is about to go up in smoke,' I say. 'There's no trip switch to cut out the power. How much are you using?'

'Around 30,000 kilowatts,' whispers Bernard, watching the wires melt.

'Shit!' agrees Nigel. 'I'll get them to unplug right now.'

'Thank God we found out now,' says Bernard. 'That would have had half the village up in a puff of smoke.'

'Do you think?'

'It was about to blow. You'd better send a few butlers down here just to make sure the straw doesn't catch fire while the thing cools down.'

'Shouldn't we call the fire brigade?'

'And ruin a fabulous party?'

Bernard and I walk back to the marquee to witness the wine merchant thankfully driving up the drive.

'I'll organize the alcohol and sort out another power source for the bloody ovens,' Bernard says. 'You check on the bride. The cars will be here in half an hour and Mike's still got the family snaps to do. Also you'd better check that he has a wet-weather spot. Does the mother have anywhere in mind?'

Back in the kitchen, Alistair is dressed in his morning suit, looking around for the buttonholes.

'Aha!' he says, pointing at me a little exuberantly. 'You'll know where they are!'

'The pink roses are in the hall,' I say. 'Ready to take up to the church for the ushers and the groom.'

'I bet they're having a lovely lunch in the pub,' he says longingly.

'I'm not feeding anyone,' declares Louise, walking into the kitchen.

'Who said anything about food?' Alistair replies, looking his ex-wife up and down.

She is dressed in the smallest, tightest French-blue suit I have ever seen. Cinched in at the waist, it has red piping around the edge of the jacket and pockets, and it stops a good three inches above the knee. She has bare legs and a scarlet handbag with matching scarlet shoes. On a girl of twenty-five the suit would be a statement; on a woman who is definitely twice that age it is a goddamn proclamation.

I have often found that mothers of the bride dress one of two ways on their daughter's big day. One is the demurely attired practical dresser, who pops on something pretty with a nice hat, but whose main aim is to keep the show on the road and make sure that everyone else, especially the bride, is having a good day. The other is the showstopper mother who is fighting her daughter for the limelight. Determined to be noticed and to claim pole position on the big day, she will pour herself into something ludicrously tight or obscenely short, in order to make her point. I can't tell you how many pairs of ropy old Stilton legs or empty-shopping-bag breasts I have seen work the aisle.

I remember one wedding we did a few years ago, where the bride was just about to get into her rather large and rather beautiful wedding dress when her mother burst into the room in some skin-tight slinky number. Unfortunately her zip had broken and she was stuck in the gaping dress. So while the bride stood there in her underwear, two bridesmaids and I rolled around on the bed with the mother for a good twenty minutes, trying to release the zip. Eventually the bride gave up waiting for any help and ended up trying to dress herself. It was only when she asked for help with her buttons that anyone remembered she was there.

Louise is certainly going to get noticed today, as is Katie, although I am not sure that was her intention. Trisha walks in in a yellow plunge-neck suit with a knee-length skirt and high golden sandals. She and Louise look each other up and down, trying to work out who has done better in the style stakes.

'Darling, there you are!' declares Alistair. 'Where have you been? You look stunning. As do you, darling,' he says quickly to Louise.

But before the ex and the current squeeze can size each other up too much, the bride makes an appearance in the hall. The floor-length Annabel Rogers dress and thankfully new veil look beautiful. The dress fits her perfectly, the shoes are the right colour, and the veil sits confidently on the top of her head. It's a stunning combination that flatters and looks fabulous. It's just the hair and make-up that are a catastrophe. She has heavy blue eyes, a dark-pink mouth and a poodle of curls at the front of her head. Alice is a beautiful girl; she has a pretty, innocent, charming face, and she looks like she's been in a fight with a clown. The room falls silent. No one quite knows what to say and my heart breaks for her.

'That dress looks fantastic,' says Louise, finally finding a drop of maternal blood.

'The shoes are lovely,' says Trisha, joining in.

'Darling! You look wonderful!' declares Alistair, raising a glass of champagne.

'Absolutely,' I agree, desperately trying to sound positive.

'Do you think so?' asks Alice. 'Honestly?'

'Fabulous!' asserts her father and the bride promptly bursts into tears.

'Don't cry!' shouts Vicky, running across the room with a make-up brush. 'I've just spent three sodding hours doing that!'

Alice's make-up pours down her face in navy-blue streaks. Black mascara circles form under her eyes. The more the make-up runs, the more she cries. It's a bloody disaster.

'Careful of the dress!' I say. The last thing we need

is big black blobs on the dress. The face we can rescue, the dress we can't.

Louise rushes over to put her arm around her daughter and Alistair searches for his answer to all life's problems – a glass. Vicky cracks open a packet of tissues and I make lots of placatory noises. Thank God Bernard is not here to witness this. There is nothing he hates more than a bride in tears. It is the one thing we always try and guard against on the day, as no one wants a snivelling, puffy-faced bride walking up the aisle. But I would say about 30 per cent of them do cry on the morning. It's nerves, lack of food, and the inevitable sharp comment from their mothers that set them off. Thankfully Alice's make-up was so poor, this must be a blessing in disguise.

Eventually Alice calms down and is sent back upstairs with a glass of champagne as the cars pull up outside the house. We have booked two large Mercedes for the family and a white open-top Rolls for the bride. I have to say that there are so many bridal-car companies around, run by a hundred local businessmen, that I never particularly care how the bride chooses to get there. Just so long as the driver turns up looking smart, and doesn't break wind or break down on the way to the church. Although last year we had a chauffeur have a stroke while the bride was in church. It was a little tricky, to say the least. Bernard called the ambulance and we popped him in the back as the bride and groom came out of the church. Fortunately, Bernard was able to drive the happy couple back to the house while the ambulance took the driver to hospital. Sadly, he didn't make it.

Mike is beginning to get a little twitchy; he has about seven minutes to secure a few family shots before the first wave leave for the church. He is pacing the gravel drive like some prize stallion.

'Can we maybe do some bridesmaid shots and mother-of-the bride shots?' he suggests. 'Outside on the terrace?'

Finally he manages to grab Louise, Grace and Liberty and get them outside, and he is just beginning to place them around one of the planters when the first drops of rain start to fall.

'It's raining,' says Liberty, scrunching up her face and looking at the sky.

'No, it's not,' replies Louise, poised, posed and breathing in, ready for her close-up.

'Is,' says Liberty.

'Fucking not,' replies Louise. 'Smile everyone!'

'Absolutely!' agrees Mike. 'Everyone ready?'

Mike gets his shots and even manages a few sensationally stiff snaps of Louise, Trisha and Alistair before Alice's reappearance. Devoid of much of her make-up, with a simple shiny gloss on her lips, she looks a thousand times prettier – radiant, even – and clearly feels it.

'OK.' She smiles at Mike. 'Where do you want me?'

The rest of the party leave for the church, while Mike gets the last few photos of Alice and her father. Spots of rain continue to fall, but no one seems to mind. They are all subscribing to that particularly English attitude to the weather: if you don't mention it, it isn't happening.

Having allowed a good ten minutes since the advance party set off, Bernard arrives with the fabulous bouquet of pink peonies and roses and suggests that the bride should start making her way to the church.

Alice looks stunning as she gets into the Rolls, the raindrops stop and she sits grinning in the back, surrounded by puffed-up layers of silk. This is it. The big day is about to begin in earnest. Alistair slips in next to her and Mike starts snapping away. They are just about to set off when a convoy of minibuses comes cruising up the lane.

'Shit!' shouts Bernard. 'I'm sorry,' he says. 'It's more catering staff. It's the second shift. You'll have to wait for a few minutes. You don't mind, do you?'

Alice, her father, Mike and I watch as the vans

come up the narrow lane, get stuck and then start reversing backwards and forwards and backwards and forwards, trying to make the tight right turn into the drive.

'You'll be fine,' assures Bernard, looking at his watch. 'You've got plenty of time.'

'Oh well, while we are here,' suggests Alistair, reaching into his pocket, 'we may as well have a sharpener.' He pulls down the mahogany tray in the back of the car and wipes it with the cuff of his morning suit. He then unfolds a small white envelope and pours out a pile of white powder on to the tray. Then he takes out a credit card from his top pocket and racks it up into two neat lines. He rolls up a twenty-pound note and hands it to his daughter. 'Ladies first,' he says.

For a moment I see Alice hesitate, but it is not for long. 'Ah – thanks, Dad,' she says, popping her peonies to one side. She leans in for a snort. 'You think of everything.'

'No pictures,' jokes Alistair, waving his hand at Mike, who for the first time since I have known him is actually lost for words.

Saturday p.m.

Bernard and I only just make it to the church before the bride. We have a bootful of umbrellas in case of a deluge, and our phones at the ready in case of delinquency. In fact we are both more than a little worried about how Alistair might behave in the church. I have seen people do lots of drugs at weddings – I've seen a bride pop an E before going down the aisle, I have seen couples chop out lines before the dinner, but that is the first time I've ever seen a father and daughter share a line before the church, or indeed share before or after anything.

Bernard doesn't quite know what to do or where to put himself. He mutters and mumbles all the way to the church. I don't know what has shocked him the most – the fact that Alistair offered his daughter drugs, or that a girl so seemingly square and bourgeois as Alice would take Class As in broad daylight in front of so many people.

'Mind you,' he finally concludes as he parks our car, 'if I had a mother like Louise I might want to anaesthetize myself on my wedding day. Talk of the devil,' he adds as we walk towards the church carrying the brollies. 'Check out the garb,' he mutters through his service-industry smile. 'Who knew there were smart gloves to match?'

Louise is pacing up and down outside the church, swinging her hips, rather like a hooker plying for clients. A pair of matching red-lace gloves complete the full coordinated look. At least the ushers appear to be enjoying it. There is much elbowing and gawping when her back is turned.

'One can only hope that is the reaction she was after,' says Bernard, watching a couple of pink-faced boys snigger into their orders of service. 'Good afternoon, Louise,' he continues. 'The bride is on her way. If you would like to take your place at the front?'

'Just a few more minutes,' she says.

I take a look inside the church to check everything is as it should be. The place is packed and the atmosphere is very jolly and upbeat. There's a heady mix of dresses and coats and hats and fascinators; they are all so bright and colourful, like Dolly Mixtures in a jar. The elderly are seated towards the front of the church and the back is packed with the young, chatting and gossiping, catching up as they lean against the font. Alex and Trudi have done wonders with the flowers. On either side of the aisle, bunches of sweet peas, pinks and roses hang in clusters off the end of the pews. And there is a huge display of pink and lilac flowers in a plinth by the altar. Standing by the altar, looking itchy and nervous, is Richard. I give him a small encouraging wave from the back of the church and, catching my eye, he comes rushing towards me.

'Oh, thank God you're here,' he exclaims, smelling slightly of ale. The ushers' lunch was clearly a success. 'The vicar hasn't turned up yet and I don't have his number.'

'Oh shit,' I say. 'I am not sure I have.' My heart starts to race. This is the first wedding I've had with no vicar, and unlike chauffeuring it is not a job that either Bernard or I could fill. Surely the prospect of the Queen of Sheba, 1 Corinthians and *The Prophet* can't have bored him so much that he's decided not to show? I scroll through my telephone numbers and draw a blank.

'Did the wine arrive?' asks Richard, wringing his pink sweaty hands.

'Yup,' I reply, still looking through my phone. 'The champagne and white are on ice.'

'Thank God for that,' he says. 'At least we can all get drunk, even if we don't get married.'

'There it is! Numbers dialled. I knew I called him yesterday to find out where to collect him from.'

'Thank you!' he says, squeezing my hand.

I dial the number and Reverend Dave picks up almost immediately. 'I am on my way,' he says. 'I have been stuck in some traffic for the sodding village fête.'

'That's great news.'

'I'll be with you in five,' he says. 'I'd better get my skates on. Derek is coming in straight after us, there's a funeral up next.'

'On a Saturday?'

'Don't ask me,' he says. 'It's not my idea. Anyway, sorry to inconvenience you with a death, they tend to be a little unpredictable.' He hangs up. I get the impression that he really doesn't want to do this service.

Alice's car rounds the corner and I shove Richard back down the aisle. She and her father are sitting in the back with a couple of rictus grins gripping their faces. Fortunately the rain has stopped, so we can keep her in the car for a few more minutes waiting for Reverend Dave to arrive. They are unsurprisingly a little twitchy as they sit there.

'How long do you think we'll have to wait?' she

asks, chewing her lip. Even though she is obviously quite wired, she is looking stunning. The windy car journey has blown out the curls at the front of her hair-do and her make-up is much softer than before. Her pale-blue eyes blink at me from under her veil. I have half a mind to pull her out of the car, take her by the hand and make a run for it over the fields.

'Not long now,' I say, scanning the lane. Thankfully there's a screech of brakes and a metallic-blue Mini careers into view. I can see a billowing white gown through the open window. Reverend Dave pulls up in the car park, takes the keys out of the car, chucks them in the air as he leaves the driver's door open and strides purposefully into the church. He turns at the end of aisle, gives me a broad grin and nods to the organist to start winding up the pre-processional.

It is at this precise moment that Louise decides to make her entrance. She slips the short red veil on her hat over her eyes and, with a swing of her no longer fecund hips, sashays down the aisle. The organ music stops. The congregation holds its breath in expectation and the sound of Louise's heels echoes around the church.

Fortunately, Alice is too busy smoothing down her dress and arranging her veil to see her mother's moment of glory. She is too twitching with nerves and cocaine to see beyond her own satin shoes. Alistair's not helping matters by insisting that he stand on the left instead of the right. Grace is trying to help her sister, while Liberty is standing about rather sheepishly with her back to the wall of the church. It is not until Bernard and I line everyone up to move off that we realize why: her dress has ripped all the way down the back, leaving her white shoulders and lemon-yellow teen bra visible for all to see. Neither Bernard nor I mention it. What is the point? There is no way she can pull out now. She will just have to stand there with her back to the congregation throughout the service.

The organist strikes up the opening chords of the Queen of Sheba and they are off. Like stampeding buffalo, Alice and her dad bolt for the altar and make it there in less than a minute. Alistair hands her over to the vicar and is seated between the ex and the current squeeze well before the music finishes. Alice just stands there with her head down. And poor Richard didn't get the chance to admire his future wife's approach, for no sooner had Dave given him the nod than she was standing by his side.

Dave opens with a polite and engaging welcome, a well-worn number two in his collection, I suspect. And we move swiftly on to 'I Vow To Thee, My Country'. Which Dave can sing with his eyes closed, so he does. Alistair makes a right tit of himself stumbling through 1 Corinthians. I can't work out whether it is the booze, the coke or his vanity which prevents him from wearing reading glasses and so renders him illiterate. Either way, Dave has clearly never heard a reading like it, though he looks engaged and smiles throughout. Whoever said you couldn't reinvent the wheel?

Bernard and I are standing at the back of the church when Dave asks if there is any unlawful impediment why Alice and Richard can't be married. There's a small snigger that goes around the font and some gauche looks, and then my mobile phone goes off. The whole church turns to stare at me as I blush scarlet and slip out the back.

'Hello?'

'Hi there, it's me!'

'Caroline!'

'I was just wondering what you were up to this evening. I am on my own, and I was wondering if you fancied coming over for dinner and maybe a chat about my party. What do you say?'

'I say I am at a wedding, working.'

'Oh,' she says.

'Where else do you expect me to be on a Saturday night in June!' I say, and hang up. When is she ever going to get the hint that no matter how many baby showers or birthday parties she gets me to organize, I am not going to sleep over.

I step back into the church just in time to witness Andrew fumble for the rings and Richard and Alice stammer through their vows. Richard is louder and more sure of himself than Alice, who sniffs and stumbles over her own name. Dave then pronounces them man and wife and invites Richard to kiss the bride. A ripple of applause goes through the church, catching a couple of smokers out the back by surprise. They stub out their fags on a couple of handy gravestones and sneak back inside, to take up the applause like they have been there all along. Alice and Richard head to the vestry to sign the register while a big-breasted soprano keeps the rest of the church entertained with a rather poor 'Ave Maria'.

'Jesus,' whispers Bernard, as we both slip outside to check on the cars and the weather, and to put a quick call through to Nigel to see if things are on schedule. We have an ETA of about twenty minutes, so he should have all his flutes and canapés at the ready. 'That has to be one of the more terrible services I have ever been to. We didn't have anything to do with it, did we?'

'I gave them a list of suggested readings and hymns and music, and they have just chosen the top one off every list,' I say. 'Or at least that's what it feels like.'

'That poor vicar is going to fall off his perch with boredom!'

'Not long now,' I say, giving the thumbs up to the chauffeur, who is smoking by the gate to the church.

He flicks his cigarette on the ground and walks towards me. 'D'you know what?' he says. 'I have seen all sorts in the back of that car. Brides being sick because they are pissed, hungover or just nervous. I have seen the father and daughter polish off the best part of a half-bottle of brandy on the way to the church. I have even had a couple shag on the way back from the church. But I have never seen that.' He sniffs. 'I didn't know where to look.'

'Straight ahead?' suggests Bernard, looking up at the sky. 'It's going to bloody rain.'

The reedy strains of 'Dear Lord and Father' drift down the path towards us.

'Not long now,' I say. 'I think we should get to our posts.'

'Ten minutes,' Bernard says down the telephone, before hanging up. 'I'm just off to get a few more umbrellas from the car.'

By the time he's back, the organist is banging out the opening bars of Vivaldi and the bride and groom are striding down the aisle, followed by the attentive and ever-snapping Mike. Just as they reach the entrance to the church, there is a rumble of thunder and the first few heavy splatters of rain. The congregation pours out of the church, applauding and cheering and throwing fistfuls of rose petals. Alice is buzzing, loving her moment and rushing from cheek to cheek as all her friends queue up to kiss the bride. Bernard tries to follow her with an umbrella, but he can't keep up. The result is that Alice's face and shoulders become splattered in rain and then covered in rose petals, which stick to her skin like splashes of paint. It is not the look she was after, but there is little anyone can do at the moment. Richard is otherwise occupied, having his hand practically shaken off by all his mates. Alistair tops up the alcohol in his system with a quick slurp from a miniature brandy he has in his pocket, and while Richard's mother walks slowly towards the car, her hand tucked firmly underneath Granny's armpit, Richard's dad, a short bald man who exudes an unfathomable pomposity, stands around next to his second wife, Bev – a grey-permed carbon copy of his first. Katie and Liberty make a mad dash for the car, while Grace smokes a cigarette and bats away the early attentions of an alcohol-fuelled usher. Louise is in a bit of a flap. Rain was not part of her plan and she doesn't quite know where to put herself. She fusses around and forgets her umbrella.

'For heaven's sake, Louise,' shouts Bernard across the crowd. 'Put one up yourself!'

'I've been trying to get her to do that for years,' replies Alistair, unscrewing his bottle again. 'Might give her a sense of humour.'

'Oh shit,' I say, just loud enough for Bernard to hear me. 'Look.'

We both turn to see a large funeral cortège making its mournful way up the lane towards the church.

'Oh bugger,' says Reverend Dave, appearing next to me. 'That's a bit of a clash of atmospheres.'

'Also, we don't want the bride to be blocked in by the hearse,' says Bernard, his eyes narrowing. 'I think I'd better sort this out.'

'Um . . .' starts Dave, but it is too late. Bernard is already walking down the path towards the cortège to take command of the situation. Unfortunately, he appears to have forgotten that he is wielding a pink-plastic princess brolly above his head, which could somewhat undermine his authority. Dave and I watch as he ingratiates himself with the grief-stricken widow and her three children. Somehow he manages to persuade the driver of the hearse to drive past the church, so that the white Rolls can depart. It is an extraordinary sight as the multicoloured wedding party crosses paths with the black-clad mourners. Richard and Alice are perched in the back of the white car, each sporting a leopard-print umbrella, as they slowly crawl past the long line of black limousines that are parked up against the bank.

'All we need now is a christening,' says Dave, 'and our work is done.'

By the time Bernard and I get back to the house, after quickly filleting the church of all its bridal flowers to make way for the funeral, the wedding party is in full swing. Mike has managed to take an unifying set of photographs of the bride and groom with various dysfunctional members of their family, and is now trying to get as many jolly party shots as possible. The weather has thankfully cheered up a bit and the champagne is flowing. Alice and Richard are on meet and greet, shaking hands with everyone and lapping up the compliments and congratulations.

'Excuse me?' I turn around to find Carol blinking at me from underneath the shiny brim of her pistachio-coloured hat. 'This is Gran.' She indicates towards a more decrepit version of herself, sitting on a chair taking in the view. She has a cup of tea on her lap, and her ankles, which are the same width as her knees, are crossed. 'She has many problems,' shares Carol. 'But the most important one is that she is a diabetic, so on no account is she allowed to drink any alcohol.'

'OK,' I say. 'Does she know this?'

'She is very well aware of it. But she likes a tipple, so keep an eye on her.'

'Righty-ho,' I reply. 'I shall inform the staff.'

'Thanks very much,' replies Carol, immediately leaving Gran on her own as she goes off in search of some company and canapés.

Bernard is patrolling the place like a meerkat on crack. I keep seeing his face popping up, scanning the marquee and surrounding garden for problems and hitches. He is Nigel's eyes and ears, and his constant trips backstage keep everyone on their toes. He pre-empts the lack of prawn-and-coriander kebabs on the terrace and the dearth of cold champagne on arrival. The guests are obviously terribly thirsty, although strangely not for the elderflower fizz with real blooms that is slowly warming in the weak afternoon sun. The Parma ham and asparagus is being consumed almost as soon as it gets out of the kitchen and the smoked salmon rolls are being picked off at the pass. The party is becoming more lubricated, the noise level is increasing, the laughter is getting louder and everyone is clearly so much more entertaining than they were forty minutes ago.

'This isn't quite as bad as I expected it to be,' says Grace, sidling up to me at the back of the marquee. 'I think people are having a nice time.'

'Great,' I say, as I check that the placement cards are straight on the tables.

'Well, everyone except Carol, I think,' she says, taking a sip of her champagne.

'Really?'

'She keeps trying to talk to Mum, and Mum just keeps ignoring her, like she genuinely can't hear her.' She smirks. 'You should have heard Mum this morning, telling Dad that after today she never wants to see that family ever again. She keeps saying that if she can get through the day then she deserves a medal.'

'And does Carol know?' I ask.

'Know? Mum says it in front of her. Richard and Alice are going to be dodging bullets all through dinner.' She smiles. 'That should be entertaining.'

'Ah, there you are,' says Bernard. 'The bride needs you. Also keep an eye on Granny – every time a drink is put down on the table next to her, she bloody pinches it.'

'OK. Where's the bride?'

'Round the back.'

I walk through the tent and down the tunnel, past Nigel, who is controlling his waiters like super-charged synchronized swimmers, conducting their entrances and exits with a nod of his stooped head. Eventually I find Alice behind the Portaloos, hopping from one foot to the other.

'Hi,' she grins. She is a little edgy. I wonder if she's been with her dad again. 'I need the loo.'

'Right,' I say, somewhat taken aback. 'You are right by them.'

'I can't use those, I might get blue chemicals all over my dress,' she sniffs. She has definitely been with her dad.

'How about the house?'

'They are locked. Mum locked them to stop people having sex in them,' she says, rubbing her nose. 'Bernard said something about a bridal potty?'

'Oh that,' I sigh. Bernard does keep a bridal potty with him, which is basically a large child's potty for use when the size of the bride's dress prohibits her from sitting on the lavatory.

'He says it is in his tent.'

'The admin tent?' I ask.

'That's it,' she nods. 'Please hurry, I am desperate.'

'Follow me.'

Just behind the two catering marquees is a tiny tent where the staff have put their coats and bags and where Bernard has organized a small desk for himself with a chair and a place to charge his phone. At larger or celebrity weddings, this is a more solid structure that can be used as a mini satellite office during the build-up to the wedding. Here, however, it is a dumping ground for staff rubbish.

'There!' says Alice, spotting the potty in the corner. 'Now what?'

'Do you want to pee here?' I ask.

'It's as good a place as any,' she replies, clearly desperate.

'OK,' I nod, getting down on my knees.

'Hang on,' she says. 'Let me get my pants off.' I turn my back to much huffing and puffing and ruffling of silk. 'Ready,' she says, standing there clutching a pair of white lace knickers in her hand.

'Right, then,' I say, getting back down on my knees. I grab the potty and shove it under her skirt. 'OK then—'

She squats down a tiny bit, appears to concentrate for a minute and then she releases. I was expecting a gentle girly tinkle of some sort, but she is like a horse. A great jet of warm urine fills the potty and splashes all over my hand, sleeve and arm. Whatever desire I had for the girl disappears in an instant.

'I am sorry,' she says as she finishes. 'Did I get you?'

'No, no,' I reply. There is no point in embarrassing the girl.

'Do you have a tissue?' she asks.

'Yup.' I pull out a Handy Andy.

'Cheers,' she says, as she hands me her tepid pants.

'Can you look after these? I can't be bothered to put them back on again.'

Bernard is utterly nonplussed when I tell him the bride has just pissed on my hand.

'Think yourself lucky,' he says, monitoring events over my shoulder. 'Sad fucks pay thousands for water sports. Anyway, it happens all the time. That bloody granny!' he hisses. 'She's just swiped another glass. What time is it now?' he asks, not bothering to look at his own watch.

'Just gone six,' I say, dutifully checking my own, thankfully on my dry wrist.

'We should be having the speeches now,' he says. 'I am going to talk to the groom.'

It takes another ten minutes before the wedding party gathers in the marquee and the noise dies down enough for the speeches to begin. I can see Nigel pacing like a stallion out of the corner of my eye, but there is very little that either Bernard or I can do.

First up is Alistair. As the father of the bride, his job is to thank the assembled company for gathering, say something sweet about his daughter and toast the happy couple. He weaves his way through the crowd with a tiny scrap of paper; the man is very obviously drunk. The worst pissed speech I have ever heard was delivered by a best man so plastered that he lay down on three chairs to speak. Alistair is not that bad, but he is not far off.

'Ladies and gentlemen,' he slurs, hitting his nose on the mike as he lurches forward. 'Thank you for coming.' He then sniffs into the mike and appears to lose his train of thought entirely. 'Um, welcome.'

'Get on with it!' yells a sweaty bloke at the back.

'Oh!' he says, sounding genuinely taken aback. 'My first heckle.'

'Hurry up!' shouts another pink-faced youth nearby.

'Oh, a second!' He wobbles slightly. 'Welcome,' he starts again. 'To this very happy day!' There is a ripple of applause. 'I'd like to say some lovely things about my daughter, because she is so lovely.'

'Hear, hear,' agree a few in the crowd.

And so he staggers on for another two excruciating minutes, forgetting what he wants to say, stumbling over his words and slurring the name of his ex-wife. Finally he toasts the happy couple, and everyone is mightily relieved to see him go.

'One really must question the quality of his cocaine,' Bernard whispers in my ear as Alistair vacates the stage. 'Usually it makes you sharp as a chat-show host.'

Richard is up next, ready to thank everyone all over again and raise a toast to Liberty and Grace. He apologizes in advance for his speech, because his sweaty hands have caused the whole thing to run, so he says he is going to keep it brief.

'Thank God!' shouts a wag at the back, and in the far corner of the marquee I can see Nigel mop his sweaty brow in agreement.

Richard battles on with all the wit of an accountant, which is what he is. He regales the crowd with pleasantries about Louise, during which she preens, puffing her bosom out over the top of her jacket. He then turns his attention to his own mother, who smiles, despite the derogatory snorts coming from the ex-Mrs Oxford. Paul is pleased with his mention, Alistair is too drunk to hear his thank-you, and both Trisha and Bev are irritated to be omitted from the roll call of the important. By the time he gets around to thanking the bridesmaids, the level of mumbling and murmuring chat is beginning to rise at the back.

A few of the more drunk and shameless disappear for a fag in the garden as Andrew steps up to the mike. He is not the most inspiring-looking of characters, with his weak chin, side parting and pink complexion, so you can hardly blame them. He clears this throat.

'I suppose it was love at first sight.' He smiles. A few diehard romantics cheer. 'When Richard walked into the bar at university.' Suddenly everyone is paying attention. 'Maybe it was his generous smile or sharp wit, or his enormous zest for life, but either way we have been joined at the hip ever since. And the things we have done together, the things we have been through. Other couples can only really dream of the relationship that we have. Like when we went white-water rafting in the Amazon and I got soaked and you – Rich – you took off your jumper and gave me your T-shirt!' He laughs and looks across at Richard. 'You have been such a good friend to me. So many things. So many good times and so many bad. Like when I had my appendix out and you came to the hospital and brought me grapes . . . You ate them all, of course, leaving me only the pips as a reminder of your presence.' He laughs again. 'You're so funny. I love it when you crack a joke and your lips smile before the punchline, or when . . .'

'This is weird,' I whisper to Bernard.

'It's marvellous!' he replies. 'Best speech I have ever heard.'

'Is he coming out to the groom?' I ask.

'Sounds like it to me,' he nods. 'Look at Nigel.'

Over at the other end of the marquee, Nigel is standing in the doorway, surrounded by chefs and waiters, who are totally riveted.

'Anyway,' says Andrew, clearing his throat, 'what I

really wanted to say is that Alice is very lucky. If she only knew half the man I know then she will be a happy lady. Rich is so sensitive and kind and funny. She will be very lucky – yes, very lucky indeed.' His lips purse. 'So I raise my glass to the happy couple. I love you.' He looks across at Richard. 'Um – both,' he adds quickly. 'Thank you.'

The muttering and the applauding fight each other for dominance as he leaves the podium. No one can quite believe what they have just heard. Did he come out? Did he just say that he was in love with the groom? Both Richard and Alice stood stock still as he raised his glass to them. They neither looked at each other or at him. They both stared into the middle distance, unable to decide what the hell to make of it all.

'Ladies and gentlemen – dinner is served!' announces Nigel with a dramatic clap of his hands.

Everyone ambles over to their places; the bride and groom make their way towards the top table and the butlers fan out into the room, carrying fish starter selections on their square plates.

I watch Alice knock back a whole glass of champagne in one swig, before she straightens her veil and finds a weak smile to put back on her face. The girl looks miserable. She has her new father-in-law on one side of her and her new husband on the other, both of whom are talking to other people. Richard is trying to charm the increasingly drunk and annoyed Louise, while Paul is doing his best to entertain Trisha, who by some quirk of fate and seating has managed to make top table.

The starters are down and the wine has been poured and Bernard is looking a little less uptight.

'What the fuck?' he suddenly says, looking up at top table. 'What's happened to Granny?' I follow his gaze to see her passed out head-first in her supper, with Alistair, who is sitting next to her, looking completely the other way. 'Shit,' adds Bernard. 'Is she dead?' Carol is the only one who notices Granny's predicament; she leaves her seat and removes the old woman's face from her food. Wetting a napkin, she wipes her face down and seemingly revives her in the process. 'Oh, thank God,' says Bernard, clutching his chest. 'She is back with us.'

Backstage things are heating up, quite literally. The ovens are on full-blast, warming the pre-cooked lamb, and there are cauldrons of boiling vegetables awaiting placement on the plates. There's a queue of butlers waiting, the tension is mounting and the air is redolent with steam and sweat.

Finally the lamb is served, a little drier than Nigel would have liked, but who cares about timings when the best man is outing himself in his speech? The butlers pour the quite decent red wine that Bernard managed to source this morning. And I weave between the tables, checking on the service. I spot Grace sitting between two boys who both have their heads in her cleavage; she raises her glass at me and gives me a wink and a wave. Reverend Dave is on the next-door table with Liberty on one side of him, who is picking the peas out of the assortment of vegetables, and an earnest female on the other side who I can hear discussing her theology degree. The poor man continues to sip his water and looks like he wants to kill himself.

Over on top table things are looking ever more strained. Richard and Andrew are having an intense conversation. Louise and Carol have moved their chairs back slightly so they have more room to insult each other. Alistair is openly flirting with Bev, and still no one is talking to Alice. She stares ahead, flicking her food around, then suddenly gets up from her chair. She walks straight towards me, looking extremely stressed.

'Do you have a cigarette?' she asks, her jaw practically clamped together.

'But you don't smoke,' I reply.

'I do now!'

As we stand outside, under the pale-blue evening sky, she takes a deep drag on her cigarette.

'Who the hell have I married?' she asks, exhaling. 'His parents are hideous, the best man is in love with him, and half his friends keep giving me the nudge-nudge-wink-wink, like I am supposed to know a whole load of stupid secrets that they keep alluding to. I think my husband is gay,' she says, looking totally shocked.

She wouldn't be the first, obviously. I have organized two marriages that were never consummated – they both ended in divorce through lack of interest. The first was because the groom was actually gay, but the second groom just didn't fancy his wife. He later remarried and has two children with another woman. I don't know what happened to the bride.

'Just because the best man is in love with the groom doesn't mean the groom is gay,' I say, trying to sound positive. 'A lot of people find their love unrequited.'

Alice is not listening to me. She stubs out her cigarette and walks back into the marquee. I follow her, only to catch the tail end of an argument that has kicked off between Louise and Carol.

'If my son is a poof, then your daughter is a slut!' shouts Carol, standing up from her seat with her hands on her hips. She reaches across the table and picks up a full bottle of red wine. I think for one terrible second she is going to chuck it at Louise. Instead she turns to Alice, who is standing right next to her, and slowly and very deliberately empties the whole bottle down the front of her dress. The whole reception falls silent as they watch her. Alice is so shocked that she can't move. The only person who reacts is Grace, who runs screaming through the tables to pull her sister out of the party.

It takes the sisters about fifteen minutes of persuasion before they let me into the locked Portaloos. Alice is hysterical, her make-up is all over her face and her hair is everywhere; her sister has been scrubbing at the dress with Molton Brown soap for the last ten minutes and has only succeeded in sealing in the stain. I pour a bottle of white wine over the red and some of the pink fades. But the frock is ruined. Richard keeps hammering on the door, shouting apologies for his mother and informing us all that she has been removed from the party. But Alice still won't let him in.

Three cigarettes later, Alice suddenly decides to clean her face and rejoin the party. The relief on Richard's face as she finally opens the door is endearing, yet she brushes off his overtures and entreaties and takes hold of her sister's hand before walking back into the marquee.

The Taylor Six have already struck up and are valiantly trying to keep the party going. There are a few revellers swinging their hips to the toe-tapping tunes, the most exuberant of whom is Alistair, who seems to have his hands all over a firm twentysomething backside while grinding his hips into her thigh. However, despite Alice's valiant attempts to get her own wedding back on track, the joy has kind of gone out of the occasion. The wedding cake remains uncut and half the symphony of summer puddings sit on the tables untouched. The couple do manage a dance together, although it is obviously not the first.

So by the time the buses arrive to take the guests back to the village, they line up quite keenly. It is Bev who asks if anyone has seen Granny, as the marquee begins to clear. Bernard looks at me and I roll my eyes. The old bag could be anywhere. We both set off into the shadows, recruiting Nigel as we go. In fact it is Nigel who finally finds her, passed out like Jesus Christ in a bed of white arum lilies.

'Louise is going to be furious,' I say, hoiking the woman off the floor. 'I don't understand how anyone this old can get this pissed.'

Bernard and I frogmarch her to the bus, where an anxious Bev is waiting.

'Oh, thank you,' she says. 'You all right, Gran?' she shouts.

'Me teeth,' says the woman through flapping lips and gums. 'I've lost me teeth. I was a little bit sick around the back.'

Bernard rolls his eyes and marches back behind the Portaloos.

'Bag!' he says. I hand him a plastic carrier as he bends down and starts to rummage in the chunky pile of puke by the wheel. 'This is beyond the call of duty,' he says, inhaling through his mouth. 'Here they are,' he says.

He walks into the loos and I watch him rinse the teeth under the tap, then I follow him as he hands them back to Gran, who is now sitting happily on the bus. She mumbles a sort of half thank you and slips them straight back into her mouth.

Bernard and I knock back a few stiff vodkas and smoke four cigarettes in quick succession.

'I love a wedding,' declares Bernard, throwing his cigarette butt into a bush. 'All human emotion is on display. Are you coming to clear up?'

'One more cigarette,' I say, staring up at the stars. 'It is such a lovely evening.'

Bernard disappears, leaving me standing at the bottom of the garden by the stream. There is a rustle in the bushes and a familiar figure arrives.

'There you are,' she says, the moonlight catching her very pretty smile. 'I have been looking for you for ages.'

'Really?' She licks her lips. I can feel my heart beating faster. 'Can I help you with anything?' I ask.

'Actually, you can.' She moves a little closer to me. I can hear the rustle of her dress.

'Yes?' My mouth is totally dry. I swallow. 'What can I do?'

'Come to bed with me.'

I hesitate, not sure I've heard her correctly. 'I am sorry?'

'Come on,' she says taking my hand. 'I won't ask again.'

It is six in the morning and I am woken from my nice warm large double bed by the sound of a straining engine. I unwrap myself from Grace's warm soft embrace, step over her pink frilled bridesmaid's dress and wander stark-naked over to the window. The dawn is just breaking over the fields and in the middle of the lawn is a large blue van, trying to drag the Portaloo trailer across the soft, damp grass. The engine chokes and coughs with the strain; the trailer skids and stalls and then suddenly there is a loud cracking sound as the three-Portaloo unit detaches itself from the van and tips up into the air. There's a loud whooshing noise as a blue river of sewage and sods of toilet paper pours across the lawn, engulfing an ornamental cherry in its wake.

'Granny's tree!' comes a scream from the next-door room.

My mobile immediately starts to buzz in my jacket. I look at it and recognize Louise's number. I think for a second about ditching the call. But I can't. '*We have control, from the first piece of paper to leave the office to the last piece of rubbish picked up off the floor at the end.*' Bernard's motto rings in my ears.

'Good morning,' I say, picking up.

'Is it?' snaps Louise. 'From where I am standing the shit has almost quite literally hit the fan. It's all over the lawn. It's pouring towards the stream and, most hideous of all, it's covered Granny's tree!' She is beginning to sound quite hysterical.

'Don't panic. Leave it with me,' I say, staring back out of the window at the huge, glutinous, all-engulfing electric-blue lake. For once she is not exaggerating. I hang up. I sigh, look longingly across at the gently snoozing Grace and start scrolling through the numbers on my phone.

And so begins another busy morning at the coal-face of the ultimate service industry.